Memories Cast in Stone

Mediterranea Series

GENERAL EDITOR: Jackie Waldren, *Lecturer at Oxford Brookes University; Research Associate CCCRW, Queen Elizabeth House, Oxford; and Field Co-ordinator, Deya Archaeological Museum and Research Centre, Spain.*

This is a new series which will feature ethnographic monographs and collected works on theoretical approaches to aspects of life and culture in the areas bordering the Mediterranean. Rather than presenting a unified concept of 'the Mediterranean', the aim of the series is to reveal the background and differences in the cultural constructions of social space and its part in patterning social relations among the peoples of this fascinating geographical area.

ISSN: 1354-358X

Other titles in the series:

Marjo Buitelaar
Fasting and Feasting in Morocco: Women's Participation in Ramadan

William Kavanagh
Villagers of the Sierra de Gredos: Transhumant Cattle-raisers in Central Spain

Aref Abu-Rabia
The Negev Bedouin and Livestock Rearing: Social, Economic and Political Aspects

V. A. Goddard
Gender, Family and Work in Naples

Sarah Pink
Women and Bullfighting: Gender, Sex and the Consumption of Tradition

Memories Cast in Stone

The Relevance of the Past in Everyday Life

DAVID E. SUTTON

Oxford • New York

First published in 1998 by
Berg
Editorial offices:
150 Cowley Road, Oxford, OX4 1JJ, UK
70 Washington Square South, New York, NY 10012, USA

Berg is the imprint of Oxford International Publishers Ltd.

Library of Congress Cataloging-in-Publication Data

A catalogue record for this book is available from the Library of
Congress.

British Library Cataloguing-in-Publication Data

A catalogue record for this book is available from the British Library.

ISBN   1 85973 943 1 (Cloth)
         1 85973 948 2 (Paper)

Typeset by JS Typesetting, Wellingborough, Northants.
Printed in the United Kingdom by WBC Book Manufacturers, Mid-Glamorgan.

For the two Sams, past-present and
present-future

Contents

Contents

Acknowledgements

My interest in modern Greece began with a book of ancient Greek mythology which my parents would read to me at bedtime when I was eight years old, and visits to the Parthenon and other ancient sites on holiday a few years later. It wasn't until a three-month study-abroad program on Kalymnos, between high school and college, that I became enchanted with modern Greece. One aspect of this enchantment was my intimations of how Greeks today saw their past, and it was this question which brought me back to Kalymnos to conduct doctoral fieldwork in the early 1990s.

This book is about contemporary life on the island of Kalymnos, and how people filter the present through ideas about the past, whether the past be 20, 200 or 2,000 years ago. However, it is not a book of history, nor are Kalymnian ideas about the past used to reconstruct Greek history, modern or ancient. Rather it is about the ways people on a very un-insular Aegean island use the past to interpret, evaluate and judge issues pertaining to today's present. It is to those who wish to understand "historicity," or the felt relevance of the past in everyday life, that I address my efforts.

I have many people to thank for their help in the creation of this book. My greatest debt is to the people of Kalymnos, whose humor and patience at my mistakes of language and etiquette, and their tolerance of my questions made my many visits to the island from 1980 up to the present so rewarding. One of the few ways I can return their kindness is to show my allegiance through regular visits, like a migrant (ξενιτεμένο) Kalymnian, and by writing about their special sense of historicity. I would especially like to thank Katerina and Yiorgos Kardoulias and their daughter Katina and son-in-law Nikolas, for their long-lasting friendship and constant aid and support since my very first visit to the island. At their house I always feel I am at home (στους δικούς μου), and I cannot imagine having come this far without them. Perhaps one day we will arrange the marriage contract (συνοικέσιο) for our children. I also owe a deep debt of gratitude to Angeliki and Yiannis Roditis for their warmth, support and encouragement, and for the graciousness with which they accepted me and my family into their home. Also for the diligence with which they have kept me in touch with the island through their frequent mailings (pestellẃmata) of newspaper clippings and Kalymnian figs and mountain tea, the latter so that I would not forget the taste and smell of the island. I'm also grateful to Yiannis for the use of his artwork in this book, and for his cover design. Similarly, to their son Dimitris, for his always appreciated companionship, debates and insights, I am most grateful. Dimitris also provided considerable technical assistance on the computer matters so essential to a research project these days, and took considerable time in helping me to gather and assemble the photographs used here, and providing me with last-minute checks of facts and translations. To Nina and Manolis Papamihalis, and Nina's mother Irini, for their friendship and care of my family, for keeping me up-to-date on neighborhood gossip, and for being the first on Kalymnos to read my dissertation. Too many other Kalymnians were helpful in one way or another to list them all by name. Instead, I want to express my heartfelt thanks for the legendary hospitality (φιλοξενία) of Kalymnos.

I am also grateful to those scholars in Athens who gave me support and encouragement in many different ways. In particular I would like to thank Anna Frangoudaki, Argiris Fatouros and Nikiforos Diamand-ouros. Nick Germanacos deserves special thanks for setting me on this path. It was through his study-abroad program on Kalymnos, and his inspirational course on modern Greek poetry, that my interest in Greece and the meanings of its past for the present was first aroused. Finally, I appreciate Kostas Mitropoulos' permission to reproduce his cartoon, and thank him and Dimitris Mitropoulos for providing me with this cartoon.

I wish to offer many thanks to all those who read this book in its various stages and advised me on my research. The caring support of my dissertation committee at the University of Chicago, James Fernandez, John Comaroff and Michael Herzfeld (from Harvard), was invaluable during all stages of the process – I cannot thank them enough. I wish to state my deep appreciation to Jim for his father-like support over the years, and for teaching me of "revelatory incidents," "the play of tropes" and "the return to the whole;" to Michael for casting a guiding light on the relationship of Greek ethnography and anthropological theory, and for the "embodied knowledge" imbibed through the many gourmet meals he prepared in his kitchen where I hatched out the contours of my project; and to John for provoking my interest in historical consciousness, and for his always insightful criticisms.

I put many friends and colleagues through the arduous task of reading and criticizing drafts of chapters along the way, and through the equally difficult task of keeping my spirits up in difficult times.

Thanks go alphabetically to Keith Brown, Tom Burgess, Renate Fernandez, Renee Hirschon, Alan Lenhoff, Michael Scott, David Slater and Rob van Veggel. Particular thanks for their good grace at my constant pesterings, and their insight into and enthusiasm for my project go to Jane Cowan, Nick Doumanis, Antonio Lauria ("big Andonis"), Neni Panourgia and Peter Wogan. What a long, strange trip it's been.

Most importantly, I offer my gratitude to the two women in my life. To my wife, Bethany Rowe, whose patience and humor, advice and support, love and kindness during the long process of this book, is beyond description. Also for her careful eye for detail, which showed both in proofreading these materials, and in keeping me conscious of the material world of Kalymnos. And to my mother, Connie Sutton, who first afflicted me with the "culture" bug, who took me to many "fields" before Kalymnos, who has guided me through the often murky waters of anthropological theory and practice, and like a good mother has been merciless in her criticisms of this manuscript.

The research on which this book is based was supported by the following granting agencies: The Fulbright-Hays Doctoral Dissertation Research Abroad Fellowship, The Dissertation Fellowship of the Joint Committee on Western Europe of the Social Science Research Council and the American Council of Learned Societies, and the Sigma-Xi Grants-in-aid-of-Research Program. I am grateful for their support.

Chapter 2 is a revised version of an article that appeared in *Journal of Modern Greek Studies* (Sutton 1994) (copyright © John Hopkins University Press). Chapter 3 is a revised version of an article that appeared in *Anthropological Quarterly* (69:66–78) under the title "Explosive Debates: Dynamite, Tradition and the State" (Copyright © 1996 American Anthropological Association). Chapter 8 is a revised version of an article that appeared in *American Ethnologist* (24:837–852) under the title "Local Names, Foreign Claims: Family Inheritance and National Heritage on a Greek Island" (Copyright © 1997 Catholic University of America Press). All are partially reproduced here with permission. The map appearing on p. xii is reproduced with permission of the Department of Geography, University of Chicago.

Finally, the converting of my dissertation into this book was done with support of the Democracy 2500 Fellowship in Aegean Studies at St Peter's College, Oxford. To the donor of the scholarship, as well as to the Master of St Peter's John Barron, to Henrietta Leyser, and to all the college fellows I offer my thanks.

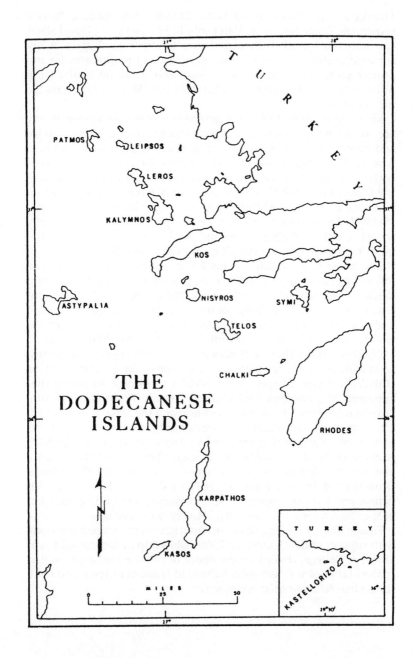

THE
DODECANESE
ISLANDS

Source: Kasperson (1966: 9)

Introduction

It's painful and difficult, the living are not enough for me
first because they do not speak, and then
because I have to ask the dead
in order to go on farther.

George Seferis, *Stratis Thalassinos Among the Agapanthi*[1]

I

Santayana's dictum that "he who forgets the past is destined to repeat it" was the last resort of the frustrated history teacher when I was in high school. This reflects the fact that *history* in US popular culture is viewed as something with no intrinsic bearing on the present. The expression "that's history," means it's over, finished, no longer an actor on the present stage. In a century dominated by a Fordist vision of mechanical reproduction, one is reminded of Henry Ford's derisive remark, "History is bunk!". Studs Terkel, the historian of popular memory, has diagnosed US society as suffering from a collective Alzheimer's disease, where "yesterday's headline is forgotten as a new one is emblazoned today."[2]

This culturally constructed view of history stands in stark contrast to that expressed by Seferis' poem above. I first encountered this poem while on a study-abroad program on the Greek island of Kalymnos during my senior year in high school. The poem and my experiences on the island became a touchstone for me that suggested an attitude toward the relationship between past and present different from that with which I was familiar. It was my perception of this contrast that stayed with me and motivated me to undertake a study of historical consciousness on Kalymnos, to give ethnographic flesh to the idea that there are different ways of constructing the relationship between past, present and future.

As I began my graduate education in Anthropology in the mid-1980s, the issues of history and historical consciousness had gained a renewed importance in anthropological theorizing. There was much

1

talk, on both sides of the disciplinary boundary, of the possibilities and prognosis for a *rapprochement* between anthropology and history. Geertzian interpretivism and the text metaphor had been adopted by a number of historians, while Hayden White's theories of "tropological" approaches to the past had gained an eager anthropological audience. In an influential article entitled "Theory in Anthropology since the Sixties" Sherry Ortner (1984) claimed that the development of a theory of historical practice was the key task for anthropology, a way of resolving the theoretical impasse between structure and event, rule and process. At the same time, the worldwide growth of nationalism and other forms of identity politics in the late 1980s meant that an understanding of the uses and abuses of the past in service of present purposes was placed high on the agenda for anthropology.

This boded well for my interest in developing an anthropological understanding of historical consciousness. And yet the idea that anthropologists could formulate a singular theory of historical practice, devoid of culture and context, seemed to smack of anthropological imperialism of times past. Surely, as my original sense of US and Greek historicities led me to believe, there were culturally diverse ways in which the past was seen to inform action and consciousness in the present, different rules for use of history, as Appadurai (1981) suggestively put it.

Some anthropologists did begin to look at the cultural construction of "historicities." However, initial attempts seemed caught in old dichotomies – history versus myth and linear versus cyclical – taken from earlier studies on the anthropology of time. Sahlins, for example, made a salutary call for the analysis of the ways "different cultures constitute their own modes of historical action, consciousness, and determination – their own historical practice" (1985: 33–4). However, his principal example contrasted the Ilongots and the Maori in terms of their performative vs. prescriptive structures, that is their linear versus cyclical ideas about the past. While few contemporary anthropologists characterize whole societies as linear or cyclical, they continue to use these terms (or variations on them), to characterize different *aspects* of a society.[3] The continued use of this guiding metaphor seems to impoverish, rather than enrich, our understanding of different attitudes toward the past that occur cross-culturally. Thus I had more sympathy for Renato Rosaldo's (1980: 54–5) grappling with the representation and understanding of historical consciousness:

> It makes a great deal of difference . . . whether one speaks about history as a river running slowly to the sea or as the fierce gales of change, an irretrievably lost moment, a seed grown into a blossoming flower, the good old days, an ugly duckling become a swan, a green betel quid chewed into red saliva, a walk along the path of life, or an oscillation

between the focus of inward movement and the diffusion of outward dispersal.

Without the context-dependent richness of different cultural accounts of historical practice, we will continue to reproduce sterile theoretical dichotomies. Rosaldo's call for a thick description of attitudes and idioms by which the past is conceived and cut-up is therefore crucial for understanding the cultural differences in the ways historical consciousness is structured. Nevertheless, it is difficult to find in recent ethnographies a focus on the different categories of the past that make up historical consciousness.[4] Many anthropologists focus on the *content* of disputed histories, and attempt anthropologically informed reconstructions of histories in order to challenge national history or other dominant versions of the past. If we are to understand how local, national, class and gender histories compete for dominance, and why these histories are seen as relevant to people's everyday lives and everyday practices, we must be sensitive to these multiple categories, metaphors and terms. For "History" or even "histories" do not encompass a people's way of linking past, present and future. Linnekin, for example, suggests some of the different understandings of the past and of culture encapsulated by seemingly similar concepts in Pacific societies such as *kastom*/custom, "Maoriness" and "the Samoan way" (1990: 162). Even within cultures, the past comes in many different containers bearing differing labels – from "history" to "tradition," from "custom" to "heritage." These important distinctions are frequently omitted from current accounts of the uses of the past in the present. This is particularly true insofar as analysts often implicitly share many of these categories – tradition, modernity, history – in their own theoretical discourses, and thus tend to miss the different valences these categories may have in different cultural contexts. In this book I attempt to analyze some of the different terms used to talk about the past on Kalymnos, to see what differing contents they yield, what different mental spaces they mark out, how they compete and overlap, and how they are associated with gender and other social divisions.

Counter to my expectations of endless stories of war and occupation, for many on Kalymnos the past simply meant "the good old days" (τα παλιά τα χρόνια literally: "the old years"). Unpacking these good old days proved challenging, since they sounded so similar to familiar discourses. But the analytical rewards were rich. Thus in Chapter 2 I counterpoise Kalymnian views of "modernity" (εκσυγχρονισμός) and the old years. I examine the ways these terms are debated, revalued and surpassed in Kalymnian discourse. Herein lies a lesson for any analyst who still wishes to use the term *modernity* neutrally and descriptively. In Chapters 3, 4 and 5, I examine several present-day practices in the light of their status as "custom" (έθυμο) or "tradition" (παράδοση), while recognizing that other practices, such as dowry, which would seem to exemplify the domain of custom, are given other labels by Kalymnians. I show how Kalymnians, sometimes according to age or gender, attempt to justify or dispute present-day practices with these labels. I also discuss why such justifications are rarely sufficient in the current constellation of values. In Chapter 6 I contrast custom and tradition to local categories of history, to argue that while the content of history may be debated on Kalymnos, the meanings and uses of the concept are widely accepted. In Chapter 7 I continue my discussion of history through a concrete example of its usage in understanding an ongoing world crisis, namely the war in the former Yugoslavia. Finally, in Chapter 8 I examine specific discourses on history as "heritage" (κληρονομιά), in the context of the conflict over the naming of the "Former Yugoslav Republic of Macedonia." I suggest that these explicit discussions of heritage disguise other, more intimate categories concerned with concepts of kinship and family inheritance practices. This account emphasizes the different categories of the past that inform the historical consciousness of Kalymnians and that are brought into play as Kalymnians seek to interpret their everyday experiences in the present.

II

Some clarifications of my initial contrast of US and Greek historical consciousness are required, lest the reader suspect I am engaging in the same binary thinking that I have been criticizing. In US culture, of course, the past *is* at certain times perceived as still alive and effective – in public, "historical" contexts. Battles over the past are clearly in evidence: in debates over Smithsonian exhibits on the bombing of Hiroshima and American Westward expansion, and in the respectful interest in the Holocaust Museum and the Vietnam War Memorial in Washington DC.[5] But what was striking to me on Kalymnos were not such public commemorations of the past, which are part and parcel of the building and maintaining of every nation state. Rather, it was the role that the past played in the mundane venues of everyday life.

Thus it is the relevance of history to the present that is at issue in this study. Richard Parmentier (1987: 15) captures this distinction in his discussion of the role of historical artefacts in present-day life:

> In general, we tend to carefully preserve our signs of history... by putting them in hermetically sealed environments – time capsules, archival vaults, guarded museums – so that the future events or generations cannot intentionally or unintentionally change their

physical shape . . . But in Belau and in many preliterate societies, signs
of history . . . are [also] deployed in social action.

It was because of Kalymnians' references to the past in their daily
experiences, in understandings of actions and motivations, and in
patterns of argument and understanding of the new, that I felt the
issue of cultural differences in historical consciousness could fruitfully
be explored on Kalymnos. Indeed it was the way that some Kalymnians
wished to cast the past "in stone," while many others envisaged a
more active role for the past, that captured my imagination. What
were the grounds for a relevant, or an irrelevant, past on Kalymnos?

Part of our shared interest in the past, no doubt, stemmed from the
fact that the Hellenic past was often at stake. The modern Greek state,
as it shakily found its feet in the nineteenth century, attempted to
build a culture and a national identity in which individual actions
and behaviors were legitimate only insofar as they could be related to
similar behaviors in the Classical Hellenic Greece of more than twenty
centuries before. Post-war ethnographers of Greece recognized that
the past played an implicit role in the present for Greeks, and that it
raised important issues for the question of Greek identity. However,
they tended to relegate discussions of the past to brief introductory
or concluding comments in their texts. This treatment of history
developed from a concern to establish modern Greece as an entity
worthy of study on its own terms, without reference to its glorious
ancient past.[6] However, changing theoretical currents led a new
generation of anthropologists to place issues of the Greek past at the
center of their research agendas on modern Greece. They therefore
examined official versions of Greek history in order to extract their
ideological implications in the present and the changes they implied
for evaluations of past historical periods.[7] The most influential of these
accounts is Michael Herzfeld's study, *Ours Once More* (1982a). Herzfeld
traces the conflicting interpretations of the past among nineteenth-
century Greek scholars and folklorists to the influence of Western
Europe and the Philhellenic movement in the Greek War of
Independence. He describes the modern Greek state as attempting to
balance the images of Classical Greek heroes against images of wily
and resourceful Greek bandits and tricksters from the more recent
past (the years of Ottoman rule).

These works on the modern Greek past adopt the ideas of recent
approaches to the "invention of tradition" and "imagined communities." Such approaches have explored some of the different uses
of history or traditions which "appear or claim to be old [but] are
often quite recent in origin and sometimes invented" (Hobsbawm and
Ranger 1983: 1). Anderson used the term *imagined communities* to
suggest the way nations create a sense of connection and common

destiny among people who have never met each other but believe themselves to be inheritors of a shared past, and to possess a common heritage both biological and cultural.[8] He argued that "narratives of national identity," in which history is traced back from the present moment, are a crucial component in constructing a nationalist consciousness. Interestingly, while Hobsbawm and Ranger, as well as Anderson, stress the importance of history (i.e. ancestry/heritage) for nationalist imaginings, they also point out that the significance of history changed as nationalist projects shifted. Hobsbawm suggestively compares the much greater role given to history in the construction of German as compared to French nationalist identity in the nineteenth century (1983: 272 ff.). Anderson similarly notes that New World nationalisms initially imagined a radical break with the past, a "blasting open of the continuum of history" (1991: 193).

In the 1980s and early 1990s, these two concepts – "the invention of tradition" and "imagined communities" – formed the basis of much of the interesting work on history in anthropology.[9] However, several problems arose from such studies. Firstly, excessive emphasis was placed on the construction of the past from above: its creation was viewed as an élite project controlled by intellectuals and national leaders, who then disseminated the results to the masses. As Ranger notes, in his recent (1993) reformulation of the "invention" concept, such a view tends to deny any agency to the people, who, seemingly, passively accept such inventions. In fact, as Ranger illustrates extensively with regard to colonial Africa, the non-élite engages in a much more complicated process of recasting and reshaping past practices as they adjust to shifting hierarchies of power.

When we look at modern Greece in these terms, we must perform a difficult balancing act in order to capture the interplay of forces. We must recognize the interconnectedness of social processes across national borders and cultures – the shaping influence of Western European projections on modern Greek consciousness – while at the same time not reducing local historical consciousness to a reflection of, or resistance to, Western impositions.

The second problem with such approaches is their tendency to posit a split between authentic customs and invented traditions, so as to debunk the latter.[10] While such debunkings are useful and even liberating in the context of nationalistic histories, they often assume a true history exists beneath the invented myth, waiting to be revealed by the careful scholar. Friedman asserts that even Anderson's use of the more suggestive "imaginings" tends to posit such a mystification in "constru[ing] the modern nation as an imagined community, as a symbolic organization creating a collectivity *for which there is no concrete social base*" (Friedman 1992: 849; my italics). The idea that invented or imagined pasts can be replaced by "truer" scholarly accounts leads to numerous political ironies. Shaw and Stewart (1994: 23) observe the continued imperialistic implications of such a project:

> anthropological hegemony now entails taking apart practices and identities which are phenomenological realities for those who use them ("your tradition is invented"). In our enthusiasm for deconstructing syncretic traditions we may have invented another kind of intellectual imperialism.

It seems to me that what is at issue here is the question of continuity: what kind of historical continuities can politically committed scholars accept as meaningful, and which can be dismissed as "fabrications of nationalism or other power structures"? Some have suggested that the key issue is that anthropologists must not give solace to nationalist or primordialist explanations. And yet, can we apply exclusively political criteria to the scholarly choices we make in our studies of continuities? Stewart (1995) goes to the heart of this issue when he asks: Do we, as anthropologists, feel more comfortable with the claims to continuity between ancient Athens and the contemporary Greek homosexual movement than we do with similar claims to continuity with the ancient past made by Greek nationalists?

One way to approach this issue is to turn the focus to the significance of continuity and rupture with the past in people's everyday lives and practices. Here I had suggestive guides from a number of anthropological studies of Greece published in the late 1980s and early 1990s which have begun to look at some of the uses made of memory for constructing gender, class, political, regional and personal identities. These studies help to untangle how national questions of continuity between past and present are conceived and constructed at the local level. For example, Seremetakis has examined how village women use mourning rituals to construct female histories of their villages; histories which challenge men's perspectives on issues from lineage violence to modernization. Collard, by contrast, looks at political memories of the Greek Civil War (1945–1949), which have come to serve as metaphors for present-day disorder in a mainland village. She writes, "Many current agrarian disputes are often couched in terms of the Civil War when, it emerges, they involve contemporary issues. Disagreements among kin also tend to be attributed to the Civil War when more recent causes are at stake."[11] These studies portray some of the different forms in which contemporary Greeks draw upon the past. However, they all focus on specific, competing pasts, and do not ask the question central to this book: What does a given population believe to be the general relevance of the past for present-day life, and how is this played out at the national, local and personal levels?

III

The preceding remarks evoke the issue of the relationship of the "local" and the "global" terms that seem to capture our new "world order" of instantaneous movement of capital and symbols, and only somewhat less instantaneous movement of commodities and peoples across national borders and cultures. What new perspectives on old problems do the terms "local" and "global" provide? Just muses: "'Local knowledge' must be construed in a very particular way to present itself as a focus of anthropological interest in the 1990s – else one might seriously wonder what anthropology has been doing for the last seventy years" (Just 1995: 285). Is the term "local" simply a new, more politically comfortable word to replace "native" in our 1990s discourses? If this were the case, it would perhaps be time to jettison the term, and the methodologies developed to study it. For many in the discipline of anthropology, such a reformulation is being proposed: our continued relevance is premised on the ability to transfer our studies from the villages and islands of anthropology's colonial past, into the centers of power and the non-territorial processes and projects of our global world. However, I believe such a view simply reproduces the marginalization of the economic and social peripheries noted above. If one studies *only* the centers of power one runs the risk of obscuring their peripheral connections.

What, then, is the point of providing an ethnography of historical consciousness on a Greek island? I would argue that simply to promote "history from below" as an alternative to "history from above," so as to reveal "hidden histories" is insufficient. For as John and Jean Comaroff argue: "Improperly contextualized, the stories of ordinary people [from the] past stand in danger of remaining just that: stories. To become something more, these partial, 'hidden histories' have to be situated in the wider worlds of power and meaning that gave them life" (1992: 17).

Kalymnos certainly has hidden histories to reveal. It is an island in the eastern Aegean not renowned for those heroic struggles against the Ottomans recorded in school history books. Nor is it famous for the ancient ruins of the tourists' imagination. It is known in the rest of Greece primarily as the island of sponge fishermen, and is associated with the hard seafaring life conjured up by such a label. Nevertheless, a cursory reading of Kalymnian history reveals that the island has never been isolated from world events. Indeed how could it be; in 1900, because of the sponge-diving boom fuelled by the Industrial Revolution, Kalymnos achieved a prosperity that brought the island's real-estate prices as high as those in the capital cities of Europe (Bernard 1987: 175). But I did not need Kalymnian history to understand this fact. Sitting with Kalymnian men and women, calmly surveying the sea, I realized that they were as glad to have their peaceful perch from which to meditate on nature's glories as they were fascinated by discussions and arguments concerning world events and politics.[12] To write a book that did not capture both the local and the global dramas that made up the daily flow of life on Kalymnos would be to fail to represent local Kalymnian realities.

Throughout this study I have remained attentive to parallels between local Kalymnian and national Greek discourses, and have concentrated on how national issues are encompassed and understood in Kalymnian discourses and in the writings of Kalymnian intellectuals. Along with many Kalymnians, I became an avid consumer of Greek national newspapers and other forms of Greek mass media, since these are key sources for the opinions discussed, debated and digested on Kalymnos. Thematically, I have combined a focus on local detail with an interest in this larger picture. Thus, in Chapter 2 I present Kalymnians' own anthropology, their view of their place in a world of other islanders, Athenians, Turks, Europeans and Americans. In Chapters 3, 4 and 5 I look at Kalymnian responses to European integration and to changing gender-roles as represented by Europe and the United States. Chapters 7 and 8 focus on Kalymnian interpretations, based on their views of history and change, of such regional and international events as the naming of the Former Yugoslav Republic of Macedonia and the disintegration of Yugoslavia.

IV

Any book that takes historical consciousness as its subject must be clear about what is meant by "consciousness." At certain points I have focussed on explicit discourse – the way Kalymnians talk about the past in anecdotes, everyday conversation and more extended narratives (as well as the explicit discourses of the Greek mass media and of local historical/folkloric writings). In analyzing these discourses I have looked for the tropes, the figures of speech used by Kalymnians to create a sense of wholeness in their own lives and to relate their stories to the "master narratives" of the nation.[13] While my commentary on these narratives is meant to place them within the context of Kalymnian social life, it does not intend to reduce them to their message. For history is more than a message; it is a telling. On Kalymnos, a seemingly trivial detail such as, "I was eating a bowl of lentils when Yiannis suggested we visit the old cemetery," may evoke a whole set of associations: the time of year, the religious connection between lentils and fasting, the knowledge of places and modes of production, the standard ways of preparation, and the sensual aspects evoked by reference to this common Kalymnian fare. Furthermore, while Kalymnians recognize that histories are often organized around the repetition of key themes through time, they also believe that these repetitions must be elaborated for their fine distinctions, their differences that enrich a common corpus. Thus I have tried to evoke in my own narrative some of the contextualized richness of Kalymnian stories.

But, as Marx, Freud and Durkheim have, in their different ways, demonstrated, consciousness is far from encapsulated by explicit discourse. The study of less literate contexts reveals, unsurprisingly, that historical consciousness comes in many forms other than articulated written or oral histories. In her work with an indigenous group in the Ecuadorian Andes, Rappaport (1994: 76) states:

> I was struck by how people perceived many current practices, agricultural and political, ritual and interpretive, as being the stuff of which history is made . . . The present-as-past in Cumbal is most effectively represented through non-narrative genres of expression, such as ritual and elements of material culture, that recall the past without enumerating it.[14]

Similarly, I look at the ways that discursive, narrated historical consciousness is sometimes supplemented by, sometimes contradicted by, ritual and kinship practices. For example, I examine the role played by ritualized dynamite-throwing in subtly bringing to mind different periods of the island's past. These periods often remain unarticulated in everyday conversation because direct articulation would explicitly question the relationship between Kalymnos and the local and national authorities. In Chapter 8 I explore notions of continuity with the recent and ancient past that are implicit in Kalymnian kinship and naming practices. I look at how such practices also remain in the realm of the non-discursive, because explicit acknowledgement of them might imply "backwardness" in the area of international relations. These examples and others show how ideas about the past are grounded in everyday human activity. This juxtaposition of the discursive/abstract and the sensuous/concrete is one of the defining features of an anthropological understanding.

V

This book relies heavily on conversations (sometimes taped, more often informal) with Kalymnians both in standard modern Greek and occasionally in the local Kalymnian dialect. During the course of my research I might start my day with a trip from my neighborhood to the commercial center of town. While shopping for daily goods I would engage in conversations with shop owners and their customers, sometimes stopping to listen in on coffee-shop debate. After lunch at home with my wife and son I would go out in the afternoon, often accompanied by my son, to one of the houses in the neighborhood where my presence was accepted as a normal event. This was a particularly good time to talk to married women, whose shopping and cooking duties were largely accomplished after the serving of the main meal (between midday and 2 p.m.), and who could thus find a quiet moment to reflect while the rest of the household slept. I usually spent my evenings taking notes and perusing the daily paper in search of potential topics for conversation the next day. Evenings were also useful occasions to observe Kalymnians socializing in groups, as neighbors visited each other on business or to chat. This was often a time for stories about the past to be told and retold. It was also the time when young Kalymnians would go out to bars for music and tongue-loosened conversation, followed by a late-night snack at one of the fish restaurants that line the harbor.

In addition to these daily rhythms, one was always prepared for unusual events: a speech in the harbor by a visiting political or religious figure, a lecture on the latest researches of one of the island's numerous local historians, an evening liturgy at the local church, or a funeral procession, announced by the ringing of bells throughout Kalymnos. Daily rhythms were, of course, punctuated by the prospective expectancies of religious holidays which shape Kalymnian perceptions: the impatience during lent for the coming Easter celebrations with all its ritual and gustatory elaborations; the prospect, especially for women, of a trip to a nearby island shrine or a remote shrine on Kalymnos in honor of a particular Saint's "name-day," more secular excursions to one of Kalymnos' numerous beaches or to a more fertile neighboring island to gather one's yearly supply of grape-leaves. Then there was always the unexpected event that burst on the scene: rumors of a crying icon of the Virgin Mary which can disrupt the schedule of the islander and the anthropologist, as the curious rush to the scene to see with their own eyes, while others simply regard such reports as proof of a coming secular or religious catastrophe, or of Kalymnians' perennial gullibility and "backwardness." These are some of the rhythms with which I lived and worked during my stay on Kalymnos.

This book is based not only on my research between 1992 and 1993, but also on my longer acquaintance with Kalymnos. My first trip to the island was in 1980, for three months on a high school study-abroad program that ran on Kalymnos from the mid-1970s through the late-1980s. That program was my first time as a participant-observer on Kalymnos, as I learned about the island not only through study, but by being apprenticed to Kalymnian craftspeople and sharing in their daily lives. Part of our assimilation into the community was to be "baptized" with a Greek name. The name chosen for me, Andonis, has stuck with me since then, and most Kalymnians still know me only as "Andonis the American." I was apprenticed to a family of leather tanners who had recently seen their son off for a year of work abroad as a seaman. His name was also Andonis, and his mother joked that I would fill his place in his absence. What seemed at the time a quaint coincidence, can have much more fateful significance, as I later learned, and as I explore in detail in Chapter 8. My friendship with that family became one of the motivating forces in my continued interest in Kalymnos, and my Kalymnian "mother" still locates the root of our relationship in that happy coincidence of names.

Over the next twelve years I made several visits to the island to maintain and extend personal ties formed on this first visit. My extended acquaintance helped to transform my status for a number of Kalymnians from that of "outsider" (ξένος) to that of a contextual "insider" (δικός μας άνθρωπος). This, in turn, permitted me to enter into a number of Kalymnian homes and to observe closely and be made privy to certain types of family interactions normally hidden from outsiders. In part because of this long acquaintance, I was able to interact with Kalymnian women, both married and unmarried, to the same degree as Kalymnian men. Although I engaged in the usual participant-observation of public family rituals and public events such as religious and national holidays, the major source of my data comes from more interpersonal interactions. In my evaluation of the data I have collected, I have tried as much as possible to take into consideration the different intentionality of comments made to me as stranger and outsider, as honorary Kalymnian, and occasionally as honorary family member.

In carrying out this study on Kalymnos I sought insight into how the weight of the past was felt by Kalymnians, and how it was refracted through the socio-political structure of their society. This was a personal as well as a theoretical quest. In this age of constant move-ment at hyperspeeds, of perpetually fractured wholes, I sought to return and remember a place that had been meaningful to me. More than the place, I sought to reconnect with a group of people who had earlier touched my life and to answer for myself Seferis' question (from *The King of Asine*):

> does there really exist
> here where one meets the path of rain, wind and ruin
> does there exist the movement of the face, shape of the tenderness
> of those who've shrunk so strangely in our lives

To the Kalymnians who helped me see that the past could make a difference in the present, I am grateful.

Notes

1. All citations of Seferis' poems are from Seferis 1967.
2. Terkel 1988: 2. Elsewhere Terkel (1975) has argued that people in the US are "conditioned not to have a sense of history," but only of chance and personal destiny. Rejection of any historical determination has been perhaps the major problematic in twentieth-century Western-art. Hayden White, for example, has described the deeply hostile attitude of twentieth-century modern Western art and literature to historical consciousness and the past more generally. He notes, "It could even be argued that one of the distinctive characteristics of contemporary literature is its underlying conviction that the historical consciousness must be obliterated if the writer is to examine with proper seriousness those strata of human experience which it is **modern** art's peculiar purpose to disclose." As he cites Joyce: "History is the 'nightmare' from which Western man must awaken if humanity is to be served and saved" (1978: 31 cf. Terdiman's (1993) excellent discussion of modernity as "memory crisis"). On Fordism, see Harvey 1989.
3. See Sahlins 1985: 52 ff. Different approaches to the issue of history seen as linear and cyclical can be found in Bloch 1977, Peel 1984, Hill (ed.) 1988, Connerton 1989, Pina-Cabral 1989, and in the Greek context, Hart 1992. Lee (1959) exemplifies earlier approaches to the issue.
4. Handler's (1988) sensitive account of nationalism in Quebec is an exception in this regard.
5. See Bodnar 1992.
6. Friedl 1989: personal communication. Cf. Campbell 1964: 1–6. Campbell, for example, begins his ethnography with a sensitive depiction of the political and intellectual disputes over the historical origins of the community he studied, before moving on to the task at hand: describing their present day way of life. Ten years later, du Boulay (1974) presents a static "portrait" of Greek village life, with history relegated to a concluding chapter. These attitudes toward history no doubt reflected the shared assumptions of the varying approaches – structural-functionalist, structuralist and Geertzian interpretivist – that were current during the 1960s and early 1970s.
7. See, for example, Danforth (1984), Herzfeld (1982a), Just (1989) and Kyriakidou-Nestoros (1986).
8. Anderson's insights into nationalist imaginings owe an unacknowledged debt to earlier anthropological work on collective consciousness and collective representations.
9. A review of some of the literature is provided in Foster (1991) and Ranger (1993).
10. See, for example, Hanson 1989 and the debate surrounding his "Making of the Maori" (Hanson 1991; Linnekin 1991; Wilford 1990). Also see Keesing (1989), and the discussion of all of these authors in Friedman (1992).

11. Seremetakis 1991; Collard 1989: 98. Other recent approaches to memory and the past in Greece can be found in Dubisch (1995), Herzfeld (1987a; 1991), Hirschon (1989; 1993), and Panourgia (1995). Given my interest in the past, one may wonder why I did not employ the more formalized techniques of oral history. Oral history and "narrative analysis" form the basis of a number of recent books on Greece by non-anthropologists (Doumanis 1997; Hart 1996). Although oral history is being employed more and more to illuminate the present as well as the past (e.g. Samuel and Thompson (eds) 1990), the tendency, once again, is to focus on alternative reconstructions of specific pasts. Thus Doumanis reveals some of the tensions and contradictions, often unstated and unrecognized, between oral and written histories of the Italian Occupation of the Dodecanese, while Hart similarly presents an alternative gendered history of the German Occupation and the Greek Civil War. Such approaches provide suggestive insights into the ways that people use the past in constructing present-day identities. Once again, however, the analytic emphasis of oral history tends to be on presenting new readings of specific histories, rather than on exploring historical consciousness or the relevance of the past to the present *per se*.

12. The precariousness of this sense of peacefulness was brought home to me in early 1996 when Greece and Turkey nearly went to war over the uninhabited Greek island of Imia, located just two miles from Kalymnos.

13. On "the whole" see Fernandez 1986. Borneman (1992: 37–8) defines master narratives as follows:

> The state, in constant interaction with its citizens, seeks to unite these disparate experiential tropes into a single frame, a shared history of the nation; it does this by providing its own preferred master narratives . . . In sum, master narratives serve as public matrices for the creation of collective conscience; they give an overarching meaning to a series of experiential tropes, and hence are politically contested frameworks for constructing historical accounts.

14. There is a rich and growing literature on such non-literate, or non-articulated historical consciousness. Classical landmarks include Rosaldo 1980, Price 1983 and Comaroff and Comaroff 1987.

Kalymnos: The Barren Island

Kalymnos: rock and light.
Kalymnos: salt air, drying octopus, sunset.
Kalymnos: the island of the faithful and brave.

On Kalymnos you meet history.
On Kalymnos Hestia cooks for you too.
On Kalymnos the impregnable fortress of monasticism.

Kalymnos: the capitol of the sea, the border of the world.
On this island the sun cast all its light.
lanes sprinkled, tradition.

> from *Kalymnos*, Archbishop Nektarios 1986 (my translation)

Even today, many of the houses of Kalymnos still are painted blue and white, the national colors of Greece, a vivid testimony to the long years of spirited resistance to foreign rule. That the memory of these difficult years lives on was forcefully brought to the author's attention when he was mistaken for a German and stoned in the streets by the children of Kalymnos.

> Kasperson 1966: 91

The History

On the wall [of the fortress-city of Rhodes] two armies are fighting with wooden swords – a dozen children in paper hats against half a dozen bareheaded ones. They are not Knights and Saracens, as one might think, but British and Germans. The battle sways backwards and forwards . . . High up against the sun an eagle planes above us, watching history plagiarizing itself once more upon these sun-mellowed walls.

> Lawrence Durrell, from *Reflections on a Marine Venus*, 1953

Although Durrell was writing about Kalymnos' neighbor, Rhodes, he believed this "historical plagiarism" to be a property of the Dodecanese islands, which lived, as he describes it, in the "historical present," where time is abolished, and "there is no past, present or future."[1]

15

History, in this formulation, doesn't repeat itself. Rather it plagiarizes: it takes from the past, in acknowledged and unacknowledged ways, that which is useful in the present. As I offer a background history of Kalymnos (and the surrounding islands in the Dodecanese chain), in a book with history as its subject, I am made particularly aware that history is not just a jumbled collection of things past. It is one story, or many, often conflicting stories, told with particular purposes in mind. Like a well-made Kalymnian story, and based partly on Kalymnian historians' own telling of their history, my brief review is not meant to be comprehensive, certainly not "objective," but is organized around themes, premised on the idea of repetition (a topic I investigate at length in Chapter 6 onwards). This concept of repetition is not based on the mechanical Fordian notion of perfect reproduction which erases the need to remember the prior model, but on Durrell's sense of plagiarism.

The twelve islands off the coast of Turkey which constitute the Dodecanese have a distinctive history in relation to the rest of Greece.[2] Although they were loosely part of the Byzantine Empire until the beginning of the thirteenth century, the empire scarcely administered the Dodecanese. Instead, from the fourth century onwards, they faced constant pirate raids which caused the decline of the economic and demographic fortunes of the islands. After the sack of Constantinople in 1204 AD had further weakened the Byzantine Empire, the Dodecanese were ceded to (more accurately, taken by) Venetian and Genoese merchants. These merchants ruled until 1310 AD, when they were replaced by the Knights of Saint John. The Knights taxed the population heavily, but they also built fortifications, curbed piracy, and brought a degree of prosperity to the islands for the two centuries of their rule before they fell to the Ottoman Empire in the 1520s and 1530s.

Ottoman rule was extremely light in the Dodecanese. Except for Kos and Rhodes,[3] they were given the title "privileged islands" by the Ottomans. These privileges were decreed by imperial orders (*firmans*) which formed a charter of local autonomy. The content of this autonomy is described by Booth and Booth (1928: 32) as follows:

> In matters of personal status, such as religion, marriage, divorce and inheritance, all the islands enjoyed complete freedom. Educational institutions were left under the control of the Orthodox community, and no attempt was made to interfere in questions of language. Rhodes and Cos had Turkish governors with a certain control over local administration. The other islands conducted their own affairs through elected councils called Demogerontia, the only limit of their freedom being the payment of "maktou," a yearly tax levied by the Turks to cover the cost of protection.

Each island elected its own "council of elders" (δημογεροντία) which, with a number of other annually elected bodies, administered the secular affairs of the island. Thus the Dodecanese had a highly developed system of democratic elections which can be traced back to Roman times, if not before.[4]

Despite their privileged status, many Dodecanesians joined in the War of Independence in the 1820s, and succeeded in liberating the islands. The Greek government sent a temporary administrator to Kalymnos in 1828. This administrator seems to have spent most of his time trying to keep public order, and to instill in Kalymnians a respect for the law by comparing them to their island neighbors (Patellis 1994: 44). This mistrust of centralized authority is a theme I shall examine at length in Chapter 3. Kalymnos' experience of central Greek authority was brief, it lasted a mere two years. In 1830, Greece traded the Dodecanese back to the Ottomans in exchange for Euboiea, largely at the behest of the British Foreign Office. Thus the islanders tasted the Great Power machinations which were to plague them and the rest of Greece up through the 1990s.[5]

Ottoman rule became more severe in the nineteenth century, as administrators attempted to squeeze higher taxes from the islands. During the mid- to late nineteenth century island leaders on Kalymnos, and other islands, made great efforts to preserve their privileged status through negotiations with the Ottoman Sultan.[6] Local Turkish administrators' focus upon tax matters is unsurprising given that the nineteenth century was a period of growth and prosperity for the Dodecanese, unparalleled since ancient times. But it also reflected the *tanzimat* reforms, i.e. the concerted efforts of the Ottoman rulers to streamline their imperial system during this period.[7] Kasperson distinguishes the sponge-diving islands from the rest of the Dodecanese at this time as follows: "During the nineteenth century . . . the sponge-fishing islands spearheaded the resistance to the Turkish occupation. Educational and cultural achievements, voluntary theaters and intellectual organizations, and local community government were most fully developed on the islands of Symi and Kalymnos" (1966: 170).

By 1912 the population of the Dodecanese was at its peak at 150,000. However, in this year Italy invaded, and seized, the islands in the course of its war with the Ottomans over Libya. Subsequently, Kalymnos set up its own government and bureaucracy, which included government seals that read "State of Kalymnos." At the same time Kalymnians let the Italians know of their wish to be made part of Greece, and they received a number of reassurances from the Italian admiral, Viale, that they would remain "free."[8] The islanders assumed that they had been relieved of the Ottoman yoke, but the Italian government had other plans. They hoped to use the islands as a bargaining chip: first in their negotiations with the Ottomans over

Libya, and similarly in their negotiations over Greek expansion into Albania during the Balkan wars. During the first years of Italian occupation there seemed a strong possibility that Great Power negotiations would lead to a granting of the Dodecanese to Greece. However, Italy eventually decided that the islands were "a pawn [which she could not] let slip from her hand."[9] Italy believed that the Dodecanese might also prove useful as a stepping-stone for Italy's commercial and military aspirations in Asia Minor. Thus, instead of their promised ceding of the Dodecanese,[10] the Italians instituted thirty years of harsh rule over the islands. This rule was particularly severe after the beginning of the fascist period in Italy in 1926, when Italy began to introduce assimilation policies.

In the early period Italian rule consisted of rigorous taxation, press censorship, secret police, and the exclusion of Greek labor from public works. After 1926, when Italy introduced active policies to make the Dodecanese into Italian islands, some restrictions were placed on the use of the Greek language in schools (it was outlawed after 1937). All references to the Greek nation were also proscribed. Attempts were made to separate the Dodecanese diocese from its leadership in Istanbul, and to bring it under greater Italian control. Finally, land left uncultivated for three years or more was occasionally appropriated for settlers from Italy.[11] In this period active resistance to Italian rule became most pronounced, the most notorious act of resistance was the Rock War of 1935 (discussed fully in Chapter 4).

The centralization and military focus of Italian administration meant that Rhodes and Kos regained a certain prominence during the Italian occupation. Leros, which neighbors Kalymnos to the north, also became significant owing to its apparent strategic military value. Extensive development occurred on these three islands, including the construction of roads, administration buildings and public facilities. Many of these structures still exist, marking these islands as more "developed" and less backwards than Kalymnos. Many Kalymnians believe that these other islands were developed so extensively because their inhabitants didn't resist Italian rule as strenuously as the Kalymnians. For some it is a source of regret, expressed in the idea that "if we had accepted the Italian rule more peacefully, we wouldn't have the terrible roads that we still have today." Kalymnos suffered economically under the Italians in other ways. In particular, the Kalymnian sponge industry was adversely affected by restrictions on exports and the closing of North African seas. Some of the smaller islands were more affected than Kalymnos; however, Kalymnos lost 35 per cent of its population to migration during these years before the Second World War.[12] Without the benefits of development Kalymnos had strong reasons to resent Italian rule.

Resistance activity in the mid to late 1930s enabled Kalymnians to

successfully avert plans to change the structure of the leadership of
the Orthodox church. As a part of their protest Kalymnians kept
churches closed after 1935 until the outbreak of the Second World
War, and held services in secret. Italian rule lasted until the fall of
Mussolini in 1943, when the islands were briefly occupied by Germany.

The German occupation was a period of extremely harsh, arbitrary
rule in the Dodecanese, and famine led many islanders to flee through
Turkey to the Middle East. On Kalymnos the lack of agriculture led to
severe famine conditions. However, considerable espionage activity
was undertaken by Dodecanesians during this period.[13] After the
German retreat, the islands enjoyed a brief respite of local autonomy,
followed by a two and one-half year military administration by Britain
while the fate of the islands was being decided. Some islanders still
had unfavorable memories of the British who were seen as insensitive
to local concerns, and were popularly referred to as the "red-asses"
(κοτσινόκωλοι).

The Soviet Union played a critical role in pushing for the islands to
become part of Greece rather than to be returned to Turkey. This
contrasted with Great Britain's more ambiguous role which attempted
to keep the islands under British administration. Dodecanese unification with Greece was formalized in 1947 under the Treaty of Paris,
when the Dodecanese became the last territorial acquisition of the
modern Greek state.[14]

In the post-war period, Kalymnos has consistently supported
political parties of the center and center-left. Support for right-wing
parties has been much lower on Kalymnos, in comparison with Greece
nationally and other Dodecanese islands (see Table 1). Kasperson argues
that the Dodecanese experience of foreign rule has consistently created
support for the liberal tradition in Greece (associated with Eleftherios
Venizelos), and votes against right-wing parties. He notes that in 1961,
when the right-wing E.R.E., led by Konstantinos Karamanlis, carried
the country with a 17 per cent margin over the Center Union, their
victory in the Dodecanese was by a scant 365 votes (1966: 91). On
Kalymnos, however, the right lost by nearly a two-to-one margin.
Locally, the only period in which Kalymnos elected a mayor from the
right was from 1959 to 1963. Since the fall of the Junta in 1974
Kalymnos has had twenty-two years of unbroken mayoral rule by the
socialist PASOK party. Kasperson associates these political patterns with
the fact that sponge-diving led to higher levels of education on
Kalymnos, and a wider contact and concern with the outside world.
As he writes (1966: 91):

> A noteworthy characteristic of political behavior in the sponge islands
> of Symi and Kalymnos is the far greater importance of ideological issues
> in electoral choice. In the elections of 1963 and 1964, the "triumph-of-

Table 1. Voting results of Dodecanesian Sponge Islands, 1961–1964[a] (in percentages). *Source:* Kasperson 1966: 92

Per cent change,	Election of											Per cent change, 1961–1964[b]		
	1961				1963				1964					
	E.R.E.	Center Prog.	P.A.M.E.	Ind.	E.R.E.	Center Union	E.D.A.	Prog.	E.R.E. Prog.	Center Union	E.D.A.	E.R.E.	Center Union	E.D.A.
Dodecanese Islands	48	47	5	–	34	56	4	6	32	68	–	–16	+21	–5
Sponge Islands (Kalymnos, Symi, Chalki, Astypalia, Kastellorizo)	38	58	4	–	28	67	3	2	22	78	–	–16	+20	–4
Kalymnos	33	62	5	–	25	70	4	1	19	81	–	–14	+19	–5

[a]*Source:* Nomarchy of the Dodecanese.

[b]Percentage changes are not strictly accurate because of the shifting coalitions of Greek parties. In 1964, for example, E.D.A. did not oppose the Center Union in Constituencies where they had not offered effective opposition in the past. The progressives, led by Spyros Markezinis, have contested elections as an independent party and in alliance with both the Center Union and E.R.E. Nevertheless, the figures do represent a reasonably accurate indication of party support over these years.

democracy" call of Georgios Papandreou struck a very responsive chord in these islands. This greater concern with ideological issues is probably a result of higher educational levels, greater communication with the outside world, and the historical resistance to political suppression.

Anti-monarchism was also higher on Kalymnos than in Greece as a whole. This is indicated by the plebescite taken on the return of the king in 1974, in which Kalymnos voted 85 per cent against the king, as compared to 70 per cent nationally. Kalymnian historian Yiorgos Sakellaridis proudly boasted to me how Kalymnos had known social-ism long before it was instituted in the West: that the local government since the Ottoman period had provided free doctors, free education and other social services.[15] He claimed that a member of the British Labor Party had visited Kalymnos at the end of the Second World War, and had seen in the Kalymnian public records expenditures to pay for a woman to breastfeed a baby whose mother could not. The politician said that if his party came to power in Britain they would institute such a program, that they could learn much from Kalymnos.

As already noted, the majority of Kalymnians have supported the socialist party PASOK throughout the 1980s and 1990s. In the most recent national election in September 1996, PASOK polled just over 50 per cent of the vote on Kalymnos, while the right-wing New Democracy party polled under 33 per cent, as compared to national figures of 41.5 per cent and 38.1 per cent respectively. This was a considerable decline from the 1993 elections, in which PASOK won 59.5 per cent of the vote on Kalymnos, and New Democracy 33.9 per cent (the corresponding national figures for 1993 were 46.9 per cent and 39.3 per cent). This decline can largely be attributed to the formation of a new party in 1996 by former PASOK minister Dimitris Tsovolas. This party, which claimed the "true" mantle of PASOK creator Andreas Papandreou, polled 8 per cent on Kalymnos, considerably higher than its national figure of 4.4 per cent (see Table 2). Though many factors may account for these patterns, the fact that PASOK's populism has consistently been framed in a rhetoric of decrying the "powerful", i.e. Western governments and wealthy interests within Greece, plays no small part in its appeal on Kalymnos.

I would like the reader to take a few main points from this brief history for the purposes of what will follow.

- The Dodecanese islands have for centuries been under the control of foreign rulers. At different times this has necessitated different strategies of submission, negotiation and passive or open resistance. But it has always meant that the fate of the islands was not under the control of its inhabitants, and that decisions made in far-off places had direct impact on the lives of these islanders.

Table 2. 1996 National Elections.

Kalymnian voting, by sex, by party (based on an 87% sample of the total recorded)

Party	Men	(4257)	Women	(4502)
PASOK (socialist)	48.5%	(2063)	51.2%	(2304)
New Democracy (right)	32.5%	(1383)	34.1%	(1536)
Dhikki (pasok breakaway)	9.7%	(411)	6.7%	(301)
KKE (communist)	3.6%	(154)	2.9%	(131)
SYN (eurocommunist)	2.5%	(106)	2.7%	(123)
Political Spring (nationalist)	1.8%	(75)	1.8%	(82)
Minor Parties	1.5%	(65)	0.6%	(25)
No Party	2.6%	(114)	2.1%	(96)

National percentages vs. Kalymnian percentages, not sex divided.

Party	National %	Kalymnian %
PASOK	41.5%	50.4%
New Democracy	38.1%	32.8%
KKE	5.6%	3.3%
Synaspismos	5.1%	2.5%
Dhikki	4.4%	8.0%
Political Spring	2.9%	1.9%

- The nineteenth and twentieth centuries in particular have been a period in which these islanders experienced acutely how the "civilized" nations of Europe can "play games" at their expense, and how they must always be ready for the opportunity to manipulate these larger powers in pursuit of their own concerns.
- This has led to a strong desire to make sense of international politics, and to understand in both diachronic and synchronic terms what they could not directly control. This understanding is very much a part of present consciousness, as I will argue in the course of my analysis. It informs the way Kalymnians imagine the present as much as the past and the relation between past, present and future.

The Island and its Economy

Unlike its neighboring islands, Kalymnos is mostly bare rock. It is 49 square miles of rock sitting a few miles off the coast of Asia Minor; the third largest (in size and population) of the Greek Dodecanese islands. Less than a fifth of its land is arable, and this is mostly concentrated in the village of Vathi and scattered along the west coast of the island. Kalymnos has therefore always made its living from the sea, and its fame is as the "island of sponge fishermen," for sponges have provided the island with a source of livelihood, and sometimes wealth, for centuries. The first real boom for the Kalymnian sponge industry was in the nineteenth century at the time of the Industrial Revolution, when demand for sponges led Kalymnos to prosper to such a degree that, as noted before, by 1900 land prices in the main town of Pothia were comparable to major European cities (Bernard 1987: 175). Some other factors contributing to this nineteenth-century boom were the healthy boat-building industry throughout the Dodecanese, and the well-established Kalymnian diaspora in Europe and the Middle East which was able to promote the export of Kalymnian sponges and other local products such as tangerines (Logothetis 1983). The Italian Occupation (from 1912 to 1942) was, as noted, a period of general decline in the sponge industry and of population migration (between 1912 and 1947 the population dropped steadily from 23,000 to just over 12,000 before a post-Second World War increase).[16] Some of this decline, however, can be attributed to price decreases caused by over-supply in the European markets.

Of all the islands engaged in the sponge trade, Kalymnos fared best. As a larger island, Kalymnos' economy was more diversified: it included trade, a small citrus industry and a cigarette-rolling industry employing 800 women before the Second World War.[17] The sponge industry survived largely owing to Kalymnian willingness to venture farther into the non-Greek world in search of sponges and markets (Kasperson 1966: 76). Prior to the Second World War several thousand Kalymnians established a community in Tarpon Springs, Florida, based upon sponge-fishing in the Caribbean; and at this time Tarpon Springs became the world's largest sponge-producer. For Kalymnos itself, this was a period of considerable prosperity, described by Bernard (1987: 178) as follows:

> Between 1910 and 1940 Kalymnians produced more than eighty metric tons of sponge a year. A 5.5 per cent municipal tax on sponge sales produced revenues of more than $45,000.00 a year . . . The sponge merchants grew very wealthy. The richest of them all, a Mr. Boubalis became a legend in his own time, building an old-age sanitarium, a hospital, two high schools, a grade school, and an orphanage.

After the Second World War the Kalymnian sponge-industry went through an initial increase after wartime curtailments, but the development of industrial synthetic sponges severely restricted the world market for natural sponges in the late 1950s. Between 1950 and 1968 sponge-fishing and processing went from providing 60 to 70 per cent of the Kalymnian economy to 30 per cent (Bernard 1987: 200). The deficit was picked up for Kalymnos largely by remittances from migrants in Australia and the US (18 per cent), and from Kalymnians in the merchant marines (22 per cent). The situation with regard to sponges remained fairly stable into the 1980s, but a disease that afflicted sponges in the mid-1980s perhaps struck the death knell for sponge-diving on Kalymnos: total sponge production fell from 30,000 metric tons in 1986 to 3,000 in 1992. Tourism has grown significantly, but it has not become the major industry of the island as it has on many other Dodecanese islands. Instead, organized fishing has become an economic replacement for sponge-diving. It currently employs about 1,200 men, approximately 25 per cent of the working population on Kalymnos. Unfortunately, over-fishing seems to be a growing problem, but some hope that the new industry of fish hatcheries will come to the rescue.[18] These hatcheries are estimated to produce between 500,000 and 1,000,000 fry that are raised for export to the European Community.

Throughout the twentieth century Kalymnos has been among the most densely populated of the Dodecanese islands, and this is despite the fact that its mountainous geography makes large areas of it uninhabitable (Agapitidis 1986: 18). A significant number of the male population is currently, in the 1990s, employed in the building industry as laborers, masons, carpenters, electricians and plumbers. Since it is the goal of parents to build a house for each of their children as a lure for them to remain on the island, it seems that this industry will remain secure as long as there is prosperity on Kalymnos. Another reason for the importance of house building is the increasing number of foreign (non-Greek and non-Kalymnian) wives (and some husbands) living on Kalymnos, for whom housing must be provided. In 1994 a social group was formed by these foreign wives, called "The Neighbors," which has organized and funded a number of events and projects, including the rebuilding of a central playground. At present in 1997 the group has approximately thirty members, largely from the United States and Scandinavia. However, local estimates put the number of non-Greek wives on Kalymnos at around one hundred. This influx of foreigners can be traced to contacts through tourism, and to return migration; and it has clearly had an impact on many local practices and ways of thinking as will be seen in the course of my analysis.

There has been a steady increase in the numbers of Kalymnian women seeking employment on the island. Those who do not work in family-owned stores generally find employment, along with men, as workers in banks, private offices, schools and other office work. There is much resentment towards the publicly employed office workers, especially on the part of the self-employed middle classes (for example, shop-owners and those who work in the tourist industry). Their complaint is captured in the common suggestion that people try and get places in the public sector in order to sit and do no work (ψάχνουν γία μια θέση για να κάθονται). This is also the source of some intergenerational tension, as older people suggest that the younger generation looks for these jobs out of laziness.

Those who have higher education, the men and women who return from schooling to live on Kalymnos, either become doctors, lawyers or teachers. Alternatively, they set up their own tutorial schools (φροντιστήρια) in foreign languages or in mathematics, to compensate for what is felt to be the inadequacy in public education on Kalymnos and in Greece. Although the era of sponge-diving may be over, most Kalymnians remain optimistic about the future. This optimism is borne out by the fact that Kalymnos is the only Greek island with an economy not reliant on tourism that increased its population during the 1980s. This has had an effect on my analysis: the role played by tourism in the objectification and commodification of the past, while touched on occasionally, is not a major focus of this book. The evocation of the atmosphere of the past is crucial to recent tourist attractions throughout the world and such processes are especially significant in Greece. Here tourist interest in ancient Greece makes up for Greece's contemporary "dearth of power and prestige, on the one hand, and lack of a cheap labor force, on the other hand ... Having put the ruins of its history on tour, Greece thus features the culture of ruins as *its* most recognizable *modern* signature."[19] On Kalymnos a new magazine published by the mayor's office entitled *Kalymnos Today* (1997: 15; my translation), is particularly frank about the relationship between tourism and culture:

> Present, past and future dictate our historical identity. The projection of our cultural energy should not be interpreted today simply as folkloric leftovers, closed off [from the wider world], but as a viable condition motivated by a contemporary understanding: uniting tradition with the productive axis of tourism, an energetic intervention of local tradition in our tourist policy. Culture as consumable good, culture as capital.

As such a statement indicates, tourism is clearly a useful site for the study of transformations in the meanings of "tradition" and "culture," and it is this sense of the past as capital, or something that you can own that I explore in my discussion of "heritage" in Chapter 8. If I had worked on Kos or Rhodes, with their plethora of ancient remains, or any of the surrounding smaller islands whose economies have been reduced to reliance on the tourist trade, an analytic focus on tourism would have been necessary. However, there are the marks of special pleading in the official statement above. For, while Kalymnos receives its share of the tourist market, it has neither the ancient ruins, nor the clean, secluded beaches so attractive to Western tourists seeking refuge from "modernity." Furthermore, Kalymnians are proud of the fact that their economy and continued prosperity still derives significantly from productive labor from the sea, rather than from tourism and the perceived servility and laziness it breeds.

This brief review of economic changes on Kalymnos in the twentieth century hopefully provides the reader with a sense of what the Kalymnians mean when they suggest that they can survive and prosper on their "rock," their "barren island" (άγονο νησί). It is easy to see why biological metaphors come to mind for those writers, Kalymnian and non-Kalymnian, who try to capture Kalymnian identity. One writer, reporting on Kalymnos for the national magazine *New Ecologist*, refers to the "endogenous [native] dynamism" (ενδογενής δυναμική) of Kalymnos. Metaphors of biology and character aside, Kalymnians are proud that they can change with the times while preserving in living form (as opposed to the museum-like monuments of neighboring Kos and Rhodes) something of the "history" and "tradition" that connects them to a past they feel to be so continuously relevant.

Yet the changes have been enormous and they seem to demand an intellectual response from the Kalymnians. They fuel what is perhaps a longstanding debate about the place of the past in the present on Kalymnos. And this debate goes to the heart of my subject matter in the chapters which follow.

My Arrival

Just as we can no longer write "historical background" without a sense of irony, post-modern anthropology has alerted us to the ideological presuppositions of claims to "being there" of arrival stories.[20] What follows does not attempt to encapsulate an objective description of Kalymnos; rather it describes some of the personal spaces and paths by which I experienced the island. I have further juxtaposed my own impressions with some Kalymnian representations and experiences of the physical landscape of their island.

While my first arrival on Kalymnos is lost to me in a haze of adolescent memory, it seems that I am forever returning to the island. Not unlike the many Kalymnians who are born on the island but who leave in pursuit of work, my return to Kalymnos is the sweetest experience. Fumes from the trucks parked in the hull of the huge ocean liners that make the fourteen-hour trip from the port of Piraeus (near Athens) to Kalymnos threaten to overwhelm me, overloaded as I am by suitcases and packages brought back from abroad for my Kalymnian friends and "family." Increasingly I find that my packages cannot compete with the goods carried in these trucks, which make available to almost every Kalymnian those magical consumer goods from the West. Other goods are brought in trunks by Kalymnians returning home. In the past, when travelling to and from Europe, Australia or the United States was a major undertaking, and boats from Athens infrequent, the migrant's return was an important local event. Young boys would wait down by the harbor to find out about a migrant's return, then rush to the family's house to announce the news, giving them time to prepare and receiving a tip for his efforts. As Kapella (1987: 42–6) describes it, "the news of arrival [συγχαρίκια] that you manage to receive or to send are some of the memories that remain alive forever."

The return to Kalymnos always brings back floods of memory for me as well. But memory must test itself against a constantly changing landscape. Kalymnos, that rock of seeming resistance to human designs, is in fact in constant flux, as houses, stores and churches spread across its landscape, finding their way into the most unlikely places. There, against a rock face barely approachable by land or sea, shines the white stone of an unpretentious but beautiful chapel. What human will and determination brought the materials together to construct this monument? Herein lies some of the secret, Kalymnians will tell you, of how Kalymnos has survived and flourished, changing and unchanged, against all odds. However, tourist films about Greece, including one recently produced about Kalymnos, tend to linger on this landscape – house-fronts, churches, boats docked in a wind-swept harbor – as if the makers of these objects had absconded. It is as if someone had carried out the fantasy often expressed by Kalymnians complaining about their gossiping neighbors, to "turn over the island and shake out all the people, and then Kalymnos would be a nice place to live." It is more likely that such empty landscapes conform to a tourist imagination, with a background of boozouki music and a few people added in later for local color. The actual sights and sounds that I associate with Kalymnos, of bustling activity, noisy motorcycles and trucks bringing goods through the narrow streets, are not recorded in these films.

The Human Scape

As the boat docks one is met by a crowd of competing taxi drivers, many of whom attempt to lure the tourist to the chosen guesthouse of a mother, aunt or sister.[21] Others are left to transport their fellow Kalymnians and their many possessions. On returning from a day excursion I made with three women to the neighboring island of Kos, the taxi driver complained bitterly about fitting the 300 pounds of grape leaves we had picked that day into the nooks and crannies of his vehicle. One woman commented to him, "How can we expect to be part of Europe, if we provide such grumbling service." The taxi driver did not miss a beat in his response, "*Europeans* would not be trying to transport 300 pounds of grape leaves in my taxi!" The question of the European identity of Kalymnos reappeared in numerous forms throughout my research.

Coming off the dock, you enter the town of Pothia. The view to your left encompasses a pine-covered mountain, to your right rises a mountain of stacked homes. One layer of homes meets you streetside, but when you climb thirty stairs or so, you will enter the home of another, often extended, family. This family might also have another entrance to their home on another street that runs higher above. Porches and common staircases, worn and steep, act as roads to separate homes and properties.

An unusually wide road meets you as you turn right off the dock. It arcs to the right and runs alongside the harbor showcasing sailboat and tourist ferries. Gleaming white yachts from neighboring countries dwarf the adjacent colorful blue, yellow, red and sea-green fishing boats double and triple parked, an immediate indication that since the 1980s tourism has made some inroads on Kalymnos. The harbor road is wide enough to accommodate two-way traffic, double parking and even pedestrians, and it is one of the busiest streets on the island. This road was widened substantially in the mid-1990s, and on a return visit there in 1996 many Kalymnians of different political persuasions proudly pointed to the harbor road as the fruit of a particularly energetic mayoral administration. It is here that much social activity takes place, from political or religious rallies and speeches to national parades, featuring the Kalymnian philharmonic, to the "bride's bazaar" (νυφοπάζαρο) where every Sunday evening young men and women dress up in their best clothes and venture out, often with their families, in order to see and be seen. It is here that I saw my first Greek state ritual, "Ohi day" on October 28 1980.[22] The photographs I took then could almost be exchanged with the ones I took twelve years later. While much of the landscape has changed, these celebrations have taken on the dull, unchanging nature of state ritual which is remarked upon by Kalymnians and myself.

As you walk along the harbor road the sea is on your right, and to your left is coffee shop after coffee shop, restaurant after restaurant – each establishment differentiated only by its style of table and chair or different colored cushions as each restaurant or coffee shop offers the same menu and might be only further distinguished by its regular customers. The chairs all face toward the sea, ostensibly to watch the traffic at the harbor, which is very light during the middle of the day, but mainly to register the activity on the street as men gather for coffee and women do their daily shopping.

The majority of the island's shops run along a very narrow and busy one-way road that branches out of the harbor road. The harbor road circles around the Kalymnos court-house and if one chose to continue on this road one would pass through another stretch of restaurants and coffee shops, a small daily farmers' market and finally, as the road slopes sharply upward, a neighborhood on the other side of the valley similar to the one in which we began. This road continues along a breathtaking stretch of unpopulated, sparse mountainside for about twenty minutes by car to reach the agricultural side of the island, the community of Vathi.[23]

The road that branches out of the harbor road begins on the other side of the court-house, and offices of the regional governor (Έπαρχος). This building, along with the customs-house and the town hall are among the few erected by the Italians during their years on Kalymnos. This seems sparse when compared to Kos, Rhodes and even Leros, but as with roads and other projects Kalymnians told me, sometimes approvingly and sometimes disapprovingly, that "we didn't let the Italians build on our island." This claim, and its ramifications in terms of local identity, are discussed in the next few chapters.

Next to the court-house is the church of Christ, the most prestigious church in Pothia, where swank weddings and memorials are held, and from which speeches are made on national holidays. In this church the Italians attempted to hold services in April 1935, and thereby precipitated the events of the Kalymnian women's Rock War. Beyond the church is the unprepossessing front of the mayor's office, the political hub of Kalymnos. It is here that disgruntled citizens come to use their connections (μέσα) to get something fixed, as I had to do when a careless developer cut the water-main to my house. I was shunted from office to office, and my predictable problems revolved around who was responsible and who could authorize repairs. It was only when I reached the vice-mayor (near the top of the hierarchy), who had been informed that I was writing a book about the island, that my problem was dealt with. Many Kalymnians at the time urged me to include this incident in my book, as an indication of how things do or don't get done on the island.[24]

The road that branches out of the harbor road begins on the other side of the court-house at the fish and meat markets right on the harbor and continues directly north through the dense retail center of Kalymnos; sweet shops, vegetable stalls, clothing, shoe and toy stores, grocery stores, souvenir shops, electronic stores all compete along a snaking, extremely narrow street about half a mile long. Bread shops are hidden on narrow side-streets, seemingly as a reflection on their lessening status in a market where foreign goods are at a premium. In the 1990s the main grocery store at the taxi stand sells canned goods from all over Europe and America. Ten different varieties of chips are available for Kalymnian children to choose from. The one foreign beer available in 1980, Amstel, now jostles for space among a wide range of beers and sodas, while the Greek brand, Fixx, is now nowhere to be found. The fruit and vegetable stands also reflect these changes. Once they only sold those fruits that were in season, now they offer such formerly rare items as bananas, pineapples, mushrooms or Israeli sweet potatoes to the demanding Kalymnian shopper. Foreigners comment on how they used to bring crates of fruit back with them from trips abroad: Americans brought the first taste of avocados or persimmons to the island. They note that in the 1990s even ginger and soy sauce are readily available, if one has hankerings for Chinese food. However, one cannot make simple assumptions about the effect of such imports on the Kalymnian palate. Many of the new items – fruits, chips and sweets of various kinds – are eaten only as snacks. The main meal of the day, with all its social implications for bringing the family together, remains relatively unchanged. Some use new products, such as expensive French Roquefort, as part of the constitution of a middle-class identity, while others without such aspirations have domesticated Roquefort – one man pounds Roquefort together with feta to make a newfangled version of a traditional Kalymnian cheese-spread (κοπανιστή). Another young man, a computer programmer about to marry into one of Kalymnos' *nouveau riche* merchant families, tells me that he likes to try new food when he travels abroad, but is a vociferous conservative when it comes to Kalymnian cooking. He declares, "I'm a localist – I eat the local food wherever I go, but when I'm on Kalymnos I want to eat locally as well!" As with other places, Kalymnos incorporates and accommodates the global market-place.

Cars and trucks traffic along this main thoroughfare surprisingly fast, and shoppers must always be on the lookout and ready to walk single file or to step up quickly onto the narrow stone walkway in front of most stores. The road widens and forks at the taxi stand: one may either continue north or circle around toward the harbor. Perhaps most striking to me when I visited the island in 1989 after a seven-year absence was the profusion of "video clubs" offering an eclectic mix of mainstream American and Greek films, predominated by sex and violence.[25] I'm not sure if I'm more overwhelmed by this cultural invasion, or by the building mania that has gone on in my absence. Houses have sprung up everywhere, not only in the already crowded capital, but in previously unpopulated areas of the island. It seems that almost every parent is financially able to provide houses for each of their daughters, and perhaps for their sons too. Many houses are half finished, or have the concrete beginnings of a second story propped indefinitely on a functioning first floor, giving one the sense that there is more building going on than an island with a population of 15,000 could possibly support. These concrete outcroppings reflect the conventional wisdom on Kalymnos: money is safer spent on housing than languishing in the bank (even at the 18 per cent interest

The harbor of Potnia: view of the courthouse.

Women shopping from a fruit truck.

prevalent in 1992). If you don't have enough money to construct an entire house, invest in the foundations, and a year or two later perhaps you will have enough to finish the job.

Apart from a couple of different shops, from a stationer's to a video store, the main retail district of Kalymnos town ends here, with the former residence of the post office on the left (recently moved and expanded) and the telephone office on the right. Beyond this one enters more exclusively residential districts. If you take a sharp left at the first street approximately one hundred yards up from the telephone office you enter the neighborhood of Ayios Mammas. Here the road is wider, the houses are large, and even though homes are close, neighbors are not living on top of each other, although families often are. Here there is room to have a couple of fig or olive trees, perhaps some chickens and even a goat or two.

This road forks also, and the right passage ends a little further along in a tall steep stairway, reminiscent of the times before there were cars and motorbikes on Kalymnos. The other street curves gently to the east, passing behind a church-run orphanage for girls and up past a couple of two storied elaborate summer homes, with fresh smooth plaster painted in contemporary muted shades of beige and brown, outfitted with expensive solar water-heaters and screened in windows.

These expansive and expensive houses contrast greatly with the smaller homes directly north whose shutters have been painted frequently, in kelly green and sky blue. Their windows have no screens and freshly laundered jeans often hang dripping across the front porch. Doors and windows stand open and inviting as the sounds of food preparation signal breakfast time.

At the square (*platea*), a gypsy has stopped in front of the sweet shop to sell men's bikini briefs out of a large wooden handcart. A couple of the women whose homes look onto the *platea*, or who were near enough to hear the seller's cries, gather to look at what he's selling, but more often, to take a couple of minutes out from hanging their laundry or sweeping their porches, to gather with other women and talk. The woman whose fruit stand is also on the *platea*, leaves to help her husband unload another truck full of potatoes into the lower half of a two-story home she has recently built as part of her teenage daughter's dowry. The new home for her daughter is not ten feet away from her own home, and is equally close to three of the girl's other relatives.

Of the three recognized roads that intersect in the *platea* of Ayios Mammas, one is a major thoroughfare which heads off toward the hospital and the inner island, and one leads directly for 200 yards or so into the churchyard. Even at this early hour women can be seen on their way up to the churchyard to tend to the gravestones of their families – to clean them and make sure that candles remain alight. In the evening one might see the little cramped figure of the widow who is paid by relatives who are unable to tend daily to their gravestones, climbing up the steep pathway, one hand grasping a cane as she prepares to begin her nightly task of lighting the candles.

The third road, which leads up to the mountains, steepens slightly after one passes the electrical shop across from the sweet shop. One passes a tiny road on the left, which is only wide enough for a motorbike, and like the many pathways on Kalymnos, one wonders whether it is a street or a neatly kept passageway which leads into a cluster of homes belonging to a large extended family. If one is accustomed to streets being named and numbered it's hard to know for sure – there are not more than a handful of street signs on Kalymnos. You might see an interesting house in the distance while out walking yet not know how to get there. Once you get further inland houses are often built at strange angles, as each tries to compete for a better view, and sometimes the only way to get to a home appears to be through someone else's yard. Often the passageways needed to access streets must be purchased; ownership is usually hotly disputed.

As one continues to climb one must stand to the side of the street to make way for a large gypsy truck – the back is open and laden with cheap carpets. A woman and two children sit in the back, while a man in the cab shouts his wares over a loudspeaker. Two women, sisters-in-law, have just emerged from the little pathway. They are carrying buckets full of leftover vegetables and bread for their goats on the mountain and they pause to barter with the man. They only stop briefly as they have many things to do today and the trek to feed the animals will become uncomfortable in the summer heat if they dawdle too long. In earlier times this road used to be a river which extended all the way down to the orphanage.

When I first visited the island in 1980 it was a dirt road that seemingly led nowhere. However, I would trudge up it on a daily basis to the house of a family of leather tanners to whom I had been apprenticed as part of the study-abroad program. It has since been paved over to allow easy passage to students' mopeds as they go to hang out at the high school that suddenly appears at the end of the long incline. This is where we made our home for fifteen of the eighteen months of my fieldwork. I chose this neighborhood because it too was a return. From 1975 until 1989 it was home to the program for American students which introduced me to the island. It was chosen by the program director because it was among the more "traditional" neighborhoods on the island. Whilst for me the people of Ayios Mammas tended to be well-disposed and accustomed to foreign students frequenting their shops and prying into their lives. Some I had formed friendships with on earlier trips, others who I only vaguely remembered, claimed to remember me well. My connections to this neighborhood provided at least a small, shared basis of memories from which to begin that process of exploring the past together upon which I now embark.

Notes

1. See Roessell 1994.

2. The Dodecanese islands include the major islands of Rhodes, Kos, Kalymnos, Karpathos, Kasos, Leros and Patmos and the smaller islands Simi, Halki, Tilos, Nisiros, Astypalea, Kastellorizo and Lipsi, plus a few uninhabited or sparsely inhabited islands.

3. The Ottoman Empire granted special status to those subjects who voluntarily surrendered as opposed to being conquered. Kos and Rhodes, as centers of the military power of the Knights of Saint John, fought vigorously and exacted a considerable toll against the Ottoman army before they were taken. They were thus treated more harshly than the other islands who voluntarily surrendered.

4. See Wambaugh 1944: 16.

5. See Booth and Booth 1928: 33.

6. See Frangopoulos 1952; Sakellaridis 1986a.

7. On Dodecanese prosperity, see Kasperson 1966: 150. On the *tanzimat* reforms see Hourani 1981: chapter 3; also Augustinos 1992: 189 ff. on Ottoman Greek community reactions to these reforms.

8. For a discussion of this period on Kalymnos, see Maïllis 1992. For an overview of Italian designs in the Dodecanese see Doumanis 1997.

9. Italian Foreign Minister San Giuliano, cited in Bosworth 1979: 318. On Italian plans, see Bosworth 1979: 320 ff.; Booth and Booth 1928: 278–9.

10. Great Power negotiations at the time also considered the possibility of returning the islands to the Ottomans, or of making them independent, but under Ottoman suzerainty. For a full discussion of the diplomatic wrinkles, see Bosworth 1979: chapters 9 and 10.

11. On labor and land policy see Booth and Booth 1928: 183; Kasperson 1966: 160. On linguistic and educational issues see Kasperson 1966: 21; Zairi 1986.

12. On changes in the sponge-industry see Bernard 1987; Kasperson 1966.

13. On the famine see Kapella 1983; Billiri 1982. On resistance activities see Tsoucalas 1989; Frangopoulos 1986.

14. For a documented account of the events leading up to Dodecanese unification with Greece see Frangopoulos (1952 vol. 3; 1994).

15. Cf. Kasperson 1966: 149–52.

16. See Agapitidis 1986; Korkoli 1990.

17. Bernard 1987: 176; and for a detailed account of the cigarette industry see Sakellaridis 1986b.

18. On these recent development, see Mertzanis 1994.

19. Leontis 1995: 66. Cf. Graburn's (1995) review of the anthropological literature on tourism and the commodification of the past.

20. Geertz 1987. For an early analysis of such arrival stories, see Pratt 1986.

21. Houses are owned by women on Kalymnos, a subject explored in Chapter 5. For a discussion of the impact of tourism on female house-ownership, see Galani-Moutafi 1994.

22. The "no" which marked the rejection by Greece of an Italian ultimatum and which launched the country into the Second World War.

23. This is the center of Kalymnos' citrus production.

24. I do not mean this as an indictment or an analysis of the workings of bureaucracy in Greece. For such analysis the reader should see Herzfeld (1992b).

25. My return in 1996 had a number of new surprises of this kind: two "cafes" purveying fresh-brewed espresso and cappucino, and a store offering fresh "American style" doughnuts.

Kalymnian Constructions of Identity and Otherness

two

> [Modernity] generates meaningful struggles because people have a commitment to the term. More than a specific set of practices, modernity is a story that people tell themselves about themselves in relation to Others. It is a powerful story because nation-states organize the body politic around it . . . As a story, it can illuminate matters and affect people's consciousness. But it can also fool and mislead us.
>
> (Rofel 1992)

Introduction

An entrée into the ways that Kalymnians think about tradition and history is to examine how they define themselves, what makes up Kalymnian identity. In using the term "identity" I am not importing a concept that is foreign to the Kalymnians themselves. Even if they do not commonly use the phrase "Kalymnian identity" (ταυτότητα), they are most eager to discuss what characterizes "The Kalymnian" (usually referred to in the masculine singular). What are his strengths, what are his faults, and what explains these traits? It is a topic that Kalymnians are quite comfortable discussing, at a time when, as Sahlins puts it, "culture . . . is on everyone's lips" (1993: 3). Here, however, I will begin with the way Kalymnians talk about "others." The structuralist insight that identity is always relational, always defined in opposition to at least one other, leads me to seek Kalymnians in their images of what they are not. Even if this way of entering into a discussion of Kalymnian identity might not be approved by my Kalymnian subjects, it is nevertheless one that they will recognize, since they too are interested in the topic of what characterizes other "peoples" (λαοί), and how they compare. To extend Sahlins' point, it is remarkable to what extent a Kalymnian laborer or shopkeeper employs terminology similar to that of an anthropologist in theorizing on his/her own, Kalymnian, character and on that of others. Those who had traveled to neighboring islands or further abroad could describe in detail various religious and other rituals that they observed, and comment on the similarities to, and differences from, corresponding Kalymnian rituals and customs. The discovery that I was an anthropologist (a term which more people understood than I had expected) often led to queries as to my view of how different cultures and peoples compared, what could be learned from each people, and which people I found to be the most true (σωστός). I found this last question particularly difficult; but it alerted me to the fact that while Kalymnian curiosity may extend further than this particular world-historical moment, there is a certain urgency to these speculations about themselves and others. It is an urgency encapsulated in the issue of "modernity" (εκσυγχρονισμός), and the relationship of "the old years" (τα παλιά τα χρόνια) to the rampant changes that Kalymnians see around them and have sometimes initiated themselves.[1] While "modernization" has been a key analytic concept in early anthropological work on Greece, it has only recently and tangentially been incorporated into more encompassing formulations of issues concerning identity and the past.[2]

In this chapter I explore how present-day identity is constructed through comparisons of a past, identified in spatial and temporal terms as "the old years," "first" (πρώτα), or "our tradition" (η παράδοσή μας), with an encroaching present, located in spatio-temporal terms as "modern." As one older Kalymnian put it, "It took hundreds of years to go from the stone age to the bronze age, but we have seen life on Kalymnos totally transformed in the past thirty years. It will be different for the present generation, but for the older generation it's hard to adapt, because we remember the way it used to be." Quite simply, Kalymnians view the question of how they have adapted and continue to adapt to modernity as the most significant moral issue facing them in the present. By hinging my discussion of these processes on Kalymnians' views of others, I will be able to explore the ways that they situate themselves in a world system that they have been drawn ever more tightly into with the recent boom in tourism, foreign products and television, and interdependence within the European Community. Thus the urgency to carve out a place within this system, and to ford the *scylla and charybdis* of either loss of identity that they fear modernity brings, or of hewing too close to the past and being left behind.

Thus, I will examine this native Kalymnian anthropology for what it reveals about the complex ways people formulate the issues encapsulated by the words "modernity" and "tradition," and their ambivalent attitudes towards these issues. The first Kalymnian others I will discuss are the "Europeans" (Ευρωπαίοι). In a way the Europeans fall most easily into a binary distinction between modernity and the past, as they are often held in opposition to the "backward" Turks. How Kalymnians locate themselves in terms of these oppositions, however, is more ambiguous. I will then discuss more tangible Kalymnian others: their neighboring islanders, for whom the Kalymnians have developed a complex characterological discourse, but who are also positioned, in shifting, contextual ways along the axis of modernity. In turning to the Kalymnians' view of "Americans" who are further away and, for many Kalymnian migrants, even more tangible than the above, I will show how the tradition/modernism dualism, even at its most elastic, fails to capture the complexities of how Kalymnians see themselves historically. I will conclude this chapter by exploring the implications of all these discourses for how Kalymnians see themselves moving into the future.

Up and Down: Europe, Turkey and the Scale of Civilization

Kalymnians ascribe to Europe the modernity that Kalymnos is seen as either lacking or in the process of acquiring. Almost any object or practice associated with Europe may be given the epithet "modern" (εκσυγχρονισμένος): a child born with blond hair is "more modern" than her dark-haired sibling. Or a teenager who wants to continue his education is more modern than his brother who wants to become a builder. Hygienic practices are a prime example of this labelling. Several people told me that Europeans bathe very frequently, and this habit is only now coming into fashion on Kalymnos. This identification of bathing with "Europeanness" was brought home to me when a neighbor was trying to convince a plumber to come and fix my hot-water system immediately. She noted that I was a "European" and thus needed to take a bath every day. There was also an implication that it would be shameful to leave the hot water tank unfixed for the "European," since it would reveal Kalymnos' lack of civilization. This example highlights how "European" is not used in any literal sense, since she well knew that I was from the United States; I was only "European" in my desire to bathe frequently. People also observe that the Italians, during their occupation of these islands, built beautiful toilets on Kos and Rhodes. Kalymnians, who resisted Italian rule and thus were cut off from European influence, remained "backward" in this regard. I also heard a number of humorous stories about ignorant Kalymnian migrants' first experience with toilets.[3] This association between sanitation and "modernization" was also pointed out by Friedl, working in Vasilika in the late 1950s. She reported the villagers' desire to acquire concrete outhouses to replace the "Turkish toilets" they had previously used. They did so not in the belief that these provided better sanitation, "but because the villagers' urban relatives have been ridiculing them for not having some kind of toilet" (Friedl 1962: 42). Similarly, while it may be the goal of every Kalymnian household to have a "modern" bathroom, bathing is not viewed as an unqualified good on an island that often suffers from shortages of water. As one older man joked: "We used to take baths once a week. Our children have made it once a day. I wonder if their children will spend all their time in the bathtub and only get out when necessary." I heard a number of similar statements that associate hygiene with the loss of sociability, identified by Kalymnians with the modern condition.

In the above examples, Kalymnians portray themselves as backward, but they do not believe themselves to be as far behind Europe as the Turks who, it is claimed, lack even the most rudimentary conveniences. Kalymnos is considered to be a midway point: it still retains many "eastern" (ανατολικά) characteristics from its years of Ottoman rule, but it is moving along the historical–geographical road to "modernization-civilization." This is a reason why the Italian Occupation of Kalymnos is often remembered favorably: the Italians are seen as having brought a civilized, European influence to the island in opposition to the years of Turkish barbarity.[4] In an example during my fieldwork in 1992, the Greek government's claim to have given respectful treatment to Albanian refugees is regarded as an indication that Greece has become more civilized and European than it was in "the old days" and more civilized than the (Muslim) Albanian government, which was in the news at the time for restricting the minority Greek party's participation in its national elections.[5] On a more mundane level: when I complained to one older man that the Kalymnians seemed shameless in making eyes at my wife, he replied that this was because the Kalymnians are not fully Europeanized, but that only the older men still did such things – the younger generation had learned to behave differently. In many such examples some part of the Kalymnian or Greek past is negatively valued in contrast to positively valued modernized outsiders, though blame is often shifted to another exogenous force, the Turks. This sentiment is captured by the oft-repeated cry about all aspects of Kalymnian life that "we are very much behind" (είμαστε πολύ πίσω) and that "it will take us a long time to catch up with the rest of Europe."

This last remark suggests a spatial mapping independent of the geographical terms. "Behind" and "in front" are used to indicate backwardness and progress, respectively. More striking is the metaphoric use of "up" (πάνω) and "down" (κάτω) to refer to Kalymnos' relationship with the rest of the world. When one travels to Athens, to Europe, or to the United States one is going "up," and the return to Kalymnos is referred to as coming "down." While this is not wholly out of line with north–south relations, I noticed that the same terms are used

when Kalymnians talk about going to Australia. However, they are
not used when Kalymnians refer to neighboring islands such as Kos
and Rhodes, which are also south of Kalymnos. Clearly "up" suggests
more "developed" or "advanced," here. It perhaps also indicates that
Kalymnians do not think of the US, Europe and Australia in geographical terms, but imagine themselves going "up" to find work and
better themselves financially in these rich countries. Kos and Rhodes
are not subsumed in this socio-economic geography since, although
more developed than Kalymnos, they are not associated with
migration to advance oneself. Athens, on the other hand, is seen in
this way. Neighboring islands are within the same moral universe as
Kalymnos; consequently, they don't require the imaginative leap that
the term "up" implies.

These attitudes are unsurprising in light of: (a) the well-documented
history of modern Greece's attempts to make itself, in the eyes of
Europe and its own Europeanized intellectuals, what it claims to be,
i.e. "modern"; and (b) the assumption that to do so it must purify
itself of its "Eastern" trappings.[6] This can be seen in the exhortations
that Greece must catch up economically with the rest of Europe, and
in the many charts showing Greece trailing the rest of the EU at the
bottom in this or that economic category. This discourse can often be
extremely patronizing in tone, as in a special supplement on Greece
from the journal *The Economist*. Readers are told, for example, that
unless the Greeks are capable of "an *unprecedented* degree of self-
discipline, the economic disappointment of the past dozen years could
slide past the point of no return. For Greece's hopes of joining the
modern world, this would be as big a catastrophe as the humiliation
the Greek army suffered in Anatolia seventy years ago" (1993: 4;
emphasis mine). The author concludes optimistically, "Perhaps the
Greeks are emerging from the long mesmerizing spell that history
has cast upon them: perhaps they are coming out of their corner. If
they are, the best way they can show it is to do something about the
economy" (1993: 4).

While Kalymnians have absorbed and reproduced some of these
views of the meaning of European modernity in relation to their own
society, they can be equally critical of these notions. Indeed, to act or
present oneself in a European manner (παριστάνει τον Ευρωπαίο) is
to put on airs, or to act like you know better than other people. Thus
one man claimed that although his neighbor put on a necktie every
morning and acted important, he was just presenting himself as
European, since his house still stank. Another more ambivalent usage
was a grandmother who referred to the beauty of her newborn
grandchild by saying that the child had "specifications from the EU."
This comment reflects the idea that the European Community tries
to hold Greece to a standard of perfection. Kalymnians relish point-

ing out how the Europeans themselves (particularly in the wake of government scandals and the rise of neo-Nazism during the early 1990s) fail to live up to these standards.

The "European system" is also identified with a modernism that has corrupted the proper, old ways of doing things. For example, in discussing the changes in the preparation of the *kolliva* (κόλλυβα, a boiled wheat and sugar concoction that is blessed by the priest and used to memorialize one's dead kin), a couple in their late sixties told me that in Athens you can buy pre-prepared *kolliva* outside the church, but that it is covered with flour instead of sugar. They explained that this is because the Athenians don't eat it as the Kalymnians do (in an act of communality in which each person feeds a spoon to his or her neighbors and to the neighborhood children), but just throw it away. Their comment on this situation was that Athens was part of the European system and that Athenians didn't do things correctly any more.[7] Here "European" is associated with a surface performance that lacks the substance or authenticity of the Kalymnian way. On the other hand, it also suggests a denial – an attempt to hide one's roots or humble origins behind a hollow façade – this metaphor applies to the personal and the national level.

The Neighboring Islands

The issue of modernity reappears in Kalymnian discussions of more tangible, closer-to-home "others": the Kalymnians' neighboring islanders. As noted, Kalymnians recount with enthusiasm and detail the rituals they have observed on different islands, and the differences between these and their own rituals. They are happy to discuss the characterological differences among different islanders.[8] Their opinions are undoubtedly tainted by the fierce spirit of competitiveness between Kalymnians and the neighboring islands, particularly Kos and Leros.[9] By talking about their neighbors, they further explore their views about what it is to be Kalymnian.

First, they regard the women of Kos and Leros as sexually promiscuous, a characteristic associated with European tourism. The issue of promiscuity is certainly of greater concern to Kalymnian men; however, it should be noted that Kalymnian women do not dispute these claims, and add their own stories of the legendary resistance of Kalymnian women to rape by foreign conquerors. The promiscuity of other islanders is associated with the men's sexual passivity and the women's sexual receptivity. This is illustrated by hyperbolic claims that every woman on Leros has two husbands (a claim that I also heard made about the Europeans), or that men on Kos don't object if you sleep with their daughters, they say it doesn't matter (δε βαριέσαι). This passivity is given historical foundation and expanded to the political level in the widespread claim on Kalymnos that they were the only island that resisted the Italian occupation of the Dodecanese.[10] In support of this, Kalymnians cite the evidence that there are no Italian surnames on Kalymnos since the few Kalymnian women who had relations with Italians were killed or exiled, whereas you will find many Italian names on the other islands.

This defense of Kalymnos' purity against outside corruption takes another form: an extreme localism (είμαστε τοπικιστές). Kalymnians often (and only half-jokingly) refer to their island as "the navel of the earth" (o ομφαλός της γης).[11] This love of their island allegedly drives Kalymnians to return to Kalymnos even after migrating and having lived for twenty-five or thirty years abroad. I do not know whether there is any statistical evidence for a greater return-migration to Kalymnos than to other islands. However, it is interesting that this Kalymnian claim seems to have gained general acceptance; other islanders who live on Kalymnos will insist it is true that on their island, by comparison with Kalymnos, people do not return home to stay after having migrated abroad. This is a source of amusement for other islanders, since Kalymnians wax poetical about an island that a Koan described as having "no nice beaches, no vegetation, just a few houses on barren rock."[12]

Another mark of this Kalymnian localism is on the landscape – there are very few Italian buildings on Kalymnos as compared to Kos, Leros or Rhodes. This may have been for strategic reasons since these other islands had greater military significance than Kalymnos, nevertheless, the Kalymnians insist it is another sign of their intractability. As I discuss below, this can be perceived as a negative characteristic: many Kalymnians complain that if they had not resisted the Italians they would possess the good roads and other public facilities enjoyed by other islands, and that other islanders correspondingly tease Kalymnians for lacking.

Thus other islanders are seen as having let foreigners in (to their islands and their bodies) and having abandoned their islands. One might say that Kalymnians regard themselves as having less permeable borders than those of their fellow Dodecanesians.[13] Other islanders are also viewed as historically passive insofar as they have not preserved their traditions and customs as vigorously as the Kalymnians. These include expressive culture – songs and dances, rituals, holidays – as well as different aspects of hospitality and sociability. I was told repeatedly that only on Kalymnos will you find people willing to treat you with hospitality, to see you as a person.[14] On Kos the people have been ruined by tourism and are only interested in you for your money. On Leros people are on the "European system" and never go out to coffee shops to engage in social exchange, but stay locked up in their homes, not willing to spend the 400 drachmas on coffee.[15] In these cases the instrumental attitude toward money is seen as characteristic of their neighbors, and once again as a European characteristic *par excellence*. Anti-sociability is also seen as a European trait, it is believed that most Europeans and Americans lead a dull, robotic life between work and television. Life in the industrialized West has been de-ritualized, and thus there is nothing in the year to look forward to, nothing to make one day different from the next. At Easter time and on other ritual occasions people would tell me to go and see all the ceremonies and to bring my wife along too, because "you do not have such things in America." Ritual practices are seen as setting off the regular routine and giving specialness to life; without these rituals "American" and "European" life must indeed seem robotic. This crit-ique is particularly interesting, since it deftly illustrates cultural presuppositions. Foreigners who have married Kalymnians and live on the island, and Kalymnians who grew up in Australia and the US, make the same accusation of dullness against Kalymnos owing to its lack of entertainment from a Western perspective, i.e. shopping, movie theaters, restaurants, etc.

Insofar as ceremonial customs are believed to have been more lively and full of joy in the past, this diminution is viewed as one of the negative aspects of modernization and the commodification of life. This is encapsulated in the opinion, expressed by many older people, that Kalymnians no longer have high spirits (κέφι). This idea is captured by Kalymnian writer Niki Billiri in her essay about Carnival on Kalymnos "then" and "now." She writes, "Carnival passed quickly this year, but nobody distinguished it from the typical days of work and routine . . . Where has our enthusiasm, our κέφι gone, and that wellspring, that motive force that made the whole island shake with laughter and joy" (Billiri 1982; my translation). In order to become part of memory special days must be marked out as different from the routine of work. Significantly, Niki Billiri told me in an interview that she felt that her work of writing about Kalymnian traditions and customs was necessary because of the European Union and the loss of specialness and identity that integration entailed.

The Kalymnian claim that they defend their traditions is similar to their claim to have less permeable borders than their fellow islanders. Kalymnians relate these claims to two traits that they consider to be constitutive aspects of their identity. The first is the hardness of their character: a result of having to eke out a living on such a barren island or to go abroad in search of work.[16] As one man put it, the Kalymnian is like a cactus growing in the desert: it must suffer under the most adverse conditions to produce any fruit. This fruit is beautiful, but it has to work very hard to achieve it. Kalymnians discuss this char-acteristic in relation to their sponge-diving past, a time when people were so tough that, it is said, if anyone came between a sponge-diver and his livelihood, the only proper course was to kill him (να τον χαλάσεις; "to spoil him"). I heard a number of stories about how Kalymnians would cut the lines, effectively killing divers from other islands who they didn't want to learn the sponge-diving trade. This hardness was equally true of Kalymnian women. When I puzzled to a young Kalymnian man about how easily an older woman talked about producing children in order to fight the Turks,[17] he responded: "You must understand, this was the generation that attacked the Italian occupying force armed only with rocks. That's the kind of mentality we're dealing with."

It is interesting to note how little sponge-diving is associated with the core of Kalymnian identity, despite Kalymnos' reputation throughout Greece as the "island of sponge-divers." While I encountered one intellectual's opinion that Kalymnos had lost its identity because it no longer practised sponge-diving, many others implicitly or explicitly refuted this idea. Most described sponge-diving as a completely inhumane job, something that "you wouldn't send your dog to do." One older man made the analogy that to suggest to your neighbor today that their son become a sponge-diver because he can make good money at it (a handful of boats still go out), is the equivalent of telling him that his daughter should become a prostitute. Sponge-diving, then, is an example of the toughness of the Kalymnian character that results from the island's barrenness. It is this hardness (of island and character), rather than sponge-diving, that constitutes Kalymnian identity.

This hardness, it is claimed, also leads Kalymnians to do everything to excess – whether it is dynamite throwing, fooling officials or other islanders in deals, even shopping. This excessiveness may be interpreted as an aspect of *eghoismós* (εγωϊσμός), i.e. the male competitive expression of self-regard that is reportedly prevalent among many Greek communities. It is interesting that Kalymnian women are also seen to embody this excessiveness and the toughness discussed above. This is apparent in the areas of shopping and consumption, which are the most frequently cited examples of Kalymnian excessiveness. Kalymnians all accept that they must buy things in bulk: for example, no one would think of buying just one kilo of oranges. Most store owners claim they can recognize tourists immediately because they buy in small quantities – only what they need for one meal. One man told me how he was too embarrassed to charge a tourist for a single apple and two bananas, and gave them to her for free.[18] Kalymnians make similar claims about Koans and Rhodians – they will buy a few kilos of lamb, just what their family needs for Easter – while each Kalymnian family will require two lambs. A Koan woman may have an extra blanket or two when guests come to stay, but a Kalymnian woman has a huge stack (στοίβα). When I questioned one man, who lived alone, why he felt he had to buy in bulk, he first hedged and said he tried to use everything, but then admitted that if you were seen buying only half a kilo of cheese someone would no doubt ask, "Is Yiannis so poor that he can't afford a kilo?" As for fooling other islanders, folklorist Niki Billiri describes the situation as follows: "Every morning the Kalymnian peddlers would come ashore in Kos, buy whatever they needed . . . and take it back to sell on Kalymnos, and they would always find a way to take advantage of them [the Koans]. The Kalymnians considered the Koans to be Cows [βόδια] and had the following saying about Kos: "O, land of Hippocrates, what donkeys you now produce" (1986: 223). This characterization of Koans as farm animals is related to the general disdain for agriculture expressed by Kalymnians. As agriculturalists, Koans are "soft" and "lazy", compared to "hard" and "adventuresome" Kalymnian seamen. Women's participation in agricultural work perhaps also marks Koan men as sexually passive: it is claimed that Koan men are so lazy they will allow their wives to do heavy labor while they sit in coffee shops.

When I asked the Kalymnians not what they thought of other islanders, but what other islanders thought of them, they claimed that they were seen as wild (άγριοι), barbaric and backward.[19] The few Koans and Lerians with whom I discussed Kalymnos held such views; they claimed, for example, that Kalymnos had no high culture, music or theater. Kalymnians regard the "Europeanization" of the other islands with a certain irony. They are quick to insist that before tourism injected easy money into Kos, the Koans were poorer and more backward than the Kalymnians. Kalymnians cite the Koans's agri-cultural lifestyle as evidence for poverty and sedateness. I even heard the suggestion that Koans used to be so poor that they would bring their babies to Kalymnos and exchange them for food. From the Kalymnian perspective the Koans may have some trappings of Europeanness, but they more resemble the backwardness and laziness that the Kalymnians associate with the Turks.[20]

If, in many cases, neighboring islanders and Athenians seem to resemble Europeans, Turks or Americans more than they do Kalym-nians, how do Kalymnians reconcile this with a sense of Greek national identity? For, as Balibar notes, the nation unifies its people "not by suppressing all differences, but by relativizing them and subordinating them to itself in such a way that it is the symbolic difference between 'ourselves' and 'foreigners' which wins out and which is lived as irreducible" (cited in Gourgouris, 1992a: 46). Kalymnians often expressed uncertainty among themselves and to me as to whether such traits as hospitality are "Kalymnian" or "Greek." This doubt is understandable since Kalymnian ideology dovetails in many respects with the national ideology, even down to their self-criticism that Greeks/Kalymnians can work together only under conditions of external threat, and once the threat is removed they bicker among themselves again. It seems that we have a similar case to how Herzfeld (1985: Chapter 1) has described Cretan mountain villagers: Kalymnians see themselves as Greeks *par excellence*, as opposed to other islanders who have lost that identity under the influence of tourism. However, the characterological differences between themselves and the Koans (for example), are not of recent manufacture, nor are they totally accounted for by the discourse of the preservation or loss of a common identity. On the one hand, this problem never arises because these identity discussions are always contextual and all the different terms are rarely brought together in a totalizing view. On the other hand, whenever the problem of internal difference is raised, it is addressed readily by Kalymnians in terms of their double myth of Greek identity: Kalymnos was settled by the Doric peoples rather than the Ionic. They claim that one can attribute to this "founding fact" many of the characterological differences between themselves and other islanders, or between themselves and Athenians, from the "harshness" of Kalymnian language, to their wild behavior as exemplified by their risk-taking lifestyle. For some, then, it is this heterogeneity at the source of Greek identity that explains the present-day heterogeneity which might otherwise seem problematic in relation to a unified national identity.

Thus far what I have described as the Kalymnians' views of other islanders corresponds to Hirschon's claim that Asia Minor refugees living in Piraeus used putative local characterological and historical differences in order to preserve their collective identity and not be absorbed into the mainstream population. She refers to this phenomenon as a type of borderline ethnic-group formation in what is fundamentally a similar population (1993: 353). While my evidence supports such a view of identity preservation to some extent, it is also interesting that Kalymnians can use these blanket characterizations for self-criticism, and as an impetus for change. The same people who might be critical of Koan laziness will also claim that the Koans seem to work together much more easily than the Kalymnians do. While Koans may take advantage of tourists (i.e. outsiders), they are not cunning (πονηροί) nor do they exploit each other and their fellow islanders as do the Kalymnians, who consider themselves notorious for such exploits. Similarly, the person who criticized the sexual promiscuity of women from other islands, on another occasion was equally critical of the Kalymnian men who had taken advantage of this through sexual adventures. These examples may be double-edged insofar as the Kalymnians criticize themselves for being more intelligent (or cunning), more individualistic and (in the men's case) more sexually potent than other islanders. Nevertheless they often represent outcries against the oppressive feeling of competition for success and money that requires these social skills and that often divides families in such a "small place" as Kalymnos.

America: Land of Lost Innocence

It is through the ideas discussed above that many Kalymnians represent "America" as an ideal contrast to Kalymnos. While their personal experience of Europe tends to be remote, many Kalymnians have lived in the United States for extended periods of time,[21] so that discussions of the United States often derive from first-hand experience.[22] In talking about "Americans" Kalymnians have a tendency to attribute to them the characteristics felt to be lacking in present-day Kalymnos but that were common in the past. Above all, Americans are said to be honest and straightforward: they believe what you tell them and correspondingly do not try to undermine each other in their work or in their political system. It is for these reasons that America is seen to have prospered – because Americans do not attempt to "eat" (take advantage of or undermine) each other and do not view each other's accomplishments with envy. Instead of trying to bring your neighbor down to your own level, as the Kalymnian does, the American will aim to excel and surpass his/her neighbor.

Americans are regarded as not overly concerned with politics. From the Kalymnians' perspective this is a positive trait since many feel that their society has been destroyed by political infighting at national and local levels. One Kalymnian who had lived for several years in the United States told me of his astonishment at how people would go to work on election day as if it were just like any other day; whereas here life stops for an election, and people on opposite sides refuse to speak to each other for weeks. Thus, America allows you to live without cunning – the trait seen both as necessary for success and responsible for corrupting social relations on Kalymnos.

Kalymnians constantly stated that their society had been ruined by gossip, backbiting, infighting and the cunning at the heart of these. A few days after my arrival on Kalymnos I met a woman whom I knew from a previous trip. When I told her that I had come to study Kalymnians and what they think about things, she responded with a snort: "What they think! All they think about is eating each other!" (πώς ο ένας να φάει τον άλλο). When people told me about something they had done that was not quite legitimate, they would say with a smile that they had followed the "Kalymnian" system. This in a sense freed them of individual guilt, because they were indulging in a flaw shared by the community. Perhaps the most common complaint I heard, particularly from Kalymnian women (old and young), was that they were tired of trying to manage their affairs with the nosiness and interference of the community, but such was life on Kalymnos.

For Kalymnian women "America" conjures up another set of contrasts favorable to the United States. Older women who may have spent twenty or thirty years in the States, before returning to Kalymnos when their husbands retire, miss the relative freedom from menial tasks that they enjoyed in America, and the more readily available entertainment such as movie theaters. They note that their husbands came back to Kalymnos to sit in the coffee shops, while they, once again, have to work all day and have no such outlets. Thus a number of older women told me that they would have preferred to stay in America. Younger women in particular look to America for the freedom of movement and freedom from comment on their behavior that they do not have in Kalymnos. This problem is not restricted to women. For example, a divorced man in his sixties complained that in America he could have remarried, but here in Kalymnos people talk; they wonder why you got divorced and whether, in remarrying, you will be making the same mistake again. Thus it's not so easy. As the expression goes: "Kalymnos is a small place" (είναι μικρό το μέρος), followed by a shrug as if to say, "What do you expect?"

Although America, Europe and neighboring islands are all employed in different contexts as a foil for those parts of Kalymnian society people want to criticize, each is used in a different way. Neighboring islanders, as the "others" Kalymnians know best, are given the most elaborate characterological treatment. They provide Kalymnos with an anatomy of how various foreign (European, Turkish, American) traits "look" when grafted onto a common Greek body. Europe provides the "modernist" future that Kalymnians see sometimes positively, sometimes negatively, most often with ambivalence. But "America" represents Kalymnos' past, the good old days, when people were more straightforward, did not fight over party politics or try to undermine and "eat" each other. America provides spatially the distance that "the past" provides temporally – a purchase on the present.[23] This represents a surprising inversion of my expectations which may be explained in part by the experiences of the generation of migrants who had returned to Kalymnos since the 1970s having spent twenty-five to thirty years in the US. They left after the Second World War when Kalymnos was impoverished, but proud of its resistance to the Italians and Germans and of its newly acquired freedom. Those who had returned had usually accomplished what they had set out to achieve: to make money and return home, rather than make a life for themselves in the US. After a relatively prosperous experience in the United States in which they had primary contact with the flourishing local Kalymnian community, and had never fully entered into American society to try to marry, rise in status and power, or to experience its peculiar inequities, they returned to an island in the midst of its own economic boom and concomitant changes. As one Kalymnian intellectual complained to me, "it's the return migrants who are the most against change, since they haven't lived the changes and want Kalymnos to be the way it was when they left it."

Progress and Decay

These issues raise the larger question of what are regarded as forces for change on Kalymnos. Kalymnians have the dual sense that group identity is something inherent (as noted above, they trace many of their characteristics to their Doric ancestry) and something that can be lost. Change is both a promise and a threat. Many see current changes coming from the influence of tourists and foreigners living permanently on Kalymnos. There is a sense that people can slowly lose their Kalymnian identity by observing these foreigners and adopting their habits and mores. For better or worse, the possibility of change is seen to have been given to the younger generation: they are the ones who interact with tourists, who inter-marry with foreigners, and who are raised on products imported from the West. The feeling of ambivalence is universal. Older Kalymnians perceive themselves as the last representatives of the "traditional" Kalymnian way of life, but they also applaud many of the changes in the younger generation – their broadmindedness and willingness to question what was taken for granted in the past. One man in his forties spoke with admiration of how foreigners and Koans go out and see the world: "Kalymnians only know how to work, and while I cannot change that for myself, I am teaching my children not to have that mentality." However, this man also feared that the European Union would entail the economic takeover of Greece by foreign, tourist developers. The young, too, act and express themselves with considerable ambivalence. A man in his late twenties who had dated a number of women tourists complained that he couldn't order a drink in Greek in many bars on Kalymnos. This complaint about the "standardization" (τυποποίηση) of life under European influence was echoed by a number of young Kalymnians. But a woman in her early twenties saw the influence of foreigners through the EU and tourism as the only hope for changing the Kalymnians' backward attitudes about sexual matters.

This ambivalence reflects a larger issue: that Kalymnians operate with at least two time-lines in thinking about their relationship to past, present and future. One is the time-line of progress from a backward state. This view is not always co-opted into the modernist European discourse, it can also have a Marxist tinge, as when people recounted to me how the priests, the rich and the politicians ruled Kalymnos unimpeded in the past. Back then "we lived in darkness" (είχαμε μεσάνυχτα) but now we have woken up. One woman claimed it was the availability of television sets and the advent of television news that allowed the average person to realize what scoundrels the

Yiannis Roditis "The milkman: A beautiful image of yesterday".

Kalymnian artist Yiannis Roditis, at work in his "modern" kitchen.

politicians and the powerful really were. Another example of this is the claim made by a few Kalymnians that people need to be less cunning in the present than they did in the past. One man said this was a result of universal literacy which meant that ordinary people no longer feared being taken advantage of by lawyers and public officials, and thus didn't have to be so cunning. Another woman asserted that past poverty had led to strife but material wealth had alleviated this. She seemed to realize that this was an unusual opinion as she then suggested that things might have got better, but now they were getting worse again.

The second time-line is that of decay from a former state of grace and simplicity, a corruption by *la dolce vita* and by material desires. This view is described in the Greek ethnographic literature as closely connected to the ideology of Greek Orthodoxy.[24] However, it is not restricted to one ideology, though it does perhaps find its purist expression among the religious devotees of the island. As one particularly devout shop owner said in describing the world situation: "It is the quest for money, orchestrated by the devil that makes us worse and worse as time passes." It is accepted by the most religious Kalymnians that miracles no longer occur as they did in the past because the people have strayed so far from God. But the idea that people used to be more generous and neighborly on Kalymnos is held by young and old, religious and non-religious alike. What is interesting here is that notions of progress and decay can often express themselves in the same discourse, as is the case in the conflicts and ambivalences over modernity discussed above. Another illustrative example is how one man described the difference between Greek priests and the Italian priests who were on Kalymnos during the Occupation. The Italian priests were all more "civilized": they would stop to kiss babies and pat children on the head. The man also recalled acts of personal generosity toward him on the part of Italian priests, and one in particular who had allowed him to look into his telescope. The Greek priests, by contrast, don't have the time of day for you unless they want to collect money. He went on to comment on how the Greek Church, in comparison with its Italian counterpart, is in "the dark ages," stuck at "midnight." The Italian churches were well designed, they always had seats for everyone, and the congregation was respectful and quiet in church, not gossiping like the Kalymnians. Greek churches were just beginning to obtain seats inside and other necessary items. The man's wife said it was true that other churches may not have the "true" Orthodox religion, but they believe and respect what they are taught, while we who have the true religion no longer follow it. She quoted a biblical passage: νόμον δεν έχουν και νόμον πράττουν ([the other races] don't have laws, but they follow the laws). Here the ideology of progress is encapsulated in the claim that the Greek Church is only now acquiring the trappings of modernity that the Italian

Church has possessed for a long time. However, there is also the sense of decay. The man told me how the Greek priests have become increasingly concerned with money, not like in "the old days" when nobody had anything. This idea is also found in the wife's statement that the Greeks no longer practice their religion and have drifted away from it, unlike the "other races" (αλλόφυλοι). It is noteworthy that in all these comparisons the Italians remain unaffected by time. The Italian priests from the 1930s are compared to the Greek priests of the 1990s. Greece is perceived to be in motion, affected by various changes and historical developments, but the Italians lack history and exist as a static contrast in the creation of Greek identity.

The outcome of the Kalymnians' keen observation and their discussions of how they see themselves and their future, is ambiguous. Kalymnos' multiple others have the effect of shoring up local identity in the sense that any identity discourse does: by defining who they are not, the Kalymnians can better say who they are. But the curious effect of the Kalymnians having so many others against whom to define themselves is to leave very few aspects of Kalymnian life unexamined. Religion, politics, food, dowry, character, sex, money: Kalymnians are good anthropologists insofar as they believe that they do each of these things a certain way not because "that's the way things are" but because "that's the way we do it." Like anthropologists, they recognize that what is cultural is also changeable. With everything now up for grabs, the appeal to an imagined past, i.e. "we do things because that's the way our parents did them," must struggle for legitimacy with the appeal to an imagined future: "we must change in order to be part of Europe."

One of the few unchallenged assumptions on which the rest hinges for Kalymnians is that there is such a thing as Kalymnian identity: singular, cutting across class and gender, with its more perfect embodiment in the past, and only its prospective loss in the future. Kalymnians do not seem to confront the idea of internal difference, that there can be many ways to be Kalymnian. The absence of any consensual hierarchy of class or status has been noted in Greece (see Just 1994). Just describes the Ionian island village where he worked as "a community that recognized no group's claim to established superiority, but in which the assertion 'we are all (just) people' was endlessly repeated . . . in a world in which cleavages and animosities related not to class but to the relatively impermanent successes and failures of individuals and their families" (1994: 38). This echoes the evidence I found on Kalymnos. Kalymnians universally insisted that economic success did not confer status on its recipients. Although Kalymnians associated the former sponge-merchant families with the "first class" (της πρώτης τάξης), they argued that these families were not really "first class" because they were either morally compromised or so spendthrift that they did not benefit from their wealth. Nor were the "objective" features of class difference evident in present-day Kalymnos. These features are defined by Bennett (1988: 218) as "systematic and permanent differences in control of critical resources among groups in the population, social barriers between these groups, and an awareness by the participants of common interests within each group and different interests among them."

The Dodecanese islands, as Dimitriou-Kotsoni (1993) argues, are distinctive in comparison to the rest of Greece in that they never have had the large-scale agricultural *tsiftliks* prevalent in parts of mainland Greece, or the large property holdings which formed the bases of class distinctions between landowners and rural peasantry described by Bennett with reference to the Pelion Peninsula. However, this is not to deny the existence of class differences in the period before the Second World War on Kalymnos, when a few sponge-merchants employed the majority of the island's population (see Chapter 4). Thus, as Just (1994) suggests, the current absence of class or status difference may be a historical "hiccup," and class may be in the process of "re-formation" along the axes of education, professional status and consumption habits (i.e. cultural capital). Certainly the past twenty years since the mid-1970s have been marked by a tremendous increase in the availability of all kinds of consumer goods. In 1970 there were few private cars on Kalymnos. Now BMWs and Mercedes vie for space on the island's narrow roads alongside approximately 9,000 motor-cycles and motorbikes. If every family owns at least one form of transport, they also own at least one television and probably a video-recorder too. The structure of production on Kalymnos has also changed: Kalymnians used to be involved in relatively non-competitive work: as fishermen, sponge-divers, craftspeople and agriculturalists. Oppression, when it was felt, was perceived to be from above, for example, from rich families who served as bankers for the island at exorbitant interest rates. Now, in the 1990s, large proportions of the population are either store owners or public servants in various capacities (where the competition for "cushy" jobs is quite fierce), and a very different relationship is mandated with one's neighbors. I occasionally heard complaints that, "In American you can marry whoever you want, but on Kalymnos you marry someone for their occupation." There may exist the seeds for future status hierarchy on Kalymnos, but such distinctions have yet to express themselves in a sense of internal differences in Kalymnian identity.

Conclusion: Beyond Tradition and Modernity

Vassos Argyrou, in his book *Tradition and Modernity in the Mediterranean*, gives a somewhat different picture of the meaning of these categories in present-day discourse. In a situation where status hierarchies have become fairly entrenched, "modernity" and "tradition" are seen by Cypriots to represent statically the different attributes of the urban bourgeoisie and the rural working class, respectively. Argyrou perceives the urban bourgeoisie as embracing a Western "modernity" that will always find them trying to catch up with Western Europe. The rural workers despise their urban cousins for their lack of "authenticity" (a criticism made particularly ironic as it comes from the mouths of Western visitors as well). However, they also "secretly envy" the bourgeoisie for their privileges. Thus the rural workers embrace "tradition," but in doing so they "relinquish any claims to the privileges that [modern] life provides. By stigmatizing the culture of the bourgeoisie, the working classes signify contentment with their dominated position in the sociocultural order" (Argyrou 1996: 176). In remarking upon the way these categories entrap the Cypriots in a losing game, Argyrou makes an important point. There is a sense, as I have shown, that many of the categories the Kalymnians work with are predetermined by values that undermine their way of life. The notion that "we are very backward" posits European modernity as the only yardstick for progress, and burdens the imagination of many Kalymnians.

But here parallels between Kalymnos and Cyprus tend to break down. Owing to the lack of class stratification, at least in the way Kalymnians perceive their own situation, there is no assignation of "modernity" and "tradition" to recognizable segments of the population. This means that while there are "modernizing" and "traditionalist" attitudes on Kalymnos, there are few individuals or groups of individuals, who would be classed as either modernist or traditionalist outside of specific situations.[25] Discourses of modernity and tradition, as will be shown in subsequent chapters, tend to be dependent on context and activity. People struggle with the meaning of these categories in their everyday discourses and experiences. On an expedition to pick grape leaves on Kos I was with a couple of women in their sixties who extolled the benefits of rural life. One woman of Kalymnian background who had spent her childhood on Kos reflected that she would have had a better life if she had remained on Kos and bound to the land, instead of returning to Kalymnos for an unhappy marriage. Another woman complained of chemical fertilizers and how food no longer tasted the way it used to, though it still was a far cry from the food that her son, living in the United States, had to contend with. Their dress and their husbands' occupations might suggest that they were "traditionalist." Their discussion of agriculture soon shifted to an agreement on the practical benefits of "modern" inventions such as computers, which can keep one's accounts better than one could before. If anything characterized their attitudes towards modernity, it was ambivalence. As one woman put it, "We want these things that have ruined us – they are very useful."

In charting these ambivalences I am not disagreeing with the thrust of Argyrou's argument that in using these categories, Kalymnians potentially reproduce the conditions of their own symbolic domination. Nevertheless, I think it is necessary to take people's assessments of their ambivalences toward "modernity" and "the old days" seriously. As I have shown, Kalymnians believe that modernity brings a "robotic, atomistic" existence, and they do not envy the Europeans their perceived lack of ritual or "high spirits" (κέφι). If at times they envy "modernity," they don't usually do it secretly, as is the case in Argyrou's analysis of the Cypriot working classes.

I have argued in this chapter that Kalymnian views of others do not fall neatly into the binary categories which have plagued many structuralist discussions of identity (see for example, Thomas 1992). Who is more "modern" and who more "traditional," the Kalymnians or the Americans? A simple grid cannot provide the answer. The category of "modernity" may structure certain relations, but its content is receptive to local imagination. Some would argue that the hegemony of Western modernity is rapidly coming to a historical close (for example, Friedman 1992). Andreas Papandreou, the leader of the PASOK party that Kalymnians overwhelmingly support, hoped to find a "third road to socialism," maintaining his distance from Soviet and European Social-Democratic models. Kalymnians, in different ways, look for their own roads as well. And *pace* Fukuyama (1992), this story has not ended.

Notes

1. In a book claiming to lay out local categories of pastness, it is important to be clear on vocabulary. Kalymnians did not in normal conversation oppose "modernity" to "tradition" or "custom" (ήθη και έθιμα, literally: habits and customs), despite my earlier formulation of the issue in these terms (Sutton 1994). I realize now that the choice of this translation in my original title for this chapter – "tradition and modernity" – was more an artefact of my analytic categories than the actual words in common use. Instead they used the phrases I have suggested here: the old years, first, and the concept of "backwardness" discussed below. They did see "tradition" and "custom" as making up part of what they considered "the old years," as is noted below, and is analyzed in detail in the following three chapters which examine particular practices referred to as "custom" and "tradition."

2. For earlier approaches see Friedl 1962; du Boulay 1974. More recent formulations include Argyrou 1996; Cowan 1988; Stewart 1991: Chapter 4.

3. In the national newspaper *Apoyevmatiní* (1992) one writer complained about what he felt to be the sub-standard toilet facilities around the Acropolis, noting that "just because we are part of the Balkans doesn't mean we have to act like the Balkans." The fact that the Acropolis is what is seen first by Europeans and other foreigners visiting Greece is no doubt of prime importance in this writer's shame.

4. For a discussion of how well this selective remembrance fits with the historical record, see Doumanis 1997: Chapter 6.

5. This was prior to the Greek government's "Operation Mop-up" during which a disputed number of illegal Albanian migrants were rounded up and returned to Albania amid accusations of human-rights violations.

6. See Herzfeld 1982a; Kyriakidou-Nestoros 1986.

7. The throwing away of *kolliva* is a blasphemous act, since, like communion bread and wine, it must be completely consumed. It also suggests the breaking of kin obligations, since it is consumed for the memory of one's dead ancestors. This can be seen in connection with the fear that in going to Athens (or to any place far away from Kalymnos) one will forget one's kin obligations (I owe these insights into the *kolliva* to Laurie Hart. See also Zairi 1989).

8. Folklorist Niki Billiri (1986: 223–40) has collected numerous old sayings about the various different islanders, leading me to suspect that these distinctions are not of recent provenance. For the characterological "teasing" that goes on between different islanders when they gather together, see Skardhasis 1979: 36–9.

9. This competition was expressed to me repeatedly in the claim that when Kalymnos plays Kos or Leros at soccer, the emotions run higher than when Greece plays Turkey.

10. A claim that is also made by local historians. See, for example, Frangopoulos (1952).

11. See Skardhasis 1979: 15–18. This Kalymnian essayist sets out to prove that the reputation Kalymnians have as "boasters" (μεγάλαυχοι) among their neighboring islanders is undeserved. Not because Kalymnians don't make claims about the superiority of their island, but because those claims can be all proven to be true.

12. There seems to be a greater tendency for Kalymnian men to extol the physical beauties of their island, perhaps reflecting the fact that women stay somewhat more restricted to their own neighborhoods, and are less likely to go for a casual walk in the mountains.

13. Significantly, the word that the Kalymnians use to refer to the Koans (normally Κώοι) is Κότες meaning "chickens." One man explained the genesis of this nickname as going back to when the Italians had put the Koans to guard the island against the Germans. Instead of carrying out their duty they fell asleep and allowed the Germans to invade unmolested. This led the Italians to refer to Koan men as chickens, and worse than women.

14. A variation of this claim, that we are hospitable and our neighbors are crooks, is perhaps made by every Greek village or island in reference to its neighbors (see for example, Stewart 1991: 47).

15. Kalymnians do not see any of these characterizations as absolute, the *sine qua non* of Kalymnian or non-Kalymnian identity, but rather as statistical means. They maintain that if you find 10 per cent of people on Kos who care about preserving their traditions, there will be 90 per cent on Kalymnos.

16. It is also claimed that Kalymnian love of education is produced by this need to find employment in a physically hostile environment.

17. She was referring to the Greek government's program of paying a stipend to mothers with many children, which she said was in order to produce more soldiers for the Greek army.

18. This is in accord with Herzfeld's (1991: Chapter 5) point, that the fluidity of social relations calls for the actor never to be seen counting or calculating, but always acting without regard to small figures.

19. Again this is a familiar contrast in the Greek ethnographic literature. Both Campbell (1964: 213) and Herzfeld (1985: 6) note such distinctions between shepherds and agriculturalists, with the shepherds stereotyped as wild and uncivilized and the agriculturalists as civilized but sexually passive and morally corrupt. Herzfeld's Cretan shepherds, like the Kalymnians, relate their moral purity to resistance to foreign domination.

20. While a few people made this explicit analogy, most Kalymnians will not criticize Turks characterologically, only culturally. That is, they criticize them as a people who are "behind," but not as individuals who are lazy or shiftless. Like most Greeks, they see the Turks as having only recently acquired the trappings of civilization, before which they knew only how to make war and to rule. But most Kalymnians are also committed to the idea that the bad things done by Turkey are the fault of the Turkish government and its expansionist cravings both in the past and currently. The Turkish people, Kalymnians insist, are perfectly honorable.

21. There are several flourishing Kalymnian communities in the US, the largest in Tarpon Springs, Florida and Campbell, Ohio. It should be noted that the other major destination for Kalymnian migration in the past 35 years has been Australia, in particular Sydney and Darwin. Kalymnos and Darwin are in fact sister cities, and there is a Darwin street in the main town of Kalymnos. I do not discuss the Kalymnian view of Australians in this book for the following reasons: 1) As an American myself, it was perhaps easier for me to explore the views that people held of America since I shared with them a set of references that I did not possess in the case of Australia; 2) in many cases I found that people who had returned from Australia had had very limited contact with the English-speaking population there, and had often not learned English even after ten to fifteen years in Australia; 3) the views of Australia which I was able to elicit did not differ significantly from those which I describe for America.

22. This is a generalization. It should be noted that Kalymnians do have

personal experience with Europeans through tourism, some migration, and, for the younger generation, study abroad. Through trade and their own tourism they also have some experience with individual Turks, which, as noted above, they separate from their image of Turkish civilization and the Turkish government. Similarly they have definite attitudes toward the American government and its role in the world (a subject I examine in Chapter 7), and some are also very critical of the wrongs perpetrated by the US government against African Americans and Native Americans. But they do not, in general, transfer these views to what they think of Americans "as a people."

23. The similarities between Kalymnian and anthropological discourse come to mind here once again, since Fabian, in his now classic *Time and the Other* (1983), has described the anthropological tendency to displace in time those peoples who are spatially distant from the "center."

24. See Campbell 1966: 163; Herzfeld 1987a: 33 ff.

25. A similar point has been made by Diamandouros (1993) in his discussion of what he calls the "modernizing" and "underdog" political cultures of Greece.

three

Debates on an Explosive Custom

Into the War Zone

I was warned about renting the house across from the churchyard. When I had moved into the neighborhood of Ayios Mammas, I had been directed by friends to a large house overlooking the main town. The only drawback, I was told was "the dynamite," (οι δυναμίτες) but that was only one night, at Easter, not worth worrying about. What I had visualized as a large fireworks display, however, turned out to be a bombing. Amid cries of "Christ is risen," several hundred pounds of TNT, formed into projectiles of two or three pounds each, were hurled into the sky from the church courtyard at midnight on Easter eve, rattling our house to its foundations, cracking two window-panes and sending the window-handles flying across the room. As the explosions continued sporadically throughout the day, I felt that I had gotten a taste of life in a war zone. I later found out that the dynamiting was considered to be light that year, and that the toll of damage was nothing compared to that of twelve years earlier, when four people were killed in what later became known as "the accident" (το ατύχημα).

During the following weeks and months, as I tried to make sense of this ritual practice, I found a debate surrounded it that was nearly as violent as the dynamiting itself. The debate centered on how islanders interpreted and represented dynamite: as a well-worn Kalymnian custom with considerable historical significance, or as a "folly," a barbarous practice by a group of irrational fellow islanders. This division of opinion points to the truth of the view of ritual as "less about giving voice to shared values than about opening fields of argument; about providing the terms and tropes, that is, through which people caught up in changing worlds may vex each other" (Comaroff and Comaroff 1993: xxiii). In this chapter I continue my discussion of Kalymnians' views of their past and their present identity as seen in relation to outside forces. I do so by focussing on a specific present-day practice to see how ideas about what is "custom" are mobilized to argue for and against the legitimacy of this practice. Dynamite throwing provides a "trope" in the Comaroffs' sense, by which Kalymnians discuss and debate their identity in a changing world. At the same time, as a ritual it cuts across normal social and political party divisions on Kalymnos.[1] It cannot be neatly explained by any political, class, gender or generational split on the island. As such, it offers insight into competing discourses on the meanings of "tradition" and "modernity" which might not be accessed through analysis of these socio-political divisions.

The "invention of tradition" literature in anthropology has moved beyond the simple dichotomies (suggested by Hobsbawm) of traditions that are consciously and manipulatively invented by the State and intellectuals for the purposes of national identity; and customs that are more organically connected to everyday (peasant) life, providing continuity despite their natural changes over the years. Ranger (1993) has recently rethought the original phrase "invention of tradition," to suggest that any invention must be "imagined" as well. However, "custom" still retains for many the aura of a hegemonic, legitimizing category, similar to Bourdieu's notion of doxic societies, of that which goes without saying because it comes without saying. Yet "Custom" can also be a conscious category of debate and manipulation, as Poppi (1992) has shown in the case of Ladin carnival. Similarly, with reference to Spain, Behar suggests that custom has perhaps never been accepted passively without debate and constant reinvention. Behar (1986: 280) traces the greater degree of self-consciousness in the village where she worked to the spread of literacy in the early nineteenth century:

> Whereas in the period before the spread of literacy the villages were concerned above all to keep recycling the old texts of ordinances, in the nineteenth century there is a turn towards revising and renovating, resuscitating and reinterpreting the customs inscribed in these texts handed down from the ancestors.[2]

In my next three chapters I hope to push discussion of the invention/imagination of custom/tradition further by focussing not just on debates over traditions, but on debates about "tradition," about what this category contains, and the continued weight it has in people's daily lives. This discussion stands in contrast to my discussion of "history" in the second part of this book, a category I believe plays a much more hegemonic role in the Kalymnian imagination.

In General, Kalymnians use the words "tradition" (παράδοση) and "custom" (έθιμο) relatively interchangeably; they see them as referring to similar domains of experience, and neither term is seen as something beyond the realm of reflection. When I asked for specific

definitions, a few people gave slightly different connotations of the
terms. "Custom" refers to a habitual action that is associated with a
particular time of year or time of the life cycle. One example I was
given is: "serving doughnuts on Saint Andreas day is a Kalymnian
custom." Dynamite throwing at Easter is usually referred to as
"custom," though "tradition" and "habit" (συνήθεια) are also used.
Tradition can have a more abstract usage: it still refers to repeated
action, but not repeated in the cyclical sense of the calendar year or
the life cycle. I was offered the following example of this: "resistance
against outside invaders is a Greek tradition;" here the words "custom"
or "habit" would be inappropriate.

The Uses of Dynamite

Dynamite is closely connected to the Kalymnian orientation towards
the sea and sponge-diving. It used to be part of the divers' catch; it
was harvested from mines and torpedoes left in local seas during the
two world wars. It was known that men were killed in the process of
harvesting dynamite, but this did not deter them. As one Kalymnian
folklorist notes, "Each man has his fate, the fishermen philosophized,
since they had long been used to defying life from the time they had
started sponge-fishing" (Kapella 1987: 12; my translation). The connection between sponge-diving and dynamite is more than a material
one: they both represent an attitude of fearlessness toward danger
that is very much a part of the debate over dynamite's traditional
status.

On Kalymnos, the making of bombs is a relatively simple process.
Dynamite is scraped out of the defused mines brought up by sponge-
divers. It usually comes in large pieces which need to be pounded or
scraped into a powder. This process has its dangers: as the powder is
harmful to breathe and can be deadly if swallowed. Once pounded,
the powder is then poured into a small container – a can, a cigarette
pack, anything will do – and wrapped with tape. Then a hole is made
in the container and a detonator is inserted to make the dynamite
"live," that is, to create the conditions of heat and pressure necessary
for the dynamite to explode. Without a detonator, the dynamite bomb
is harmless. Finally, a fuse is attached, its length dependent on where
the dynamite is to be thrown – in the street, from a mountain – and
consequently how quickly it should explode. Then the fuse is lit, the
bomb is hurled, and a flash of light momentarily proceeds the loud
and reverberating explosion.

The practical use for these bombs is in fishing. Kalymnians have
long practised dynamite fishing, in which a bomb is exploded in the
water, killing all the fish in the area, which the fisherman can then
collect at his leisure when they float to the surface. This destructive

and dangerous practice has taken its toll in deaths and maimings, though certainly not to the extent that sponge-fishing did. It is illegal, but has long been tolerated, since it is not easy to catch fishermen red-handed. It is only in the 1990s that the practice appears to have started to seriously damage Kalymnian waters (see Mertzanis 1994). One dynamite fisherman complained that his take from each bomb seems to have steadily declined over the past five years.

An Easter Display

Recreational dynamite throwing is a different matter. Kalymnian skies are punctuated by occasional bursts of dynamite throughout the year. But dynamite throwing begins in earnest about two weeks before Easter. No firecracker display can compare to the sound of hundreds of kilos of TNT going off around you, magnified by the echoes from two mountain faces. The majority of throwing is done from the mountains that surround the harbor of the main town of Pothia, although some also occurs in the harbor itself. On Easter eve most of the dynamite is thrown from the courtyards of the neighborhood churches where people gather to hear the Easter service.

As Easter approaches, the occasional throwing that occurred at the harbor – preceded by someone yelling "dynamite, clear away!" – becomes more and more frequent. On the day before Easter, the first concentrated wave of bombing begins at noon, the time when Christ rises from his tomb and ascends to heaven. In the afternoon families gather to socialize and to put their lambs in large tin cans (some still use "traditional" clay pots) to cook in outdoor brick ovens. The afternoon may also be passed pounding and fixing dynamite bombs. Once they are ready, a "friendly" exchange of bombs goes on between neighbors across backyards. At a gathering of several house-builders, their friends and families that I attended, stories and plans concerning dynamite dominated the conversation: where it was proper and improper to throw; what the bishop of Kalymnos had said to try to curb the throwing this year.

The skies then remain clear for most of the evening, until midnight, when the majority of the island gathers in church for the Easter liturgy. This is when the Lenten fast is broken by most Kalymnians. As one Kalymnian explained to me, midnight marks the time when the Virgin is told of Christ's rising. Out of consideration for her, one is supposed to wait until after midnight to eat the traditional dish of soup made from the tongue, brain, organs and entrails of the lamb.

Midnight is also the signal for a barrage of dynamite to be thrown from the courtyards of churches throughout Kalymnos. The church across from our house, which is flanked by the town cemetery, was renowned for its displays. The press of bodies in the church dissipated

Easter 1995. Several thousand lbs of dynamite bombs collected on the mountain and ready for throwing.

Easter 1995. Throwing from the mountain above St. Nikolas.

the force of the explosions for those attending the service. Our house, by contrast, seemed ready to come crashing down around us. We had, out of ignorance, left our windows closed, and consequently the handles of the windows came flying off from the pressure and two windows broke. The priest who came out after midnight to read the liturgy from the second floor of the church went back inside, visibly shaken, after two or three rounds of explosions. The dynamiters considered this a victory over the priest and the church authority he represents. The bombing went on for about forty-five minutes until the police arrived. Their presence seemed to quieten things down.

The toll of damage was lots of broken glass in the cemetery, where the gravestones are topped by glass-fronted cases, in which pictures of the deceased, flowers and candles are kept. The marble gravestones have been known to sustain damage, but when I was there in 1992 they survived relatively unscathed. Apparently any damage is perceived as an annoyance, but I did not hear it referred to as a desecration. One older woman suggested to me that at least repairing the damage would make work for someone.

On Easter Sunday, more throwing is done down by the harbor, around the closed coffee shops. This is the most disreputable throwing because of its danger to passers-by and its destruction of store fronts. For that reason only throwers – mostly teenagers – and uninformed tourists go down to the harbor during the daytime. In 1992 the toll was light; only one store front was shattered. Several years before, in an effort to discourage throwing in the harbor, the mayor attempted to hold a party for the island during the daytime, with free drinks and a band. His plan was aborted when the stage the band was setting up for its performance was blown up by dynamiters who were determined not to see any curtailment of their privileges. The mayor's party is now held on Sunday evening, when the dynamiters retire to the mountains which enclose the harbor town of Pothia for the grand finale, and Kalymnian skies are illuminated by the largest and most thundering explosions.

The official attitude of local government and ecclesiastical officials towards the Sunday night display is ambiguous. While attempts have been made to control it, prior to the occurrence of "the accident" (see below), many public officials donated money towards the purchase of dynamite for Sunday's ritual. The police, as representatives of the national government, also alternate between attempts at control and implicit tolerance. I asked one police officer down at the harbor party why they didn't do anything to stop the throwing. His response was a shrug: "They're up there, what are we going to do?" In fact, I was told that several years ago a police chief did organize a group of officers to go up and try and catch the dynamiters (who have an elaborate look-out system and wear bags on their heads so as not to be identified). Once the police were within 100 yards of the dynamiters, one of the throwers shouted that he was going to start throwing. After one volley in their direction the police beat a hasty retreat. This ambiguous relation of local and national authority to dynamite throwing reflects in the present a complex history of complicity and repression, which I will describe below.

What is one to make of this thunderous display, which, after exhausting itself at Easter, continues sporadically and in small doses throughout the year at weddings, engagements, funerals, holidays and receptions for visiting dignitaries? First, it should be noted that it is something distinctly Kalymnian: I have vague reports of similar practices in other parts of Greece, but for the most part they seem to be restricted to small fireworks displays or the firing of guns, not TNT bombs. As one informant told me, one of the national Greek newspapers joked that anyone who wanted to experience what things were like in Bosnia should spend an Easter on Kalymnos.

At the same time, fireworks are used in a similar custom in many parts of Greece at Easter time. This means to the Kalymnians that the practice of dynamite throwing does not radically separate them from their fellow Greeks, but demonstrates how much tougher they are. Kalymnians' relationship to dynamite thus parallels their relationship to Greek history and identity more generally, as we saw in the previous chapter: they present themselves as always doing things "better" or "harder" than other Greeks, whether it is resisting foreign invaders or preserving their traditions. If dynamite is one defining indicator of Kalymnian character, it can be represented as proof of Kalymnian toughness (σκληρότητα) by those Kalymnians who are pro-dynamite, or of Kalymnian madness and folly (τρέλλα) by those who disapprove of it. This latter group sees bomb throwing as an unfortunate aspect of Kalymnian character, but refuses to refer to it as "custom." For those who are pro-dynamite, however, its status as tradition is virtually a given. Numerically, those against the practice represent about half the island, but with no noticeable demographic trends: old–young, rich–poor, male–female. It is interesting that women do not seem to be in opposition to it in greater percentages than men, despite the fact that dynamite throwing is the exclusive domain of men. Women are active participants in the preparation of dynamite and in watching the spectacle. Furthermore, allegiance or opposition to dynamite throwing shifts; it is dependent on the context of a discussion. Many Kalymnians are not fully committed to being pro- or anti-dynamite. Their position in any given discussion tends to depend on whether they are fondly recalling past Easter celebrations, thinking about the damage suffered to their property, or worse "the accident". Even people who shift allegiance will adopt the discourse of those who are firmly pro- or anti-dynamite in order to argue their positions.

The Throwers

Who are the dynamite throwers of Kalymnos? Most of the hardened dynamiters tend to be fishermen or builders, who have some experience with TNT from their work. However, there are also many educated office workers involved in the sport. Those who throw from the mountain tops on Easter Sunday, unlike everyday throwers, form an identity based on this collective activity. This fact was difficult to discover, since those who are involved in this level of non-casual throwing keep their identities semi-secret. This is because they know they face the risk of legal action, for the throwing and for the ways in which they obtain dynamite, which are not always legal. I first heard of these groups of dynamite throwers through what I originally assumed to be hyperbolic claims that the dynamiters started collecting material a year in advance for the following Easter's festivities. It wasn't until the second Easter I spent on Kalymnos that I understood the competitive aspect of "mountain" dynamite throwing. Originally there had been two groups or teams (ομάδες) of dynamite throwers: one threw from the mountain of Saint Yiorgos; the other threw from the mountain of Saint Stephanos. These peaks face the harbor of Pothia from opposite sides. Owing to the tragic accident of Easter 1980 on Saint Stephanos mountain, one group had gone into semi-retirement from then until 1993, when it was deemed that a sufficient period of mourning had passed for throwing to resume from that mountain. Thus, while my first Easter experience on Kalymnos (1992) seemed traumatic enough, it was not until my second Easter that I observed the full competitive reality of the Easter Sunday display. Each group would alternate throws in a call-and-response fashion, with the gathered masses of Kalymnian citizenry in the harbor below informally judging the victors by their applause.

For each of these groups the process of collecting several thousand kilos of dynamite for their yearly competition is a full-time hobby. Dynamite may be bought from sources outside Kalymnos, or it may be stolen from army installations or from public-works projects such as the airport currently being built on Kalymnos. Owing to the expense of acquiring dynamite, group members may work extra hours or even hold raffles in order to raise money for materials. Each group secures its stashes in safe hiding places, which may in fact be raided by the rival group throughout the year.

Informants (not directly involved in these groups) gave me the impression that membership was mediated through a combination of kinship and friendships, and that these groups lacked any independent existence beyond coming together to collect or throw dynamite. I do not know if I spoke to any of the members of these two groups, since they would have been unlikely to reveal their identities. One older man even warned me that if the dynamiters found out I was writing about them, they might send someone to kill me. But less committed throwers described a whole "culture of dynamite." This includes rating different qualities of dynamite, referred to in the local slang as υλικό (i.e. "material" which is, ironically, the same word used for the ethnographic material I was collecting), and different types of fuses, and ways to set off charges with different effects (such as repeated explosions – "doubles" and "triples" – or the use of nitroglycerin cord to increase the effects). Many houses also have a special tool used for the pounding of dynamite.

I went on several dynamite-preparation outings. One was with a worker who wanted to do some fishing and had bought pre-pounded dynamite for his more utilitarian purpose; one was with a group of friends who were scraping and readying a few pieces to throw in celebration of a wedding. The mixture of conspiratorial camaraderie and lack of caution in the preparation of dynamite was striking. The friends joked about being discovered and claiming to be members of the Greek terrorist group "November 17".[3] An atmosphere of toughness and playful aggression among the friends was balanced by the deliberate planning that went into deciding where to throw without endangering anyone at the wedding. The fisherman also seemed to enjoy the illicit nature of his act: he used hushed tones as he described to me what we would do while he assembled the bomb on his patio in full view of anyone who happened to pass by.[4] He took me to the inlet where he planned to throw the dynamite, and we spent at least fifteen minutes waiting to make sure that there was no one around to observe us, during which time he kidded me about whether or not I should throw the dynamite myself, whether I could handle it. The implication was that because I was a man I should be able to do it, but because I was a foreigner perhaps I couldn't.

This sense of illicit pleasure and attempts to heighten the fear around the practice are evident in descriptions I heard of what it's like to be up on one of the mountains during Easter Sunday. People walk near vast stockpiles of dynamite bombs, with detonators already attached, so the accidental setting off of one piece could blow up the entire mountainside. The danger is heightened by the fact that many of the bombs have packets of pure TNT on them to ensure multiple explosions, and this TNT can be set off by the pressure of a falling rock or by somebody stepping on it. Add to this the fact that many of the dynamiters are inebriated during the entire proceedings, and one gets a sense of the danger involved.[5] As one enthusiast describes the feeling of it:

> You hold it and you shit in your pants. You really do. When you see the
> first sparkle of the fuse, your senses are locked out . . . You can't hear it.

You can't feel anything. Somebody kicks you in the balls, you won't feel anything. And when it finally leaves your hand, and you see it going away, pffeww, the relief you feel, and then poof, you hear the–I mean, the others are listening to the boom, the only thing you hear is a light bing in your ear.

Memories of Dynamite

The Italian Occupation

The feeling of semi-illicitness is a present reflection of the genealogy of dynamite throwing on Kalymnos since the Italian Occupation, a remembered genealogy which parallels in interesting ways the history of the island itself over this period. Such remembrances can be charted, in part, according to one's view of dynamite and of politics in the present. Although Kalymnians may be correct in claiming there is no political significance to dynamite in the narrow sense of party politics, it is clear that the throwing of dynamite is wrapped up with Kalymnos' relationship to the central authority of the State. When I asked people to be specific about the changes in dynamite throwing practices over the past seventy years, I received much contradictory information, but amidst diverse accounts there was an association between dynamite throwing and political repression. Attitudes toward dynamite and state authority can be seen to encapsulate the history of the Greek state's attempts to domesticate its bandits, and the corresponding attempts by local populations to resist the imposition of state authority and law on their practices. This is captured in the claim by Cretan mountain shepherds that "the law doesn't reach here" (Herzfeld 1985: 33). This internal struggle over Kalymnos' relationship to outside authority is borne out in the historical memories of dynamite throwing, memories which reflect one's position and attitude towards contemporary practice.

For those Kalymnians who see resistance to outsiders as a positive and defining characteristic of the island, dynamite evokes fond memories of such resistance during the Italian occupation from 1912 to 1942. In these memories, dynamite throwing is seen as an archetypal example of this Kalymnian resistance to outside oppression, a resistance which, as noted above, is believed to have been much stronger on Kalymnos than on other islands. When I discussed dynamite with one Kalymnian writer, he decried its present-day damage to tourism and the environment. However, he was happy to praise dynamite throwing during the Italian occupation, suggesting the mutability of allegiance to the practice noted above. As he expressed it, dynamite was a way for the enslaved Kalymnians to say "we're alive" to their oppressors. Here it is crucial to note that dynamite throwing is centered around Easter, the principal national/religious holiday of "rebirth" in Greece. Easter is not only the victory of Christ over his oppressors through his resurrection and ascent into Heaven. It also represents the rebirth of the Greek people after 400 years of Ottoman rule. The Greek revolution is dated to have begun on March 25 which marks the annunciation of the birth of Christ. I also heard occasional associations by Kalymnians between Easter as the rebirth (ανάσταση) and the Revolution (επανάσταση). Dynamite can therefore be seen as a multi-layered symbol of these events. It is an index of war with all its firepower, and an icon of heavenly activity, i.e. Christ's resurrection. (The ascent occurs forty days after Easter, but is implicit in the celebration of the resurrection.)

At the local level dynamite throwing has an added significance. Most people believe the practice originated in the Italian Occupation. They refer to a particular, undated, defining event when Kalymnians set off dynamite on one mountain, and while the Italians were running up the mountain to investigate, dynamite was set off on the opposite mountain.[6] This is symbolically repeated by throwing from the two mountains on Easter Sunday. The image of Italian authorities running between the two mountains in a fruitless attempt to apprehend the dynamiters has a particularly pleasing quality for Kalymnians, as proof of their ability to outfox the authorities and at the same time to declare their resistance in the most strident terms. This view of the local origins of dynamite throwing is officially sanctioned by the island authorities. One of the recent mayors of Kalymnos issued an official letter (εγκύκλιο) to be used at trials for anyone caught throwing dynamite. This letter stated that dynamite throwing is a Kalymnian custom connected to the struggles of the Kalymnians for freedom against the Italians and the Turks.[7]

Several older men point to the Italian Occupation as generative of dynamite throwing in another more subtle way. In the context of discussing their childhood memories they recalled how they used to play with the "keys." These were hollow keys that boys and older men would fill with the gunpowder scraped from the tips of matches, then jam tight with a nail so that when banged against the ground it gave off a loud explosion. One man remembered these keys being so popular that there was barely a doorstep in Kalymnos that didn't have the little black pockmarks left by the keys. While the Italian authorities didn't approve this practice, they had bigger fish to fry than this minor form of entertainment.

At the same time, when people wish to decry present-day dynamite throwing, they refer to the Italian Occupation as the significant period. It is seen as a time when dynamite was not permitted, and if you were missing from your house without a proper alibi when dynamite went off you would be carted off to jail the next day by the Italian authorities. In this way, dynamite is absorbed into the two competing discourses on the Italian Occupation – of resistance and of well-ordered government – and used, so to speak, as ammunition by both sides.[8] The irony here is that, like the deeds of the Greek bandits during the War of Independence, what was once a valued practice of national resistance now stands in opposition to State authority. One man, a leading communist on the island who had suffered repression at the hands of past governments, Italian and Greek, put this matter particularly concisely: "The Kalymnians have always thrown dynamite to show their resistance; under the Turks, the Italians, the Germans and now [he smiled] under the Greeks. The Greeks won't be able to stop it any more than the rest, though [he smiled again] of course it doesn't have the meaning of resistance any more." Here any serious criticism or analysis of Kalymnos' relation to the Greek state is disguised as a joke, and thereby defused. An opposing view, which in a sense confirms this interpretation, is provided by a Kalymnian intellectual who writes in the local newspaper, *Dimokratikí Kálymnos*, (1983; my translation): "formerly, during an unfortunate period of our national life, [dynamite throwing] had some meaning. But now, living as we do in the embrace of our sweet mother [Greece], it is both meaningless and pointless." It is this very tension between Kalymnian attitudes toward independence and state control that makes dynamite such a central issue.

The Post-War Period: The Birth of a Tradition?

The next crucial period is after the Second World War, when Kalymnos, with the rest of the Dodecanese, became part of Greece, and dynamite throwing moved from being a sporadic act of resistance to the Italians to a regular practice with ritual dimensions. Two memories of this period are given here: both are anti-dynamite, though they come from opposite sides of the party-political spectrum. The first is from Yiorgos, a middle-aged shop owner who had been involved in right-wing politics, and was very concerned about his fellow Kalymnians' disregard for state law. To paraphrase his telling:

> In the period after the Second World War when Kalymnos and the Dodecanese had first become part of Greece, Kalymnos didn't take well to state authority, because they had been so long resisting the Italians, unlike other islanders who "slept with" the Italians.[9] So there was more political repression here than elsewhere, in order to make them learn to have respect for the laws: because freedom means responsibility as well. Back then if you even talked about politics, you feared that the authorities might come and get you. They even had little speedboats to patrol the neighboring uninhabited islands to make sure that fishermen

were not using dynamite. It wasn't until George Papandreou was elected
[1963] that there was a relaxation of the police state and dynamite
throwing got underway in earnest.

It is striking that even a right-wing believer in law and order expresses
ambivalent attitudes about the state repression of dynamite. It is
because of such ambivalences, shared I believe by all Kalymnians
regardless of political affiliation, that ritual dynamite throwing becomes
a way for people to explore collectively such tensions.

Yiorgos also mentioned another aspect of dynamite throwing that
is not often discussed: its economic motivation. He told me this in
explaining the origins of the "excessive" practice of throwing from
mountains. Recreational throwing was originally restricted to the kind
of church throwing on Easter Saturday described above. According to
Yiorgos, black marketeers exploited a group of pranksters eager to find
outlets for their restlessness. It was the black marketeers' idea to get
these pranksters involved in competitive mountain throwing, and they
fed them dynamite in order to get them hooked on it like a drug, so
there would always be a demand for their contraband. Even in 1993 a
few people suggested to me that it was similar powerful economic
interests that kept the police from intervening.

The second memory of this period comes from an older man, Mihalis,
who was also vehemently against dynamite. It provides a clear view
of how the topic of dynamite can intersect with, and reshape, political
memories in interesting ways. He had been complaining to me about
the problems of the Socialist PASOK government of Andreas Papandreou. Although he supported PASOK, he felt they had given people
too much freedom, and that the people weren't prepared for such
freedoms. The result, he said,

> is what you have here on Kalymnos where the authorities are now afraid
> to do anything about the dynamiters, and the dynamiters rule the
> island. Like recently when the police actually caught someone throwing
> dynamite and brought him down to the police station. His comrades
> threatened to blow up the police station, so they let him go. Papandreou
> gave people freedoms, but this doesn't mean that you can do whatever
> you want, and disregard or harm other people.

It is interesting that this man associates unrestrained dynamite
throwing with the coming to power of PASOK (1981), while most
other Kalymnians told me that it originated twenty years earlier. I
believe that Mihalis makes this connection because it was George
Papandreou, Andreas's father, who began the relaxation of the police
state which brought dynamite throwing to the fore. For this man,
however, the specific history of dynamite is less important than the
fact that dynamite is emblematic, the most unarguable example of

Kalymnian disrespect for the State law and for public order. Once again, dynamite throwing may have no specific party-political content, but for both its supporters and for its detractors it is clearly intertwined with the Kalymnians' relationship to larger forces of control and order.[10]

The Accident

> Easter, 1980. The usual group of fifteen to twenty men had gone up to the mountain of Saint Stephanos to celebrate Christ's resurrection by throwing hundreds of dynamite bombs off the two mountainsides, and lighting up the night sky. The weather was not ideal this year, with high winds making it difficult to see if a fuse was actually "live" once it had been lit. Because of this, the throwers had agreed to throw their bombs immediately, whether or not they appeared to be lit. But one thrower was a young boy from Athens, who some say was not as experienced in "mountain throwing." Making just such an error, the boy threw a lit piece of dynamite back on the pile, containing some 250 kilos of TNT. The dynamite went off before the boy's cousin, who had seen what happened, was able to reach the pile. The huge explosion killed three instantly, and severely injured four others who were in the vicinity. It took a sizeable chunk of rock out of the mountain face, and this falling rock struck and killed another boy who had been climbing up the mountain in order to watch the proceedings. While many Kalymnians rushed to the scene to aid the survivors, some were already looking for the person who had been taking photographs up on the mountain, to ask him to destroy the evidence.

The recent history of dynamite throwing is charted by all Kalymnians through "the accident." This is undoubtedly the most significant event of the recent past in the memory of Kalymnians. This occurrence turned a large percentage of the population against dynamiting, and led to official condemnation. This accident shook the entire island, and those who have recounted it to me still become emotionally overwhelmed in the recollection. People also fill their recountings with dramatic details of how the weather had been heavy all day, a strange yellow weather that suddenly cleared after the explosion. Hundreds of Kalymnians came running to the scene where, they tell me, they were greeted with rivers of blood, along with the grisly remains. One Kalymnian in his late twenties, a teenager when the accident occurred, became quite choked up in recounting the event. He said that he had to spend the next three Easters on Kos so as not to relive the occurrence, and has never even touched a firecracker since. Those who are committed throwers, however, are equally moved but view the event as an act of ignorance that they would not commit.

In the telling of this story there are variations as to the causes of the boy's fatal mistake. A number of people told me that the cause of the accident was a physical slip, rather than a mental error, i.e. the bomb fell from the boy's hand onto the pile. As one person pointed out, why would the boy have thrown what he thought was a dud back on the pile of dynamite which people were using? Here the weight of causality seems to be shifted to a physical mistake that anyone could have made, rather than the foolish mental error of an inexperienced boy. This "physical" explanation seemed to have more currency among non-throwers than among throwers; the latter are more concerned to show that if the boy had been a properly trained local thrower, he would not have made such a mistake. The fact that he was raised in Athens, and had not experienced mountain throwing, is emphasized by throwers, in order to shift the blame to an exogenous force and away from local practice. One non-participant eyewitness, who had gone up to the mountain to take pictures of the event, claims that in a sense both interpretations are true. People had indeed been instructed to throw the dynamite whether or not they could see the lit fuse. Yet people were hesitating, undecided as to whether to throw the dynamite; they were thus making jerky motions of indecision. The eyewitness did not see the fatal mistake, but hypothesizes that it was just such a moment of indecision that allowed the dynamite to slip out of the boy's hand and back onto the pile. What is clear from all this is that the process of making sense of the event still continues over a decade later.

The details of the accident are very much a matter of dispute; but interpretations of the accident's significance on the future of dynamite throwing diverge even more radically depending on whether one is pro- or anti-dynamite. For the dynamite supporters, dynamite throwing has been in decline since the accident, and the best years of dynamite throwing were before the accident. As one thrower told me, serious throwers stopped for several years in respect and mourning for the accident, during which time it was only teenagers who threw. For them, Easter 1993 represented a rebirth of the custom in all its glory, since throwing once again took place from the mountain of Saint Stephanos. Moreover, these people feel particularly bitter about the public outcry that occurred over the renewal of dynamite throwing, and the fact that money for dynamite from the local civic and religious authorities was cut off. Prior to the accident, they claim, the whole island approved of dynamiting. Thus it is the whole island which must bear responsibility for the accident, not just the dynamiters.

For those who oppose the practice, things have only gotten worse since the accident. This attitude is encapsulated in the disparaging comment, "they even threw dynamite at the funeral." One woman's memory of the accident centers around witnessing the bodies being brought to the hospital in pieces, and seeing a policeman fall to his knees and curse the bishop for approving the practice and not allowing the police to stop it a long time ago. This utterance refers to the fact that the bishop of Kalymnos would often testify in favor of the good character of a dynamiter in cases when they were caught and brought to trial. According to some who are anti-dynamite, official attempts to cover up the accident began almost immediately: the police filed the majority of the charges against one dynamiter they thought had been killed in the accident and who therefore could not stand trial (but who was in fact miraculously saved after being flown to the hospital in Athens). A report in the national newspaper *Eleftherotipía* several days after the accident notes that island officials were discussing ways to "preserve the custom" while limiting the danger of it. Here we see the source of the frustration expressed by Yiorgos and Mihalis above at the unwillingness of the local government to act as an arm of repression, or control of public order, of the national state. Once again, officialdom is caught up in the ambiguity of the attitude it should display towards a practice symbolic of local resistance to foreign oppression, and how far State power can extend without provoking violent local reaction (see Herzfeld 1985: 26–7).

For those opposed to the dynamite, the accident, in a sense, represented the victory of the dynamite forces, and of the fact that the practice would never be brought under control. On the one hand the dynamiters believe that the accident led to a severe reduction of dynamite throwing; on the other, older people who are anti-dynamite recall a more persistant cycle of increase. They remember the years after the Second World War when, for a variety of reasons noted above, dynamite throwing was relatively restricted. Women remember with fondness how boys used to throw firecrackers to scare girls, their aim being a flirtatious one – to burn the girls' stockings. But this was the extent of it. For these people, the slight decrease that occurred in the years after the accident is not as significant as the overall increase since the early 1960s.

Folly and Feeling

A key feature of discussions about the present-day practice of dynamite throwing is the debate over whether it is indeed a custom. When people wish to argue for it, they speak of it as a legitimate Kalymnian custom. When people are arguing against it, they refer to it as pure and simple "folly" (τρέλλα), a word that connotes both madness (from τρελλαίνομαι, to be mad) and a sense of useless and negative wastefulness. What is being debated here is not only the status of dynamite, but the image and role that custom and tradition play in their present-day lives.

In their description of dynamite throwing as a "folly," Kalymnians opposing dynamite evoke an image of custom and tradition which is represented by more formal and proper State and religious rituals, or the regular performances of "traditional" (παραδοσιακά) Kalymnian dances by high-school girls. Therefore, something as foolish and wasteful as dynamite could not, by definition, be part of "custom". Not surprisingly, some of the island's historians and folklorists, those most committed to the statist image of Greek identity, insisted most vehemently that dynamite throwing was not a "custom," but the insane practice of a few "barbarians". However, when they wanted to assert Kalymnian distinctiveness, even they would praise a limited version of the practice.

What is at issue for those opposing dynamite is not whether dynamite throwing was engaged in as a form of resistance against the Italians. Nobody disputes this. But the displays people remember from the period after the Second World War were severely restricted. Such limited displays would be acceptable to most. It is the excessiveness of the practice that many people object to: some note the danger involved, others the damage incurred. Still others decry the waste of money, money that could go for public works, or to buy Easter lambs for poor families on Kalymnos.[11] As argued in the previous chapter, many see doing things to excess as a defining feature of Kalymnian character and identity – from fooling other islanders in deals, to gambling and card-playing, to over-consumption of food and other luxuries. In some contexts (e.g. hospitality), excessiveness is seen as a positive trait. However, many Kalymnians view this excessiveness negatively, as the cause of many of the island's problems – from the fact that the Italians didn't develop the island because of Kalymnian excessive resistance, to present-day problems Kalymnians have working in co-operative ventures because of their excessive individualism. For those who oppose dynamite throwing, its excessive practice is no longer a "custom," but the "folly" of some Kalymnians who do not care about practical matters such as damaging other people's property, developing the island, or showing a more respectful and "civilized" face to the rest of Greece.

The supporters of dynamite throwing do not make distinctions between the "custom" as practiced after the war and as practiced in the 1990s. Indeed, they would never refer to the custom in quotation marks (see, for example, the exchange of letters in *Dimokratikí Kálymnos* 1980). When asked about origins, they either refer to the Italian period, or they say it has been going on from time immemorial (από ανέκαθεν [*sic*][12]), and in this way, they draw no distinctions between "legitimate" and "excessive" throwing.[13] Instead they justify dynamite in terms of the intense feelings that are often associated with it. For throwers, the practice can be connected to a passion or great sorrow. One word used in this context is μεράκι, which means "yearning" or "passion," but can also mean "sorrow" as from unrequited love.[14] Addicted dynamiters are said to have such yearnings that they need to exhaust them through throwing. A man with great sorrow may throw dynamite in order to get over it, as was the case of one man who was reported to have thrown 150 kilos of dynamite one afternoon because of his great μεράκι.[15]

The experience of throwing dynamite was described to me in striking terms as a sensual experience: the sight of the explosion itself, the smell of the dynamite going off around you, the thickness of the air created by the pressure of numerous explosions, and finally the sense of relief after you throw that you are still in one piece. I have been told that it is something so basic and primal that you can only experience it by throwing yourself.

The sensuality of the dynamite throwing experience parallels Kalymnian views of religious experience. I was told by many Kalymnians that sensory experience was central to Greek Orthodoxy: the sound of the singing of the liturgy, the omnipresence of icons and paintings, and the overwhelming smell of incense (cf. Dubisch 1995: 61). Kalymnians insisted that it was in these superior sensory experiences that the difference of Orthodoxy lay, when compared to what they felt was the "coldness" of western Christianity. These distinctions also accord with the general position in the ethnographic literature of Greece that ritual is much more significant than either religious dogma or loyalty to the church hierarchy in ordinary Greek experience of Christianity.[16] This is in keeping with the fact that Orthodoxy is considered Greek tradition *par excellence* in written and oral accounts of how it kept alive the "flame" of this tradition, embodied in ritual, during the long years of Ottoman rule.[17] The connection between dynamite throwing and Easter as ritual is thus very significant in lending support to the arguments of dynamite supporters. Those who watch at Easter but do not throw explain that without the dynamite, they wouldn't feel that it's really Easter. Or more positively, they say that when you hear the dynamite, then you "understand" that it's Easter. Here "understand" means to experience in an almost visceral, physical (one is tempted to say "ritual") sense, rather than in a purely cognitive way. Kalymnians living in Australia and America are known to call home on the telephone at Easter expressly to hear the dynamite exploding.

For some, religious experience is not the principal touchstone for dynamite throwing. Nevertheless, in tapping a language of feeling, those who are pro-dynamite implicitly link throwing to religious experience. These different appeals to "the feeling of dynamite" are some of the ways that those who are pro-dynamite suggest that it is something non-rational, though intimately connected to Kalymnian character (χαρακτήρας). The celebratory nature of dynamite throwing suggests another parallel: with Cowan's (1990: 132 ff.) analysis of the power of wedding dances to compel allegiance to village identity through sensuous activity:

> the eardrums ring, the body buzzes, ouzo is hot on the tongue . . . the *dauli's* [drum's] rhythms, which pulsate through the bodies of all who stand near, impossible to resist . . . participating in the dance can provoke that sense of recognition . . . that one is morally part of, just as one is now corporeally merged with, a larger collectivity, a recognition that, as a profoundly visceral knowledge, carries the force of absolute conviction.

Easter dynamite throwing shares some of this sense of collective, Kalymnian identity, which is difficult to argue with because it goes beyond intellectual choice, and is experienced as a mode of being in the world. Yet this sensual power does not mean it is simply a part of *habitus*, and completely beyond the realm of verbal reflection, as Bourdieu would have it. Appeals to the sensual, or sensual performances, must be recognized as aspects of strategies for legitimation that are, at least, partly conscious (see Cowan 1990: 130–1).

Conclusion: Custom or Character?

Thus, those wishing to support the practice of dynamite throwing attempt to move the debate beyond considerations of damage to property and monetary outlay. Throwing is portrayed as a ritual as necessary as any other part of Easter tradition. This brings us to the heart of the debate, which is as much about the meaning of "custom" as it is about dynamite. For Kalymnians, custom is, by definition, not concerned with the rational – both sides in the debate agree on this. Practices that need to invoke a "means-ends" calculus, such as dowry and inheritance practices, are not "custom," as we will see in Chapter 5. What then, according to Kalymnians, is "tradition"? When I posed this question, a common response was to refer to Kalymnian dance or traditional Kalymnian dress. Other answers looked to the unassailable practice of hospitality to strangers (φιλοξενία), which is felt to be much more strongly adhered to on Kalymnos than in other parts of Greece. Thus, tradition is perceived to most properly belong in the domain of expressive culture, a mark of distinction that sets Kalymnians off from other people in museum-like fashion.

For those who wish to oppose dynamite, its danger and its wastefulness put it beyond the realm of expressive culture. In discussion of these issues, they are in effect insisting that such a practice needs to be considered in terms of "rationality," because it is so harmful. A small, restricted dynamite display could be considered "tradition," but the practice as currently constructed does not fit within this realm. "Custom" itself is accepted as necessary only as long as it doesn't impede the "modernization" that Kalymnos is seen to need. Maria Zairi, a historian, newspaper editor and wife of the former mayor, captures this idea in a recent newspaper article entitled "Custom?" (Zairi 1995):

> Most Kalymnians, if you ask them, softly and sincerely they will tell you that they like it, they want it even if it causes problems for the whole world. Because if all the shaking didn't go on, they would feel that Easter had not come to Kalymnos . . . But for those who remain cool-headed the question poses itself differently. This custom, if it is a custom, where is it leading us, and who will censure it before it is too late?

Note that Zairi expresses some acknowledgement that most Kalymnians, in certain contexts, approve the practice, and thus she alludes to the collective responsibility that the dynamite supporters refer to. She also cites the sensory connection between dynamite and Easter, but at the same time suggests that those moved by rationality rather than feeling will recognize that the cost is too great.

Zairi admits that dynamite throwing may have become a custom in the sense of a "habit" that has been going on at Easter for several decades since the Second World War, but she also reasserts that the proper expression of "custom" is in practices of expressive culture such as the eating of lamb at Easter throughout Greece, or the cooking of lamb in clay pots specifically on Kalymnos. For dynamite supporters, on the other hand, a different image of custom as Kalymnian distinctiveness is evoked to assert the traditionalness of the practice. That is the excessiveness which, as I've argued above, Kalymnians believe to be central to their character. Other islanders may have their particular dances and costume, but Kalymnians insist that these other islanders have, in fact, capitulated to tourism, just as they did to the Italians earlier in the twentieth century. From this perspective, Kalymnians must fight to preserve the distinctiveness that is being threatened by the standardization of the world through tourism and the European Union, just as they led the resistance to the Italian Occupation. We saw this expressed in the fisherman's defiance of standardization and economic penetration through the claim that he would "kill them" before they took his boat away. It is this sense of resistance at all cost that is embodied, for many, in the excessive throwing of dynamite.

It is here that the two discourses on dynamite come together: both the implicit discourse about Kalymnos' continued refusal to recognize the Greek state as sole authority with the right to dictate the legality of local practice, and the explicit discourse over whether dynamite throwing is or is not "custom." Both of these discourses ultimately concern two models of how Kalymnians can frame their present identity: either as law-abiding citizens of the Greek state, with their own local variations of "Greekness" residing in local dance, dress and cooking practices, or as distinctive in their excessiveness, their unwillingness to bow down to any authority, whether foreign oppressors, the Greek state, the European Union or other outsiders.

If some complain that dynamite throwing damages tourism, others see it as a warning to outsiders – Greek and otherwise – that Kalymnos will preserve its resistant spirit. This was repeatedly brought home to me when people asked me whether I was scared by the dynamite throwing at Easter. They seemed quite pleased when I said yes. Here the words of Kalymnian folklorist Niki Billiri are particularly apt, they capture, once again, the ambiguities of the relationship between a resistance directed both at foreign occupiers and at State authorities. At first she told me she was strongly against the practice of dynamite throwing, at least in its present dimensions. Then, in discussing how it had got out of hand, she recalled when the then prime minister, later President Karamanlis, had visited Kalymnos in the late 1970s, and had been given a "traditional Kalymnian greeting." Billiri told me with considerable satisfaction how Karamanlis had turned to his minister, who was of Kalymnian descent, and said, "Kos and Rhodes and other islands have Europeanized [εξευρωπαϊσθήκανε] but on Kalymnos the true Greek spirit still resides."

Notes

1. Cowan has similarly shown how conflicting ideas (in her case literate and oral) compete for prominence in discussions of celebratory practices: "folkloric discourse has entered Merio Carnival experience in a diffuse sense, by providing a vocabulary and a set of values in terms of which [the townspeople] can argue" (1988: 253; cf. 1992). Cowan's analysis focusses more explicitly on issues of party politics and "high" and "low" traditions, which I did not find as relevant for my discussion of dynamite. Seremetakis (1991; 1994) relies heavily on concepts of tradition and modernity in her work on Mani. But she tends to use the terms as analytical categories rather than as debatable signs.

2. There is a certain technological determinacy to Behar's argument here, and we should, no doubt be cautious about assuming that literacy necessarily leads to a changed consciousness (for a discussion, see Collins 1995).

3. This group, which pulled off a number of terrorist operations during my stay in Greece, and which had several years previously killed the son-in-law of the then conservative Prime Minister, takes its name from the date of the uprising of students of the Polytechnic school of Athens against the military Junta in 1973. November 17 seems less associated with any particular political ideology, than with an attack on the establishment in general (Although Greek right-wing politicians have been among the victims, past targets have included financial leaders and American CIA personnel.) In this respect it makes an apt comparison to the Kalymnian dynamite throwers who are also not associated with any political party ideology, a point explored below.

4. These "performances of secrecy" (cf. Herzfeld 1985: 207–9) may be part of the establishing of one's manly competence in handling dynamite. They also reflect, I believe, the dual nature of dynamite, which I discuss further below, representing both an illegal practice and an accepted/rewarded custom.

5. This attitude toward danger resonates with the courting of risk and danger described by Bernard (1976a) for Kalymnian sponge-diving practices.

6. For a written account of these events, see Drakos 1982.

7. In one trial the defense lawyer also made the (disputed) claim that during the Turkish invasion of Cyprus, Kalymnians took up their defensive positions armed only with bags of dynamite. Here he implies that in keeping alive this "tradition" the Kalymnians are preserving a skill that still may serve them well in the future.

8. For a brilliant and detailed discussion of competing attitudes towards the Italian Occupation in Kalymnos and the rest of the Dodecanese, see Doumanis 1997.

9. See my discussion of the literal and figurative meanings of this phrase in the previous chapter.

10. The reader at this point may wonder why, if dynamite throwing is related to political repression, it has increased during periods when repression has decreased. During periods of extreme repression such as the Junta it is, of course, very difficult to engage in open acts of resistance, and a tribute to those few who do. If such acts of resistance are only taken up by the majority of people once such harsh repression begins to lift, it may be their way of saying "never again" to the repressive forces of the national government.

11. The collective monetary outlay in dynamite at Easter reaches into the hundreds of thousands of dollars, as several thousand kilos of dynamite are used at the cost of approximately $10.00/kg (a skilled workman's daily wage runs between $40.00 and $60.00). In addition, there is the expense of dynamite used for special occasions or just for entertainment throughout the year. In order to procure dynamite (and sometimes even more powerful and expensive plastic explosives) Kalymnians have been known to break into army munitions sites. There is, in fact, a standing order in the Greek army barring Kalymnians and Cretans from having guard duty at those sites. Despite this, a recent issue of the local Kalymnian newspaper (i Argó tis Kalímnou April 1994) reports that 7,000 detonators (πυροκροτητές) were stolen from an army warehouse on the

neighboring island of Kos. Kalymnian soldiers stocking up for Easter were the presumed perpetrators. Here, as elsewhere, we see that this debate is not something strictly internal to Kalymnos – it has been recognized by the rest of Greece as a distinctive Kalymnian practice.

12. Grammatically, ανέκαθεν by itself is correct usage. But the repetitive από ανέκαθεν (literally "from always from") is in fact in common circulation.

13. For the throwers and their supporters, "excessive" dynamite throwing refers to something else: the "dangerous" throwing that is perpetrated in the harbor largely by teenagers on Easter morning. Professional throwers would see this as excessive because it puts other people in danger, as opposed to the "controlled" throwing that goes on from the mountains, where for the most part only those involved are endangered.

14. This is Kalymnian usage. In standard Athenian, μεράκι connotes passion in the sense of hobby or avocation.

15. One could draw suggestive parallels here to Rosaldo's report of an Ilongot man's justification for headhunting: "He says the rage, born of grief, impels him to kill his fellow human beings . . . The act of severing and tossing away the victim's head enables him, he says, to vent and, he hopes, throw away the anger of his bereavement" (Rosaldo 1989: 1).

16. This applies equally in rural and urban contexts. See for example, Hirschon 1989; Seremetakis 1991; Hart 1992. Panourgia, for example, describes in detail the rituals of the Epitaphios, as stressing Christ as "corporeality" rather than as "divine abstraction" (1995: 151 ff.). Also see Iossifides 1992.

17. Thus Orthodoxy is assimilated to the category of "History" as well, a point explored in Chapter 6.

four

Tales of Women Casting Stones

The Shape of Power

In the previous chapter I demonstrated how dynamite is a manly substance for Kalymnians: it requires hard labor to recover it from the ocean floor, to scrape it and process it into bombs, and fearlessly to light and throw it. In this chapter I examine a differently gendered "throwing." The women's "Rock War" took place in 1935 when Kalymnos was under Italian occupation. It is a powerful example of women's collective action, which was successful in achieving immediate goals and in questioning persistent gender categories and ideologies. Its status is therefore ambiguous: as an example of Kalymnian resistance to the Italians, it has been "cast in stone" in the writings of male historians. But as an example of a specifically female power, it has become a site for reinterpretation and contested management. How this piece of the past is dealt with in the present opens up questions about women's power, women's agency and women's role in Kalymnian resistance to outside oppression. In the previous chapters it was shown that the "traditionality" of various past practices is an issue in the present-day debates about them, and also in discussions about how Kalymnos' relation to Europe, to Athens and to its neighbors is construed. So it is with respect to gender and gender relations in the present. Here the use of the past is particularly pronounced in debates over the relative powers of men and women, and the shifts and changes Kalymnos is undergoing in this domain. This chapter examines the memory of the Rock War, lodged as it is between "tradition" regarded as a female domain, and the male domain of "history." As with the issue of dynamite throwing, I begin with the question of current gender relations in order to illuminate how different pasts are mobilized for different purposes. At the same time I will further refine how Kalymnians use different categories of the past, noting their overlappings and discontinuities, and the gendered aspects of these usages.

The Rock War took place on 7 April 1935. It marked the culmination of three days of uprisings by Kalymnian women protesting against Italian attempts to take control of the Orthodox church administration. These three days had seen women, including a contingent of nuns, clashing with the Italian police force (*carabinieri*) in the main square of Kalymnos harbor. The women fought the Italians with their bare hands, sometimes blinding the Italians by throwing ashes in their faces, and using their strength in numbers to overpower them. On the third day, when the Italians called in reinforcements from other islands, the women prepared by gathering rocks from the surrounding mountains, which they hurled down on the heads of the soldiers, causing chaos as they attempted to disembark. These were some of the stories I heard, from participants and from those too young to participate, during my research on Kalymnos 47 years later.

While Kalymnian resistance to foreign domination has taken on the status of self-definition and of ritual, what was I to make of this example of women's collective action in which Kalymnian men were noticeable by their absence? Were these the same women that some men claim "were kept locked up in their houses" (κλειδωμένες μέσ' στα σπίτια) during the old days? I came to these issues already uncomfortable with the prevalent anthropological assumption of women's subordination in Greek society. The vision evoked by Jane Schneider's "Of Vigilance and Virgins" (1971) of an excessively patriarchal Mediterranean culture that enforces female passivity has become a popular stereotype, sometimes reproduced in anthropological writings on Greece. Authors have described a gender system in which men either explicitly control women's lives, or women accept a subordinate public status in order to rule within a domestic setting, i.e. they have domestic power but no prestige. A third approach has argued that women have created and therefore exercise control over their own "culture": a domain of meaning and status overlooked by earlier anthropologists, who expected to find power only in the traditional places.[1] A recent qualification of this picture has suggested the importance of patrilocal, as opposed to matrilocal, residence patterns found in different areas of Greece in determining whether women are marginalized as threatening "outsiders" or whether they can rely on the support of their own natal kin-group in disputes with their husbands.[2]

All these accounts of gender relations imply that a male "outsider" would encounter greater difficulty talking with Kalymnian women than with Kalymnian men owing to the cultural constraints of the "shame" that women must exhibit in front of outsiders. I was somewhat surprised when I found Kalymnian women of all ages and social statuses to be amongst my most lively informants. As I got to know some of them better, they proved as willing as Kalymnian men to reveal intimate details of their lives.

The second troubling surprise I encountered took the form of a joke that was circulating during the time of my fieldwork, and which was told to me by three different male informants. The joke goes as follows:

> A study is being conducted in a small village of whether men or women are in charge (κάνει κουμάντο). Those conducting the study promise to each household where the man is found to be in charge, to give a horse. To each household where the woman is in charge they promise a chicken. The researchers go through the entire village asking who is in charge, and rewarding chickens, only chickens, to each and every household. Finally they reach a house off on the mountainside where a large, heavily-mustached man sits in traditional dress, sharpening his knife [further details were added here]. When they ask him to tell them who runs his household, he responds with great offense that it should be perfectly clear that he is the boss, whatever he says, goes. The researchers congratulate him and tell him that he will be awarded a fine horse, would he like a white or a black one? He asks them to wait just a minute, calls to his wife, and says "wife, which horse shall we take, the white or the black one?"

The interesting fact about this joke is that it was told to me exclusively by men. When I followed it up by asking if it was true that women were in charge on Kalymnos, many men agreed, telling me that not only did women run things, but admitting that their own wives "rule" them as well. They acknowledged the power that emanates from the women of the household, who make the major decisions involving the day-to-day and long-term planning of the household economy. The fact that women controlled the "purse-strings" was also noted.[3] My efforts to identify other loci of power in Kalymnos drew a blank. When I tried to suggest that perhaps women were the decision-makers in the house but that men transacted important decisions in the coffee shops, this only elicited the response, "What do you mean, that men control their pockets?" (i.e. the ability to pay for coffee). Women were slightly more divided: older women in general agreed that women "ruled" but some younger women (under thirty), claimed that you couldn't generalize and had to look at each individual household. It was also clear that the older generation assumed there were power imbalances (usually favoring women), while the younger generation invoked equality at least as an ideal; although some younger men were even more insistent in stating the truth of female power. When I questioned one man in his late twenties about the issue, he quoted the saying "one cunt-hair pulls the boat," (μουνότριχα σέρνει το καράβι) to express his perception of women's abilities to get their way.

Female power, yes, but what of male prestige? Or perhaps, to invert Rogers' (1975) framing of the issue with respect to peasant France, are we dealing with a "*Myth* of Female Dominance" (as in US society, when men often condescendingly claim that the "little woman" really runs things)? In looking at the issue of women's relative power, there are several domains to be examined. Clearly there is the material domain of control of the household economy. Then there are conflicting ideological domains and associated discourses and practices. In this chapter I begin by examining some of those discourses and practices associated with the control of words, space and movement, as a background for understanding the problems and contradictions posed by the Rock War for gender categories in the past and present. In Chapter 5 I look at issues of residence, dowry and property transfer, and the reasons that these issues have become associated with the striking claim by Kalymnian men and women that "we used to have Matriarchy on the island."

Background

Mutedness?

In her study of Greek Asia Minor refugees in Piraeus, Hirschon describes the gendered significance of verbal activity as follows: "A woman's speech is held to be dangerous, her words may be irresponsible and likely to have disruptive consequences" (1978: 84). Hirschon also describes a now-abandoned custom among her community in Piraeus whereby a new bride was supposed to keep totally silent for the first few days after her marriage, until one of the groom's family gave her a gift to "get her to speak." Hirschon interprets this ceremony as reflecting the need to domesticate and incorporate the bride as outsider into the new family in this virilocal context. Such a view of Greek women's dangerous words and men's attempt to control them is echoed in du Boulay's (1974) discussion of gossip in the mainland village of Ambeli.

In Kalymnos women's words are not marked out as a threat either to their families or to the wider community. Women compete for the floor on an equal footing with men in the arena of Kalymnian conversation. While in some cases men may be freer to directly criticize their wives as ignorant, these women have an arsenal of not-so-subtle ways of saying the same thing about their husbands, although often indirectly. Thus, women may retreat under a direct verbal attack from their husband, but they will retaliate by finding ways to mock their husbands' pretensions.

A few examples will illustrate this phenomenon. A man in his seventies was telling me about the way they used to start fires on Kalymnos by using two rocks. His wife chimed in that they used a piece of cotton between the rocks. He reacted to her "interruption" by saying to me, "this just goes to show how ignorant my wife is; it's not cotton that they use." The wife held her ground briefly, insisting it was cotton and he, equally adamant, insisted she didn't know what she was talking about. She then ceded, and went into the kitchen to get on with her cooking. He continued to describe for me various technical aspects of starting fires, and then unselfconsciously said, "they use this thing, something like cotton." From the kitchen the wife repeated his words as if singing a song "something like cotton . . . " This forced the man to laugh.

On another occasion this same man had commented on his wife's ignorance in front of me and my one-year-old son. First she said, winking at me, "you see, David, I am a fool." Then she started playing a game with my son, saying, "what do Grandpa's brains do?" She moved her hands back and forth in a gesture I took to mean "Grandpa is crazy." When my son repeated her gesture the woman was delighted, and the man was in no position to respond to this children's game.

In both these cases the woman would not match her husband's insults in direct conversation (although she often would be equally critical of him when we were talking privately). However, by switching registers – using a song, a children's game and by mockingly repeating his own criticisms of her – she was able to respond to his attacks and redress the verbal balance.

It is also important to note that there are no taboos on subjects discussed by men and women: women enter as fiercely into discussions of politics as do men, and often shout them down to get their point across. I encountered no statements by men or women that women *should not* discuss politics; rather it was generally assumed that they would.

Kalymnian matrilocal residence, a topic fully developed in the following chapter, is no doubt an important factor in militating against male control of women's speech. In matrilocal situations women are part of the structure of kinship relations, and thus do not experience the loss of importance, the contingency or the muteness that they seem to do in patrilocal contexts. In the latter case, "Women are represented as mobile elements in a world of male stability, and their poetics, when they exist, are inchoate, contingent, and of a corrective nature" (Loizos and Papataxiarchis 1991: 15). Women's words are not a threat in Kalymnos in the same way that they are in a virilocal community, since women are not "outsiders" who might reveal the secrets of the inside. Their verbal articulacy is no doubt cultivated in a situation in which they are encouraged to talk by their own kin, while the husband, as an outsider, is not. I observed numerous occasions when a seemingly taciturn younger man became lively and animated at gatherings of his own kin group on holidays; while his wife, who normally dominates all conversations, suddenly took a back seat in this exceptional setting, removed from the everyday context of her own kin group.

Control of Space and Movement

If there is an area of life where men exert control over women, it is that of movement and space. Men are able to determine their wives' movements outside the house in ways that the wives correspondingly cannot for their husbands. Women who enter the outside area, for example, the road, are seen as a potential threat to family honor.[4] In some cases, men reportedly refuse to allow their wives to leave the house, even to go shopping, although such extremes are universally condemned by the community. But when women do go out, many must give a strict account of their movements. Often women only go out visiting friends when their husbands have also gone out, as it is seen as unacceptable for a husband to return home and find his wife absent unless she is taking care of some specific business transaction. A woman who had gone out for the afternoon to visit her brother showed physical signs of discomfort when her husband returned early from a hunting expedition. Even though her husband assured her that she could stay as long as she liked, she cut the visit short and rushed back, so that he would not be left at home alone.

This difference between women's freedom of expression and their lack of freedom of movement was brought home to me in discussions with a middle-aged, married Kalymnian woman who ran her own tutorial school. She is an intellectual who has written about Kalymnos, and she considers herself a feminist. When I raised the issue of the "articulateness" of Kalymnian women she heartily concurred. But when I contrasted this with their lack of freedom of movement, she saw this as something scarcely worth remarking on, and commented: "Don't husbands in America keep track of where their wives go and what they do?"

The restriction of women's movement is a phenomenon widely reported in the literature on Greece. When she leaves the house the woman opens herself up to comments by the community on her behavior: where is she going, how is she dressed, is she meeting a lover? This perspective is now being contested, as young women move into new spaces such as the Kafeteria, which have grown in number and become popular spots on Kalymnos since the late 1980s. Equally significant, young women now spend time studying in Athens or in other European countries to obtain various post-high school degrees before returning to Kalymnos to work or teach. Travel to other European countries is necessitated by the difficulty in passing the entrance exams for Greek University. A common practice for boys, and increasingly for girls as well, is to go to Italy, Germany or, before

1989, to one of the Eastern Bloc countries to get a degree. Girls often study a foreign language, which enables them to open tutorial schools (φροντιστήρια) to teach this language when they return to Kalymnos. Whether they go to other countries or to Athens, they experience a greater freedom of movement than they knew on Kalymnos, since they are usually unaccompanied by relatives. When such young women return to Kalymnos they complain vociferously about the difficulty of living in conditions of restricted movement.

However, these restrictions on female movement must be put into the general context of attitudes towards space and place that affect both sexes. Movement on Kalymnos is rarely random. It is unusual to see someone out for a stroll. Rather movement is goal-directed, oriented towards accomplishing shopping, business transactions, or specific visiting and socializing activities. People generally walk only out of necessity: motorcycles or cars are used by the majority of the population, even for going distances of a few hundred yards. My own peripatetic habits often provoked comment on the part of Kalymnians. They expressed surprise (though usually approval too) that I was able to get from my house to the town center (a twenty-minute walk) on a daily basis without difficulty. Though most Kalymnians insist upon the beauty of their island, many admitted to never having visited its different villages. A common joke I heard was that many tourists knew more about Kalymnos than its inhabitants. This lack of interest was typically explained with the refrain, "I know I should go, but what would I do there? I don't know anybody there." Those few who told me that they do wander about the island because they enjoy nature and exploration added that they were looked upon by their neighbors as "crazy."

When I discussed this subject with one man, a builder in his forties, I suggested that men were freer to explore the island than women. He said that men may be freer to go out, but that doesn't mean they explore. It means that they go to the same coffee shop to sit with their friends, day-in and day-out. If somebody suggested that they ride out to see the castle on the hill outside of town, most Kalymnian men would say, "To do what there? What's the point? I'd rather just go to my coffee shop." This same man did admit that women were more restricted in their movements. He said that this was the result of "old ways of thinking" (οι παλιές νοοτροπίες), when the Kalymnian sponge-divers used to leave the island for months at a time and didn't want their wives running around while they were gone. But, he added, thankfully these ways of thinking are changing now. During the summer it is common to see Kalymnian women frequenting the beaches of Kalymnos. Going to the beach is one leisure activity that seems to be respectable and justifiable for women of all ages, though married women are often accompanied by their children if not their husbands as well. Excursions (εκδρομές) to the beach in summer are, from all accounts, a longstanding Kalymnian tradition, though many people remember earlier times (before the 1960s) when men and women were expected to bathe at separate beaches.

My observations indicate that many women still feel the need to justify their movements to their husbands or other family members. If a woman goes visiting too often it can be interpreted as a neglect of her household duties; many women prefer to conform to these rules to avoid trouble within the family. The one area where women do not have to account for their movements is in attending church. Thus many women, in particular older married women, look forward to church holidays and the numerous liturgies held at small chapels on saints' days as a chance to escape the household, to find a little "relaxation" and "peace" away from their husbands and children. Similarly, religious excursions to neighboring islands such as Patmos (to the tomb of Saint John), Symi (for the name day of Saint Panormitis), or Mytiline (to the tomb of Saint Rafael), offer opportunities for women to travel off the island and enjoy a break from their regular routine. For many older women such opportunities to leave Kalymnos are usually only provided by urgent business that they need to conduct in Athens, by the need to take a family member to the hospital in Rhodes, or by their husband's need to migrate to another island, to Athens or further afield to find work.[5]

As noted above, the situation for young women appears to be rapidly changing, with spaces opening up such as the Kafeteria, and new expectations that young women will travel abroad without their families in order to gain an education. One eighteen-year-old woman told me that she had studied at a beauty school in Athens for two years, living in an apartment on her own. She had gone to Athens aged sixteen, having won over her father's hesitations. Although her parents had heard comments from neighbors about allowing their daughter go to Athens on her own, such things were occurring more frequently now. She added that she had a "fiancé" who worked in Ohio, but later admitted that she only called him "fiancé" so that she would be able to go out at night with her friends and be, in a sense, spoken for (i.e. not be seen as a single eighteen-year-old girl going out dancing). Here her reputation seems to depend on her intention to be married, and thus she cannot be regarded as ruining her reputation by simply having a little fun with her friends.

In summary, an examination of Kalymnian gendered patterns of speech and movement reveals a mixed picture. It clearly does not fit more traditional descriptions of male dominance in other parts of Greece and the Mediterranean. But at the same time, it does not provide a clear image of female autonomy and power. Instead, Kalymnos is caught in between conflicting ideologies and practices. Local residence patterns support female autonomy within the home. Pan-Greek patriarchal ideologies mean that women's movements outside of the home can still be seen as potentially threatening to male honor. Western influences raise new issues and possibilities for a younger generation of men and women. In the next section I turn from obser-vations of the present to a consideration of a discourse concerning gender relations of the past. Specifically, in looking at the Rock War, and the way it has been differently remembered by men and women, I will continue my exploration of present-day gender relations through illuminating the tensions provoked by the image of women acting collectively to effect change in the public sphere.

The Rock War

Unlike dynamite throwing, the Rock War (Πετροπόλεμος) is not a disputed Kalymnian custom, in the sense of a ritually repeated action. However, it is directly comparable to dynamite throwing in that it is regarded as embodying the Kalymnian tradition of resistance to outside rule. Recollection of the event by women is also significant as an attempt to claim a place in "history," a domain which men have claimed as their own. It is further comparable as an "event" to the great dynamite accident of 1980. The critical question I raise is: how does this event inform present views of women's roles in male-defined public spaces?

First, it should be noted that the "Rock War" is viewed as the most spectacular of a series of acts of resistance carried out against the Italian colonizers on Kalymnos. It was the largest and most violent protest that the Italians faced during their thirty-year rule over the Dode-canese. The Rock War occurred in 1935, during the latter part of this rule, a period that witnessed the rise of fascism and expansionism in Italy and a tightening of Italian control over these islands.[6] As from 1924 the Italian authorities had been attempting to separate the dioceses of the Dodecanese from their leadership in Istanbul, to make them into an autocephalous or independent church. This was the project of colonial governor Mario Lago. Doumanis (n.d.: 4) provides the relevant background:

> The bone of contention was ecclesiastical reform of the Greek Orthodox Church in the Dodecanese . . . The islands were basically divided into four dioceses which were under the jurisdiction of the Patriarchate of Constantinople. Lago was concerned by the prominence of the clergy in anti-Italian agitation during the first decade of the occupation, and the influence of the Patriarchate. He hoped to counter this influence and assume more control of the clergy by sponsoring the formation of a single, autonomous Church. Crucial to the success of this projected

reform was the support of the Dodecanesian higher clergy, who were
enticed by the prospects of greater autonomy, power and prestige.

While the Italians claimed that the move had purely administrative
significance, local clergy resented this potential intrusion into their
affairs. Furthermore, many Kalymnians, including the wealthy and
highly literate expatriate community in Athens and elsewhere, were
convinced that the real intention behind this manoeuvre was to put
the Dodecanese under the authority of the Pope – in effect to convert
the islands to Catholicism.[7]

The Italian plan had some support among Dodecanese church authorities. However, local clergymen, supported by the Patriarchate in
Istanbul and Dodecanesian organizations abroad, had managed to
avert these plans for several years. But by 1934 it was clear that the
Italian authorities (with the help of some members of the local church
hierarchy), were moving ahead with their plans. On Kalymnos in 1934
a number of local priests had signed an oath to do whatever they
could to overturn the Italian plans, including a mobilization of the
people. In early 1935 one priest, Papa Tsougranis, who was suspected
by the Italians of being an instigator of unrest, was interrupted in the
middle of a liturgy in the main church of Kalymnos' inland town
Horio, and informed that he was to report to the authorities. A large
group of women were in attendance at the liturgy. They realized
that their priest was going to be taken to jail, surrounded him and
accompanied him back to his house, which they kept blockaded,
refusing the surprised Italian soldiers entrance. The priest was able to
flee under cover of night and escape the island, travelling to Turkey
and eventually to Piraeus. This was the first recorded act of collective
resistance on the part of Kalymnian women.

For the next two months the Kalymnians kept their churches closed
and did not hold any services, in fear that the Italians would arrange
services in Catholic fashion. In early April 1935, the word went out
that the Italian administration at the instigation, or at least with the
active participation of two local priests (one said to be non-Kalymnian)
had ordered the churches to be opened. The bells were to be rung
announcing services at the main church in the harbor of Kalymnos.
In response, Kalymnian women, from the very old to thirteen-year-
old girls, gathered in the harbor in an attempt to block the Italian
soldiers and prevent the church bells from being rung. The women
were unarmed and were met with rifle butts, but used their numbers
to overwhelm the soldiers. One participant describes the electric
atmosphere and the sense of collective power of the first moments of
battle:

> Then came the crucial moment, when we heard the church bells . . .
> ringing. We all became enraged, and suddenly we felt a new sense of

Papa-Mihalis Tsovgranis. The priest-"hero" of the Rock War. The bust is located in the courtyard of the church of the Panayia in Horio, where yearly memorials for the Rock War take place.

Katerina Kardovlia, mid-storytelling

urgency and *power* . . . One [of us] was hit in the back, another was hit
on the head . . . all of us around me were screaming, shouting, punching,
slapping.

(Kapella 1986: 93; emphasis mine)

In all the written and oral recountings of these events I have never
heard mention of named leadership on the part of the women. What
is stressed is that the action was spontaneous and collective, the
massive response of the women who felt that their church and their
religion was under attack. Kapella (1986: 92) uses the metaphor of a
human ocean to describe the force of the collected Kalymnian women
during their first battle with the Italians: "All that crowd of women
(γυναικομάνι) was shouting, hooting, resembling a human ocean in
the midst of a storm trying to find an outlet, but no dam could hold
back its destructive (καταλύτρα) onrush."

The striking absence of men from these conflicts with the Italian
soldiers is explained in a number of accounts by the fact that the
women reasoned that the soldiers might fire on men but would
hold their fire in dealing with women. When a few Kalymnian men
attempted to join the protest, the women "all with one voice shouted:
Men, get back! (πίσω οι άντρες)."[8] Doumanis notes that the Kalymnians
saw the Italians as "soft" and "civilized" as compared to the "barbaric"
Turks who had been their previous rulers (1997: 71 ff.), and they
therefore would not fire on women. Here it was specifically the presumed Italian sense of honor, i.e. their gender ideology, which the
Kalymnian women turned to their own advantage and used as a
strategy in the Rock War.

It was equally significant that the Italians had threatened the
Church, a domain of activity in which Greek women play a leading
role.[9] In their defense of the Church, the women could claim the space
of defending the "moral community," a common strategy in women's
collective action movements. As in other moral community protests,
such as that of the Madres of the Plaza de Mayo in Argentina in
the 1970s, this involved claiming an unaccustomed spatial location.
Indeed, gendered spatial locations were reversed in the Rock War: the
women were acting in the center of town (the *platea* of Kalymnos
harbor) while the men, it is claimed, were "locked up in their homes"
like women. Another woman who participated describes the emotions
she felt as follows:

you felt ashamed to stay in your house during those days. If any woman
stayed inside because she had housework . . . as soon as they passed by
and saw you they said 'what are you staying inside for, shame on you!
Hurry up and let's go, never mind your housework, you can come back
to it again. But if they change our faith, we won't be able to get it back

again!' There wasn't anything else to be said, you put down your work and you went with them.

(Kapella 1986: 95; my translation)

During these events the normal rules of good womanly behavior were turned upside down. This reversal also allows Kapella to comment ironically on the "civilized behavior" of the Italians, who went so far as to attack a group of Kalymnian nuns and to smash the cross which the nuns were parading through the square. The movement of women *en masse* into the center of town was something that would normally only occur during ritual and religious processions, and thus it gave the protest a certain festive atmosphere, despite the danger. As one participant described her involvement: "I too was there. I followed the women who passed by my house, looking as if they were off to a carnival" (Doumanis n.d.: 9).

The Rock War itself occurred on the third day after the uprising began. The women retreated behind the walls around the square, and amassed piles of rocks that they began hurling down on the heads of the soldiers. Some men were allowed to participate in the gathering and transporting of the rocks, but the throwing was limited to women. The women had particular success in causing chaos while Italian rein- forcements, summoned from the surrounding islands, were attempting to disembark in the harbor. As participant and writer Niki Billiri describes the scene:

It was 7:30 in the morning when the ship "Ardito" arrived from Leros – full of Italian soldiers – and moored near by to the old harbor office. The crowd of women and the few men who were mixed in got stirred up as soon as they saw the soldiers, and a roar of curses and threats filled the air . . . As time passed the atmosphere became electrified. Each hand squeezed a rock and waited impatiently to begin the stoning. Then the order was given to disembark . . . What happened then is indes- cribable. The crowd, boiling with exasperation and drunk with passion, let go a rain of rocks and more rocks. The Italians, beneath this deluge of stones resembling a moving vault, fled every which way. Helmets were falling into the sea while soldiers were struck and wounded about the head and the shoulders.

(Billiri 1982; my translation)

The women's successes ended, however, when a shepherd named Kazonis insisted, over the protests of the women, on participating. Kapella's account claims that Kazonis was having considerable success using a slingshot, but the Italian soldiers saw him and several took aim at him and shot him in the head. This halted the efforts of the women who, in shock, began to lament the killing of Kazonis, and to carry his body back to his house. With their reinforcements now in place, the Italians declared martial law. That same evening they rounded up many of Kalymnos' most prominent citizens (mostly men) and took them to the neighboring island of Kos where they were tried and put in jail.

Kazonis is referred to in written texts as the martyr of the Rock War, and I did not hear anything to dispute this during my fieldwork. However, from reading the accounts one could offer a different interpretation, one that shows how his participation, over the protests of the women, was an interference that short-circuited the women's strategies and brought the Rock War to a premature end before the women could wreak even greater humiliation on the Italians. Indeed, one could interpret the shooting of Kazonis as an attempt on the part of the Italians to redefine the event as a contest between men, one which they could clearly control and contain, rather than as the popular expression of the overwhelming majority of the island's women. Doumanis argues that the Italian authorities could not accept that local women were acting on their own initiative, they were convinced that local males "had put their women up to mischief" (1997: 75). Thus, after the Rock War, they decided to imprison all the prominent male leaders (and a few women) on the island. The Italians also did a service to the Kalymnian men: in providing them the context to redefine the Rock War as their battle, not one in which they were conspicuously sidelined.

It is important to stress that the Rock War remained a victory for the Kalymnians; it achieved what it set out to do. The goal was clearly *not* to overthrow Italian rule, but rather to reject its intrusion into an area of life that Kalymnian women defined as their own. The Kalymnian churches, in fact, remained closed, and liturgies were held in secret for two years until the Italians abandoned their attempts to make the Dodecanese autocephalous. As Kapella (1986: 102) concludes: "only Kalymnos took on the weight of this inspired, suffering resistance. [The other islands] didn't share in it, but they shared the victory, the right to raise high the banner of Orthodox faith and tradition."

For women who were alive at the time of the Rock War (women now in their late fifties and older), this is the emblematic event of Kalymnian woman's strength and struggles to defend her religion and her family. Whenever I raised the issue of the resistance of Kalymnian women or even of Kalymnian resistance in general, older women would immediately respond, "oh yes, the Rock War." Women in their seventies would eagerly claim participation: they were in the "front lines" or that they led all the women of the neighborhood down to the harbor to meet the Italians. The collective nature of the struggle lends itself to such claims, since the majority of the women on the island reportedly participated. At the same time, while women asserted their individual initiatives, they simultaneously stressed the collective nature of the protest by consistently telling their tales in the first person plural.

Older women would also spontaneously raise the specter of the Rock War in everyday conversation when declaring their strength. One woman recounted to me a commercial dispute she was having with a man from Kos. When he refused to pay a promissory note he had given her, she told him, "I'll drag you through every court in this country if you try to cheat me. Don't forget who you're dealing with: we Kalymnian women who took on the Italians armed only with rocks!" In another situation when I mentioned having heard praise of Kalymnian patriotism on other islands, a woman immediately referred to the Rock War and related it to the legend of the Cave of the Seven Virgins – a story of women's bravery during Ottoman times – as one of a series of examples of the courage of Kalymnian women. In official discourse the Rock War has remained a basic reference point for Kalymnian resistance and especially for Kalymnian's unshakable Christian faith and resistance to outsiders. Thus the local newspaper refers to the "Holy Rock War" in an editorial leader about the reaction of the island to the latest religious "invaders" – a handful of Jehovah Witnesses who were attempting to proselytize on Kalymnos. Interpreted by Kalymnian women as their own war, the Rock War gives them a claim to equal (or greater) courage and bravery and equal status with men in fulfilling their national and religious duties to their country and in actively participating in local/national "history."

The significance of these Kalymnian women's memories of their active participation in "making history" stands out when contrasted to a recent study of gendered memories of the same period in Crete and Thessaly (Goltsis-Rosier 1993). Goltsis-Rosier found a striking divergence between men's memories of their participation in resistance to the German occupation and women's memories of the hardships and injustices of this occupation. Men clearly gained a sense of meaning through placing Greece's role (and their own) in the context of the efforts to defeat Hitler.[10] However, women's memories, even those who had participated in the resistance, dwelt on their role as victims of historical forces, not as participants in history. Goltsis-Rosier ascribes these differences between male and female memories as an extension of their normal gendered roles to extraordinary circumstances. She claims that men's sense of selfhood is based on constant risk-taking and "challenge," whereas women's selfhood is based on the creation of stability (1993: 42). Unlike patrilocal Thessaly or mountain Crete (which is organized on agnatic principles),[11] on Kalymnos these gender-related traits were not evidenced behaviorally or in people's everyday discourses about gender differences.

However, while older Kalymnian women perceive themselves as

historical actors, it is clear that Kalymnian men are less comfortable
with this idea. Although men do not directly dispute women's claims
concerning the Rock War, they rarely spontaneously refer to these
events. If they mention the Rock War, they tend to focus on the role
of the two men who have been memorialized – the priest and the
shepherd – and to pass over the women.[12] A few men even stated
that the Rock War had been blown out of proportion. One said that it
was foolish trouble-making, "since the Italians merely wanted to make
the church independent and did not want to change our religion."
Another man, too young to have been an eyewitness, claimed that it
was merely the act of a handful of people, caught up in the excitement
of the moment.

The Rock War is problematic for men because it seems to cross
between the categories of tradition and history. The two most extensive
recountings of the event are not written by historians, but by Kalymnos' two leading folklorists, both women. The canonical three volume
history of Kalymnos (Frangopoulos 1952) devotes less than a page to
the events of the Rock War, preferring to assimilate it within a long
account of "attempts by Kalymnian [male] leaders to deflect attempts
by the Italian colonial regime to impose taxes and educational reforms
on the island."[13] It is interesting that male writers of history have
also felt the need to change the name of the "Rock War" with its
connotations of folksiness, to the "National-Religious Awakening [or
Resistance]" (η εθνικοθρησκευτική εξέγερση or αντίσταση). This situates
the Rock War within a broader, national history, and simultaneously
downplays the women's central role in the event.

It is not only written history that has reinterpreted the Rock War;
public memorials have also done so. At the annual celebration of the
Rock War I attended in 1993, the male schoolteacher chosen to deliver
the speech was also a leading member of Kalymnos' cultural–historical
society, the Αναγνωστήριο. This celebration involved the typical
elements of Kalymnian historical celebration: the presence of the
political and religious dignitaries of the island (almost exclusively
men), the playing of the Greek national anthem by the local philharmonic band, and the laying of a wreath by the mayor of Kalymnos
on the bust of the priest, Papa Tsougranis. It was held outside the
main church of Horio (the second largest settlement on Kalymnos),
where Papa Tsougranis had been giving his liturgy when the Italians
came to arrest him. The memorial was on a Sunday after the normal
liturgy, therefore much of its audience was constituted by people
coming out of church. In the audience of approximately 200 people,
only a few were women old enough to have participated in the Rock
War. The schoolteacher's speech emphasized how the Rock War was
one of many similar acts of resistance to foreign tyranny in Greek
national history. No longer an outstanding act of collective resistance

on the part of unarmed women, the Rock War had become, in his account, an example of Kalymnos living up to the ideals of a united Greece.

The speaker's greatest praise was for Papa Tsougranis, whom he referred to as a Kalymnian Papa Flessas (the priest known as a leader of the war of 1821 against the Ottoman Empire).[14] The women who fought the Rock War receive mention in his speech only once, in the following sentence: "Papa Tsougranis, the Kalymnian Papa Flessas, inflamed the hearts of the women and led [συμπαράσερνε] them into resistance against the fascist dynasty." The Kalymnian women are depicted here as passively drawn along, or swept away (the verb συμπαρασέρνω has the connotation of being carried or led without one's willing participation), by the leadership of Papa Tsougranis, rather than engaging in their own deliberate action.

Quite a different image is given in a short, anonymous piece in the local Kalymnian newspaper of December 1992. After noting that Kalymnian women have been playing a leading role in cultural and sporting organizations on the island, the article excoriates Kalymnian men in the following terms: "This isn't the first time that we've seen such things. History tells us of the fighter, the Kalymnian woman, and of the lazy, chair-hunting Kalymnian man" (*Argó tis Kalímnou* 1992).[15] Older women to whom I read this passage immediately associated it with the Rock War. As one woman put it: "She is strong the Kalymnian woman, its in her blood. With the Rock War the women did most of it. All the islanders are all active in cultural events, they have their own organizations in Athens, but I see the Kalymnian woman as especially active."

The newspaper passage itself is ambiguous, and was interpreted by a Kalymnian woman in her twenties as referring to the everyday struggles of Kalymnian women in the past to survive amidst the myriad hardships of the island. She referred to the struggle and self-sacrifice of her grandmother and other women of her generation who raised families while their husbands were absent most of the year on the sponge boats, or returned from the sponge expeditions crippled or dead. When stripped of its legitimacy as an example of women's collective action, the specific image of the Rock War is less pertinent for younger women. It remains preserved in the consciousness of the older generation of women, but it is not clear whether it will disappear from historical memory once this generation dies out.

However, a notion of mothers and grandmothers as powerful has been transmitted across the generations. Many middle-aged and younger women had stories to tell me about the heroic or everyday struggles of a mother, an aunt or a grandmother. The most well-known person in local historical memory is probably Katerina Vouvali ("Vouvalina;" Βουβαλίνα), the wife of a very wealthy sponge-merchant who endowed the hospital on Kalymnos and a number of other public buildings. She outlived him by several decades and is therefore remembered better than him for the economic power she wielded on the island. She is commonly referred to as "the Lady" (η κυρά), a term that connotes not so much the respect she was accorded, but a recognition of her power over the island.

Memories of her are certainly mixed. She is often remembered for her stinginess, for the way she controlled the labor market, and for underpaying her workers. She is also said to have engaged in a number of illegal dealings on the island, including the unearthing of buried treasure for sale abroad. Kalymnians tend not to have much esteem for the rich, and Vouvalina is no exception. However, what is significant in Vouvalina's case is that she is remembered and admired by both women and men for her intelligence. Her intelligence was evidenced for Kalymnians in the things she had brought to the island from abroad, in her skillful management of her money, and in her ability to find the buried treasure that had eluded many others. It is noteworthy that the adjective implying legitimate intelligence (έξυπνη) was used to describe her, rather than that connoting cunning (πονηρή), which is often associated with women. This can be seen, perhaps, as an example of men praising women for successfully achieving manly behavior, a situation noted elsewhere in Greek ethnography. The occasional woman who does this is not perceived as a threat, but a validation of "manliness."[16] Her actions need not be downplayed; as tends to happen to women's collective engagement in effective action, such as the Rock War, when the majority of men stayed on the sidelines. If the tradition of dynamite throwing is a constant reminder to all Kalymnians of Kalymnian men's ability to take power literally into their own hands, the power of women to participate in acts of collective resistance finds no comparable support through repetition. Although Kalymnians of both sexes can agree that the great dynamite "accident" was a tragedy, it is a threat only insofar as essentially manly behavior was allowed to get out of hand. As an event it does not threaten gender categories, it therefore retains a largely shared interpretation. The Rock War, by contrast, suggests that women could move out of their traditional domain and achieve the same as men, i.e. wield power collectively. Thus it is preserved in the memories and writings of a few, disputed by others, and for the rest it is assimilated to the canons of legitimate history. Unlike this interpretation of the Rock War, the memory of Vouvalina, and the many mothers, aunts and grandmothers who used their intelligence and initiative to fend off adversity, has survived and been transmitted through the generations. Such images provide the present generation of women with models of hard and determined women from the past who were forces to be reckoned with.

What else can be illuminated by a comparison of women's throwing of rocks to men's throwing of "man-made" dynamite? First, when men throw rocks – as in the case of Kazonis – they use a slingshot, which accounts of the Rock War claim to be more accurate. One could interpret these contrasts in terms of women using the "natural" landscape itself as a weapon against the colonial intruders. Similarly, as an illustration of women's collective action, the analyst might assimilate the Rock War with other examples of women's protest in which women use their oppressed condition and their restriction to the domestic sphere as a means to mobilize around issues of "motherhood": to ensure their own survival and that of their children. Such forms of political mobility, exemplified by the Madres of the Plaza de Mayo in Argentina, have often had the potential to encourage women to question further diverse forms of gendered oppression.[17]

I would argue, however, that such a model does not fit well with the Kalymnian case. The Rock War was not an extension of purely "domestic" concerns, but was fought over the public, "political" issue of religion and the church, a domain where women have always taken an active, non-"domestic" role. Unlike the mobilization of women in South Africa, for example, Kalymnian women did not require a transformation of consciousness to "overcome cultural patterns that prevent women from speaking out in front of men."[18] Kalymnian women were not "muted" in their everyday lives and dealings with their husbands, but rather were accustomed to being encouraged by their kin group to hold contradictory opinions to their husbands.

A more appropriate parallel for the Rock War is provided by women's collective action and protest movements in colonial West Africa, a situation in which women's collective protests were reinforced by the relative autonomy they experienced in the structuring of their everyday lives. In these rebellions women were able to draw on precolonial histories of economic autonomy, voluntary associations, and political power in dual-sex hierarchies, strategically to counter colonial infringements. They utilized their traditional tactics, such as "sitting on a man, " in confronting male-dominated channels of local government. Women employed such strategies "when the . . . colonial institutions introduced by the British infringed on women's traditional areas of control" (Moran 1989: 450). The Nigerian Women's War of 1929, as described by Mba (1982) provides an interesting parallel with the Rock War. As with the Rock War, the Women's War was not an attempt to overthrow colonial government *per se*, but aimed to achieve specific goals: in this case the repeal of taxes on women. This was not simply an economic issue, but had political and cultural dimensions as well (Mba 1982: 296). Like the Kalymnian women, the Nigerian women took advantage of the belief that the British colonial government would not kill women. And as with the Rock War, the British colonial government attempted to marginalize the women's actions by claiming that they were only acting at the behest of "a conspiracy of men."[19] Finally, the Women's War, like the Rock War, was successful in forcing the colonial powers to abandon the plans that had sparked the protest.

If memories of the Rock War pose a threat to Kalymnian men and to their creation of local history in a national framework, it is not because of the image it offers of powerful women. It is rather the threat of women extending their acknowledged powers in the domain of "tradition", into the male domain of History. For while men threw dynamite one Easter allegedly in protest at Italian colonial rule, such protest had a purely symbolic character. It reminded the Italians that "we're alive" in the words of one Kalymnian intellectual, but unlike the women's Rock War, it did not attempt to have an impact on Italian policy, nor was it a general call to revolt. It is precisely this potential for women to act effectively not solely within the sphere of household management and the church, but in confrontation with the Italian authorities in the center of the town, that gives the Rock War both its liberatory and carnivalesque cast, and makes its memory problematic for men.

What were the sources of Kalymnian women's autonomy which, as I have been arguing, they made use of in the Rock War? To comprehend these I shall turn to practices of dowry, inheritance, and sponge-diving, and the striking claim made by present-day Kalymnian women and men that "we used to have matriarchy on the island."

Notes

1. For representatives of the first two approaches, see Campbell 1964; Danforth 1982; Dimen 1986; Dubisch 1986; du Boulay 1986; Friedl 1986; Hoffman, Cowan and Aralow 1974. For the third approach, see Caraveli 1986; Seremetakis 1991.

2. Loizos and Papataxiarchis 1991: 15.

3. Vernier (1987: 371–2) notes that women in Karpathos control their husbands earnings, and that husbands often get a daily allowance from their wives, or even their daughters, for coffeeshop and cigarette expenditures. See also Skiada's account (1990: 329 ff.).

4. Cf. Hirschon 1978; Seremetakis 1991.

5. On the church as a refuge from the home cf. Hart 1992. Visits to relatives on neighboring islands provide another opportunity for women to travel. Also

shopping excursions are occasionally undertaken away from Kalymnos. In one case I travelled with three married women to the neighboring island of Kos to harvest and purchase 300 lbs of grape-leaves for their use in making dolmadhes (φύλλα as they are referred to on the island, where they are common Sunday fare) over the coming year.

6. See Frangopoulos 1952.

7. One Kalymnian historian, Yiorgos Sakellaridis, told me that the Italians were trying to convert the Dodecanesians not to Catholicism, but rather to Uniatism, i.e. Orthodox who recognized the supreme authority of the Pope.

8. Kapella 1986: 96. See also Billiri's (1982) account.

9. For discussions of the relationship of women to Greek Orthodoxy, see Hirschon 1983; Dubisch 1991; Hart 1992.

10.   As one man put it, "It was the idea that we had to act. We were a part of history. The German advance depended on the Battle of Crete. And although we were – what were we – primitive, in comparison with the Germans . . . Yet we were significant, and nearly caused Hitler to cancel the campaign in Africa." Another man puts it more simply: "We had historical significance. We were the Allies" (Goltsis-Rosier 1993: 39–40).

11. See Herzfeld 1985.

12. Doumanis (1997: 67–80) has similarly argued that men, in their recollections of the Rock War, have attempted to downplay or explain away the centrality of women: "Male oral testimonies often reiterated the assumption that men **allowed** their women to take the center stage. They suggest that husbands sent their wives and daughters into the streets, confident the Italians would not harm them." Doumanis dismisses this view, as well as the view that the women were simply acting at the behest of an organized male leadership.

13. Doumanis n.d.: 12; see also Doumanis' discussion of the account by Sakellarios (1977).

14. This comparison was disputed by a man who attended the speech. He told me that the lionization of Papa Tsougranis was a misreading of history, since he was only one of a number of priests who had sworn an oath to defend their church against the Italian plans. And since he escaped Kalymnos after the Italians attempted to arrest him, he was absent both for the events of the Rock War itself, and for the trial and imprisonment of island leaders which followed.

15. Καρεκλοθήρας suggests the image of a man in a hurry to find himself a chair at a coffee shop.

16. Herzfeld 1985: 146. Indeed I did hear men on occasion praise a woman who showed strength of character, physical strength, or business acumen as being "like a man." In one instance in which I relayed this praise to the woman, she took it as a compliment.

17. See Bouvard 1994; Fisher 1989; Taylor 1994.

18. Seidman 1993: 309. See also Kemp 1995.

19. Mba 1982: 292; see also Ifeka-Moller 1975: 133 ff. Note that a number of women were in fact killed by British soldiers in this case.

five

Memories of Matriarchy

The historian J. Thompson writes that in the Pre-Historic Aegean we encounter matrilineal kinship, matriarchal organization, cults of matriarchal deities, and the famous myth of the Amazonian female warriors . . . It seems quite probable that the historical changes that took place in Greece and led to the passage from a matrilineal kinship organization to a patrilineal one . . . was restricted within the boundaries of peninsular Greece and there was no parallel social change in the Aegean.

(Dimitriou-Kotsoni 1993: 72)

I began the last chapter with male jokes about women's control over household finances and other significant decision-making on Kalymnos. I then showed how a historical instance of women's public power was downplayed and reinterpreted by men in the service of their own interests, which included retaining control over female space and movement. Should this all be seen as resistance, hegemony or simply a polyphony of contradictory discourses and practices?

The tantalizing quote from Dimitriou-Kotsoni suggests that in looking at these issues we may be dealing with structures of very long duration, rather than the fairly recent adjustment to economic factors such as patterns of male work-related migration, as others have argued (for example, Papataxiarchis 1995). Unfortunately, Dimitriou-Kotsoni provides us with very little evidence which might be used to substantiate her claims. My purpose here, however, is not to resolve these historical disputes, but to see what can be further learned from Kalymnians' own reconstructions of past gender relations in light of their views of the present, and of the relevance of such past reconstructions to this disputed and ever-changing present.

I begin with a description of the present scene: practices of residence and inheritance that have a distinctly matrifocal slant on Kalymnos. I then turn to memories of past gender relations on Kalymnos. These memories entail discourses of "matriarchy" which coexist uncomfortably with discourses of "patriarchy." In trying to untangle this seeming contradiction, I suggest some reasons why aspects of this gendered Kalymnian past are remembered fondly or nostalgically, while others are cast off and disparaged as "stupidities of our grand-parents." (This occurs in much the same way that dynamite, for its detractors, was seen not as "custom" but as a "craziness" that must be shed if Kalymnos was to be part of "modern" Greece and Europe).

Dowry and Matrilocality

The preference for matrilocal residence on Kalymnos gives women a strong base of support within their own kin group that does not exist for areas of Greece where patrilocal residence is practiced.[1] As Cassel-bery and Valvanes (1975) note, there is a tendency towards matrilocal residence when the house constitutes the main item of dowry. On Kalymnos, where agriculture has always been a marginal activity, ownership of a house is considered to be the most crucial item for a woman to be marriageable. The verb "to provide a house" (σπιτώνω) is often used interchangeably with προικίζω "to provide a dowry."

Since the "abolition" of the dowry by the Greek government in 1982,[2] inheritance of a house has taken on a greater significance. It now represents a transfer of wealth that can be argued for by Kalym-nians as expressing the natural desire of parents to see their children provided with the essentials for life on Kalymnos. This is opposed to land, money or a trousseau, which have now taken on the most negative and anti-modern connotations of the word "dowry."[3]

Young women may now be the main contributors of funds in the construction of the "dowry" house, normally built prior to marriage, and often attached to, or adjacent to the parental house. I believe that this "self-endowment," as Estevez-Weber (1983) terms it, is one reason that the building of a house can be thought of as not a "dowry," in contrast to land or money. Moreover, in looking at the metaphorical uses of the term "dowry," I have found that it almost invariably refers to situations of hierarchical power relations. A parent provides a dowry for a child, or if a brother provides a dowry for a sister, he is acting in the role of the father which the father is unable to fulfill. One reads newspaper references to the "dowry" that Greece is receiving from the European Union (i.e. various funds provided to the economically weaker EU countries for the purpose of "convergence" with the rest of the EU), another situation in which there is a perceived hierarchical relation. Young working women are increasingly capable of making major contributions to the building of their own houses; thus the house has become a "necessity" that each woman attempts to acquire, rather than a "custom" for intergenerational property transfer.

This stress on house-ownership is further rationalized by the widely held opinion that renting a house is an insupportable burden for a young couple. This tends to naturalize the practice into a non-dowry transaction, i.e. it is felt to be a necessity. As many Kalymnians rhetorically asked me when I questioned them about the dowry, "Don't parents provide for their children in America if they can?" Provision of a house is now spoken of as a gift rather than a dowry because, it is said, it is no longer obligatory to provide it; also because it is "stripped-down," no longer a lavish affair. As one young woman expressed it, "Yes, women get houses, but in the past the parents also gave large sums of money and the house was always fully furnished, and the groom entered his house like a lord entering his mansion. Now bride and groom furnish it together, a much more sensible system."[4] Here the image of equality is specifically invoked by a young woman: she contrasts it to the power imbalances of the past when the groom was treated as a lord (σαν κύριος).[5]

There is a vast literature on the implications of the dowry for women's status, both within Greece and elsewhere. Goody (1976) sees dowry as a mechanism for women to inherit their patrimonial "share." Whereas Sharma (1980), working in India, shows that dowry can be used effectively to disinherit daughters. In Greece, Friedl (1967) following Goody, argues for the view that dowry is a form of pre-mortem inheritance, and Dubisch (1974) views it as an important component in rural women's power.

Scholars working from a political rather than anthropological perspective have tended to see the dowry in more negative terms for women, as part of a patriarchal culture intent on preserving women's "traditional" subordination.[6] More recent work has suggested that new dowry demands in the face of the consumerization of Greek society, and the need for women to provide houses in an urban context, have made provisions for marriage particularly burdensome for young women. This indicates one of the reasons why the dowry has become a symbol of "everything that was un-modern, un-European, rural and regressive."[7] There is a certain irony in the fact that the dowry's benefits for women have been eroded by its "modernization" just as it has come to represent Greece at its most un-modern. The association of the dowry with "rural backwardness" is clearly a widespread phenomenon in Greece. This feature is crucial to Kalymnians' disparagement of the dowry and their insistence that it was not a part of Kalymnian tradition but rather, as one man put it, an ephemeral response to economic conditions imposed by the hardships of life under Italian and Ottoman rule. However, I argue below that the dowry was, in the context of Kalymnian matrilocality and matrilateral transmission, an important component of women's power on Kalymnos, despite its present, negative associations for men and women.

In the neighborhood where I lived, only three out of the fifty houses in the surrounding area had been transferred from parents to a son. In each of these cases it was because the wives involved were non-Kalymnian (two were from Australia, one was from Kos). In one of those three cases, the house had subsequently been transferred to a daughter who shared it with her parents and her husband (the typical pattern).[8] Thus it is only under exceptional circumstances, such as marriage with non-Kalymnian or non-Greek women, that their exists the situation (described by Friedl and others) of a woman who is cut off from her natal kin and resides with her mother-in-law. One older man told me that this was the reason that foreigners (in this case non-Greeks) made better wives: without their kin around, they were much more complacent than Kalymnian wives who were "always stirring up trouble for their husbands."

Women's ownership of houses in the same vicinity as their family provides them with support in disputes with their husbands. It also gives them considerable status, since they are most directly associated with the symbolic capital of houses and their transmission.[9] As a male intellectual in his forties explained to me: "through the house, women control the material transmission of the past, of tradition."

In summary, an examination of present-day gender roles and gendered power reveals a mixed picture. It clearly does not fit more traditional ethnographic descriptions of male dominance in other parts of Greece and the Mediterranean. At the same time, it does not provide the clear picture of female autonomy and power that Dimitriou-Kotsoni (1993) has argued for Fourni and other surrounding islands (north-east Aegean). In the next two sections I turn from observations of the present to a consideration of discourses of past gender relations. I believe that a consideration of these discourses will illuminate the tangled questions of authority, power and autonomy, at the same time that they help us to understand how "tradition" and other "pasts" are used in continuing debates over present-day gender relations.

Patriarchy/Matriarchy?

A constant theme in discussions and reminiscences about "the old years" was the claim on the part of both women and men that there used to be women's rule, or "matriarchy" (μητριαρχία, γυναικοκρατία) on Kalymnos. Such a claim is interesting enough in itself, and became more so when I encountered an equal number of claims that there used to be "patriarchy."[10] In some cases when the issue arose at different times the same person would make opposite claims. This suggested to me that these claims had different referents, and were being made in response to Kalymnian awareness of wider discourses concerning gender relations in Greece and in the West more generally.[11]

The claim that men used to rule on Kalymnos, occurred more specifically in the context of older people's nostalgia, as discussed in Chapter 2. It was linked to the idea of an "absolute" respect which children supposedly showed to their parents. The fact that young children were regarded as no longer demonstrating such respect to either their parents or to older people in the community, was a prominent theme in discussions of the changes Kalymnos has undergone. In particular, it was the father who was regarded as absolute "ruler," no decision would be taken without him. This discourse clearly has a conservative thrust. For men, I believe, it aligns Kalymnos with the rest of Greece where male authority is a more obvious feature of everyday life. In effect, it makes a claim to equal "honor" for Kalymnian men (see footnote 29). Women also talk of past "patriarchy," as in the following paraphrase of a woman in her seventies assessing some of the changes in women's status on the island:

> Women are able to work different jobs now. They are able to vote, and this is all very sensible. But equality threatens the family and the respect for the family unit. Because the father still must rule the home and the children must respect the father. And if the mother teaches them to respect the father, they will respect the mother as well. That's what I teach my grandchildren now, I try to make an impression on them. I'm always telling them to mind their father or "aren't you ashamed of what your father will think?" Never mind about the mother, the father must be the center of the family. I don't know, I'm just an old illiterate woman, but I think I still have my wits about me, and this is what I believe.

To this older woman it is the relationship between the father and the children that is both central to the family and the exercise of authority. Although the wife is supposed to show similar respect for her husband's decisions, statements about this relationship are qualified by the comment that he must listen to her advice and must not treat her as a servant. There is a certain self-consciousness in taking this position, as reflected by the woman's comment that she was "old and illiterate." When others expressed similar opinions, they would add comments to me such as "your wife would no doubt find me very Eastern." This reference suggests that Kalymnians are also aware of inserting themselves into a discourse of gender relations with respect to the "West," which is presumed to value equality between the sexes. Thus there is a sense in people's comments that their position is no longer fully tenable in the 1990s, that it is not in line with Kalymnos' increasingly "modern" identity. In this vein, talk of past "patriarchy" can serve the purposes of young women who want to classify their fathers as old-fashioned or backwards for trying to exert authority over them. But even the advocates of patriarchy may be feeling a waning commitment to it. For example, I recounted to a schoolteacher in his thirties (who claimed to be committed to "equality" between the sexes), the "patriarchal" comments of an older man, Yiorgos. The schoolteacher noted that Yiorgos may talk about the man ruling the family because it benefits him to say this. He identifies with the old crowd and will not come out and declare himself a modern. But he's also not going to put these beliefs into practice. His daughter is dating a foreigner, and when he talks sincerely he admits it's not such a terrible thing. Once again one perceives the varied uses of gender discourses, and their complex relation to present-day practices.

If "patriarchy" is part of the Kalymnian past which people regard with mixed feelings, but nevertheless see as "past," "matriarchy" is no less a part of that legacy. The first time I heard matriarchy explicitly referred to was in conversation with a tourist-shop owner in her thirties. She was telling me how her parents had raised her and her sisters to be different from most Kalymnians: they had worked at their father's restaurant when they were young, and their parents had given them education rather than houses "as our dowry."[12] In this context she told me: "My mother was a strong and independent woman; back then we had women's rule on Kalymnos."

Many Kalymnians ascribe the island's past matriarchy to the sponge-diving way of life. Most able-bodied men were absent from six to eight months of the year on sponge boats. Women had to make all the crucial decisions concerning the household in the absence of men. Since many sponge-divers wanted to relax and live it up when they returned to the island, they tended to spend much of their time away from home in the restaurants and coffee shops, leaving the wife in charge once again.[13] As one woman states: "The divers spent all their time at the coffee shops – music and retsina. And not home 'till the next morning. They said, we've been so long at sea, let's celebrate. And thus there was woman's rule (γυναικοκρατία) on the island." Another woman, after initially agreeing with her husband's description of strict control over women's behavior during the "old sponge-diving days," quickly changed her tune when I questioned her directly. When I asked her whether women might have been making most of the decisions while their husbands were gone, she responded that she remembered it just like that. The woman would make the pretense of asking her husband's opinion about decisions, but more often would present him with a *fait accompli*. Her mother, she remembered, sold their house while her father was gone, and then found ways of sugar-coating the news to him when he returned.

During discussions of matriarchy, I found that the strength and power of women's collective action during the Rock War was not raised. The female power referred to in the concept of matriarchy is identified with women's control over the decisions of the home, rather than over the "public," political sphere.[14]

Thus the native theory of "matriarchy" explains female power as the result of the absent husband. It is interesting to note that anthropologists have proposed similar theories in different cultural contexts to explain women's autonomy and power, and that these theories have been criticized for their underlying assumptions that female power must be anomalous.[15] It is an explanation perhaps less threatening for men, since it implies that only by force of unusual circumstances do women have the upper hand. It is also contradicted by previous research on Kalymnos by Bernard (1976a; 1976b), who claims that the wives of sponge-divers were more limited in their actions than other Kalymnian women because they had to prove their reputation to be impeccable during their husbands' absence. Bernard believes that women's power has risen with the decline of the sponge-diving industry in the early 1960s.[16]

First Daughter Inheritance

If the "absent male" theory is not satisfactory, what alternative possibilities are there? I have suggested the importance of matrilocality earlier in the chapter. However, since matrilocality exists on present-day Kalymnos, it cannot explain in itself the reputed "greater" female power in the past. One answer was suggested to me by a Kalymnian man in his forties who considered himself a feminist. He said that women controlled the transfer of material tradition on the island due to matrilineal inheritance. While women in many societies have been associated with control of the "traditional," this particular Kalymnian "tradition" was associated with women's economic and decision-making power. What he referred to as matrilineal inheritance was the custom by which the first daughter would receive the lion's share of the family inheritance. The term family inheritance needs explanation, since women owned most of the property on Kalymnos. The father was expected to earn money in order to build houses for his daughters, though he might build these houses on land owned by his wife. Land was normally passed from mother to daughter, and the mother was also responsible for the transmission of household items and trousseau items (see Kapella 1987: 20; Zairi 1992).

Under this system, subsequent daughters would be virtually ignored. As one woman described it, if the family owned twenty-five fields, the first daughter would get twenty, the other children would get one each. If a father owned a boat, or less commonly at the time, a store, he would pass this on to one of his sons. In terms of items associated with the "home," (i.e. house, land, household items) sons would not inherit at all under this system, except under unusual circumstances. It was expected that their needs would be provided for through marriage. While a family could spend money to educate their sons, it was not uncommon for the bride's family to take on the cost of educating their son-in-law as part of the dowry agreement (I heard of a case of this as recently as 1981). Ideally the first daughter would have a new house built for her from the family income. However, if this was not possible, the first daughter claimed the parental house upon her marriage, and the parents and the rest of the siblings were forced to rent a house. The house and property typically remained in control of the woman on marriage, and reverted to her in instances of divorce (even if a woman died, her natal family had entitlements to the property). Special arrangements, however, were common whereby some property or especially cash could be "written to the groom" (γραμμένο στο γαμπρό), and this could subsequently be contributed by the groom to his own sister's dowry.[17]

This inheritance system worked on a principle of female lines. This is illustrated by its direct links to the naming system, by which the eldest daughter is normally given the name of her maternal grandmother, and was expected to receive the inheritance passed on from that grandmother. As Vernier describes it: "It was said that the souls of the ancestors, who had passed on the material and symbolic patrimony of their line, entered into the body of the persons bearing their names" (1984: 40).

Vernier (1984; 1987; 1991) examines a similar inheritance system operational on the island of Karpathos, and claims that such principles were at work in a number of Dodecanese islands in the past.[18] The system that Vernier describes, however, is one of dual primogeniture where the first child of each sex inherits from their line: in other words, the father passes on his inheritance to his first son and the mother to her first daughter. Vernier outlines in detail the competing interests of the "lines," and how these spilled over into struggles over the naming of children that pitted the husband and his patrilateral relatives against the wife and her matrilateral relatives. He also notes that the economic poverty of Karpathian society meant that the remaining children were almost completely disinherited, except for a largely symbolic gift (the *xalimakia*) which often meant that these children were "condemned to celibacy" or emigration since without an inheritance they could often not find marriage partners. It is clear that a similar system operated on Kalymnos, but transmission through the male line was less common. As one Kalymnian folklorist told me, "if the father had property (περιουσία, also translatable as wealth) he passed it on to his first son." But this property would have been property or wealth in addition to what he provided for his daughters. Evidently, the father had to go to considerable expense to provide houses for *all* his daughters, and not for his sons. As Kalymnian folklorist Kapella notes, for even the poorest families on Kalymnos, the birth of a daughter signified the building of a house.[19] Often brothers added their labor to the task of providing houses for their sisters too. In this way, remaining daughters were not so completely excluded as to make them unmarriageable, as Vernier indicates is the case on Karpathos. As one Kalymnian historian told me, "on Kalymnos the system was more just [compared to neighboring islands]. The other daughters weren't completely left out, they were provided for."

The principle of the competition between male and female lines, discussed by Vernier, does not seem so obvious on Kalymnos. Rather it appears there was a strong preference for the female line. Kalymnians referred to the practice as "the first daughter" (η πρωτοκόρη), or "the custom of the first daughter," and sons were never mentioned. This favoring (which I did not have the opportunity to confirm through historical research) can be seen in the remnants of the practice in the 1990s. For many families the first daughter still has primary choice over the best house and land that the family owns. At the birth of one girl on Kalymnos (the third-born child) her eight-year-old elder brother made the following remark: "[sister's name] with the beautiful little lips, you blew it for us. You ate our dowry, the house that I liked a lot."

In talking about the custom of first daughter inheritance, male and female, young and old Kalymnians, universally referred to it as an abomination from the past that they were glad to be rid of. People focussed on the injustice of this practice and insisted that they would not perpetuate such injustices against their own children. The first daughter might still get first choice of house, but other than that property would be divided equally, with houses built for sons and daughters.[20] A number of parents stressed the fact that, unlike in the past, they would not consider giving up their own house to their first daughter to go and live in an inferior house themselves.

Vernier sees in this inheritance practice on Karpathos a system of exploitation of younger siblings by older siblings. He argues that this system was intended to reproduce the wealth of the matrilateral and patrilateral lines by reproducing the status hierarchy between siblings. In the case of sisters, the younger, disinherited sisters often became servants and agricultural workers for their older sister. I heard occasional reports of this occurring among the generation now aged between fifty and seventy on Kalymnos. Significantly, in the one case I could confirm, this was only a temporary situation: the younger sister had been promised a dowry by her older sister, but had been betrayed when the latter gave birth to a daughter and decided to transfer *all* her property to this first-born daughter. The younger sister eventually left her older sister's employ, secured a small inheritance from her mother (and financial help of a childless maternal aunt), and was able to marry. In another case, a man in his seventies told me how he threatened his mother with a lawsuit if she gave all of her land to his older sister and did not provide him with enough to build a house on.[21] Other people's stories confirmed that brothers and younger sisters would often contest what they felt to be unfair inheritance settlements. This implies that "first-daughter inheritance" was a rule only insofar as it was the predominant inheritance strategy, but it did not exclude other possibilities. I was able to trace several cases from the generation age 50 to 70 (in 1992) in which equal inheritance was put into practice between several sisters without regard to birth order. Most people from this generation referred to the practice of first daughter inheritance as something from their parents' generation and earlier, though one man insisted that some idiots (βλάκες) still practiced it in the 1990s. When I asked people what was the logic behind first daughter inheritance, I was universally told that there was no logic behind it, that it was a stupidity (βλακεία) and an injustice (αδικία) from the past. Note that stupidity has a different, and more harmful, lasting connotation than craziness (τρέλλα), the word applied to dynamite throwing.

Contemporary Kalymnians view this practice as opposed to the principle of equality between siblings, the good sense of which they take for granted. One wonders the extent to which Kalymnian views were influenced by their incorporation into the Greek state after 1948 and their submission to Greek laws of equal inheritance.[22] At the present time when "equality" is a principle on the lips of most young and many older Kalymnians, the memory of this hierarchy-creating practice serves no one well. Its significance in creating a class of women with a high degree of decision-making power and autonomy from their husbands, goes unrecognized by Kalymnian women today, even if it was an equally important factor as men's absence in contributing to the "matriarchy" of Kalymnos' past.

In a comparative discussion of historical literature on the Aegean islands, Vernier (1987) gives direct evidence for the practice of first-daughter inheritance tracing back to the beginning of the eighteenth century, and indirect evidence (travellers' accounts) tracing back at least to the early fifteenth century. He suggests that this custom,[23] and female power in general in the Aegean islands, may be connected to the frequent absence of men and gender imbalances in the population owing to various factors such as work at sea, frequent migration and piracy, though he stops short of asserting a cause-and-effect relationship. This theory does not explain why such inheritance patterns did not emerge in the Ionian islands, or other areas of the world with male migratory–fishing populations. I can only speculate as to whether male absence actually explains matrifocality, or whether it has another, more complex history. Dimitriou-Kotsoni's claim that matrifocality should be seen as part of an Aegean cultural tradition stretching back for 4000 years, linked to the lack of centralization, the political peripherality and a history of agricultural small-holdings that have been consistent features of the islands, is certainly intriguing (1993: 72–3). Her work awaits confirmation through further historical research. But it is suggestively supported by the work of one Kalymnian historian, who has shown that women in Kalymnos had a considerable degree of juridical authority during the time of the Roman Empire, in particular women had the right to emancipate slaves, and if unmarried were not considered to be under the tutelage of their husbands or their fathers.[24]

Whatever the truth of its history, the legacy of this custom is still felt today on Kalymnos, instantiated by the many "matriarchs" who hold the power of decision making in Kalymnian families. A current example concerning a marriage in 1993 is instructive. A girl in her early teens became involved with a boy ten years her senior. When the couple asked for the girl's parents' approval of their marriage, the parents said no, they should wait a few years until the girl was older and more certain. This also entails restrictions on their meetings. However, when the girl's father left on a fishing expedition, the mother and the maternal grandmother arranged for the girl to meet her lover unhindered, and to become pregnant. When the father was due to return, the grandmother instructed the couple to "steal away" (κλεφτή-κανε) to the neighboring island of Kos, as a way of publicly declaring their relationship. Immediately on hearing the news the father became outraged, and reportedly hit his wife and went on a destructive tirade through the house that landed him in the hospital. However, once he learnt the details of the situation – the fact that his daughter was pregnant and had willingly gone to Kos with the boy (had not been "stolen") he decided to make the best of it, and enthusiastically embraced the wedding. His sudden change of heart led to a rumor that the grandmother, who had a reputation for magical powers, had worked a spell on him (τον μάγεψε). The groom's mother had also opposed the marriage, and did not reconcile herself to it. Instead she threw her son out of her house thereby cutting him off from his father's business where he had been working. Nevertheless, the young couple were able to survive despite the loss of the groom's job because the bride's grandmother, who had a large inheritance, was willing to support them until they got on their feet.

This story illustrates a number of principles I have been discussing. The father may make the initial decision and he may be the authority whose approval is sought. But when the desired result was not achieved, the mother (working in concert with her own mother) helped her daughter to accomplish her desired goal. She then presented the father with a *fait accompli*, which he raged against but was eventually made to accept. The grandmother's financial power (the grandfather was alive, but not an active player in the story), also allowed her grand-daughter to overcome some of the practical hurdles of her situation. This example also is very common in that the man's authority is being exerted over his daughter. As noted above, when people spoke of patriarchy on Kalymnos in the past, they most often referred to examples of the respect of children for their father, and most commonly the father's authority over his daughters. This image fits in well with traditional Greek ethnographic descriptions of the importance of defending the honor and virginity of one's daughters lest their misdemeanors stain the family name. On the other hand, when people recalled matriarchy (as noted, often the same people in a different mood), it was the wife's ability to exert her power in spite of or over the head of her husband that was most often cited.

Images of Power

The image I have presented here (with many provisos), of female power is more of a shifting of emphasis than a radical departure from previous ethnographies of gender relations in Greece. What I would like to stress, in summary, are some of the important distinctions that my Kalymnian findings highlight. First, female power does not necessarily simply compensate for the fact that women have less "authority" than men. The power experienced by women may, given the circumstances described on Kalymnos, be more significant than the nominal authority of males. This is certainly the perception of many Kalymnians. As one man told me: "I'm among the hardest (πιο σκληρός) of Kalymnian men, and yet it's my wife who runs things in our household." The limitations of authority are recognized by all. Perhaps this should not surprise us on an island such as Kalymnos, where "authority" has always been imposed by outsiders, something that Kalymnians have learned to live with by contravening it at every turn and mocking the pretensions of all official discourse.[25] This is not to deny that in situations of external occupation, such as the Italian Occupation, men may have been even more vigilant over their daughters. I often heard the phrase "back then girls were locked up inside their houses" with reference to the Italian period. But the ways daughters have been able to circumnavigate such monitoring is equally legendary on Kalymnos. I am suggesting that on another level, Kalymnians realize such authority is deeply problematic and easy to subvert. Thus a married woman joked with her recently married niece about the girl's father's attempts to monitor her pre-marital contact with her fiancé, to the point of staying in the same room with them at all times: "he's afraid that they will have sex through the air." As the aunt (in her thirties) noted, such actions were particularly ludicrous given the fact that boys and girls are together at school, and thus can spend time together without difficulty if they wish to do so. "They will just have to do it more secretly, like Watergate" (στα κρυφά, σαν ουατεργαϊτ).

The Kalymnian men who told me the joke I began the previous chapter with are well aware of the hollowness of any claims of control or authority over others. Those men who assert that Kalymnos had matriarchy in the past and have female power in the present are claiming a special status for Kalymnos, a status which aligns it (and them) with "Europe" and "progress" in gender relations, as opposed to "Eastern backwardness." For women these claims to the past are more complicated. Some of the material sources of women's power in the past, such as first daughter inheritance and the dowry, are ideologically unacceptable in the present. First daughter inheritance is unacceptable, as noted above, because of the obvious unfairness and inequality it perpetuates. The practice of dowry is seen as another "backwards" leftover from the past, when compared to the "European" system.[26] Furthermore, the dowry has long been branded by many as demeaning to women, since it reduces them to chattel to be "bought and sold at the market."[27] The image of past "matriarchy" does not serve women well in the present either: it relies on absent husbands and the removal of men from the domestic sphere, while present ideals look towards equality and the sharing of domestic responsibilities. Consequently, the Rock War endures for older Kalymnian women as an untarnished image of their power and ability. For younger women, by contrast, the Rock War does not play such a central role in their consciousness. Rather the image and example of strong mothers, aunts and grandmothers is the legacy from the past that these women can embrace and utilize in their negotiation of their identity in the present.

These different generational memories and the different referents of "matriarchy" and "patriarchy" (i.e. husband–wife versus father–children relations) indicates that the category of "women" must always be approached with suspicion. While this may be a familiar point in writings on anthropology and women's studies, it is striking that recent Greek studies fail to make such distinctions in their accounts of "women's" power. Janet Hart (1996), for example, focusses on movement into the "public" political sphere as crucial to women's emancipation and Westernization, portraying Greek village women as illiterate and powerless. But her analysis of participation in the Greek Resistance concentrates almost exclusively on young girls, who had the most to gain from a rejection of "traditional" structures. Seremetakis (1991), by contrast, gives a very different picture of the impact of Westernization on women's power and resistance by focussing almost exclusively on older, married women. Future studies must be attentive to the multiple venues and dimensions of the construction of masculinity and femininity in the modern Greek context.[28]

Conclusion: The Value of Tradition

In light of my discussion of debates over the past moorings of present-day practices in the last three chapters, what can be said about the significance of this cluster of terms: "tradition," "custom" and "the old years"? Whether or not there ever existed a golden age talked about by the older generation when "we believed things because our parents did," it is certainly no longer true in the 1990s. It is clear that appeals to tradition or custom must nowadays compete with other values and ideologies for Kalymnian allegiance. This is apparent in the flexible definition that most Kalymnians give of the concept of custom itself: it is not something set in stone, but is simply action that has taken on the force of habit through repetition. Thus people are aware that customs may be of recent origin, as is clear in the oft-repeated phrase used in reference to dynamite: "when the custom began . . ." (όταν αρχίνηξε το έθιμο).[29] Another example is offered by a woman discussing the fact that women are restricted from entering church for forty days after they have given birth. She claimed that this custom was invented by the priests in order to degrade women; it did not come from God. Implicit in this recognition of an invented tradition is perhaps the idea that some traditions can be perceived as legitimate while some cannot. But this must be argued for in the present. This is in accordance with the work of Poppi (1992: 114) on Ladin Carnival in Italy. He argues that, "to interpret the process by which traditions are 'found' or 'created' simply as a function of the nationalistic and/or ethnic struggle (or indeed of any other variable in the formation of self-awareness) does not do justice to the complexity of the process involved." *Contra* Vansina (1990: 257), tradition is not "just a flag of convenience to legitimate a position held on other grounds." Rather it is a more weighty counter, although it does possess shifting value in a larger network of debates over the uses of the past in the present.

As noted in my discussion of dynamite, appeals to tradition have the effect of placing something beyond the rational (i.e. justifiable through means–ends argument). In general, that which is done because it is tradition is regarded as non-rational. And this is acceptable for items of expressive culture. But when I asked people what are the customs of Kalymnos, the most frequent response was Kalymnian dance or traditional Kalymnian dress. These are the items that most people feel an unqualified desire to preserve as a part of preserving Kalymnian identity – they are seen as marks of Kalymnian distinctiveness. While dynamite throwing is certainly also seen as expressive culture, its expressiveness and thus its "traditionality" are questioned by many because of its destructive nature.

When it comes to practices which have more practical import and consequences, "tradition," as a mark of distinction and something we do because it sets us apart from others, has very little weight. Rather one must appeal to other culturally defined principles: rationality, fairness, necessity. Building houses for daughters is therefore not described as fulfilling the Kalymnian dowry custom; it is seen as the perfectly logical wish to transfer property from parents to children.[30] In another example, a few people were discussing the fact that brothers commonly wait for their sisters to get married before getting married themselves. An American woman (married to a Kalymnian man) said, "Well that's the Kalymnian custom." A Kalymnian man replied, "No it's not. There's a reason for it. If the father is dead or too old, sisters need their brothers around in order to keep other men from preying on them." Clearly if there's a "logical" reason for something, then it's not a "custom." It is interesting that this comment was made by a man who was most articulate about the need to preserve tradition in order to safeguard Kalymnian identity. But even for him, in cases of major life decisions, "tradition" was not its own defense.

I could offer many more examples such as these. In most of them the thrust is the same: tradition is associated with the non-rational or the symbolic. In one case a woman defended to me her pleasure that her daughter had finally given birth to a girl after two boys. As is the general rule, the girl was named after her, the maternal grandmother. She was very pleased about this. But then, as if she needed to justify this pleasure, she told me: "It's not the name that I'm so excited about. That's silliness (σαχλαμάρες). It's the fact that a girl solves a lot of problems for the family. It means my daughter will have someone to keep her company after I'm gone. And it makes the division of the house much simpler." This is because the mother's house will go entirely to the daughter, while the sons will have to build houses on family property or obtain houses from their wives. If a third son had been born, they would have had to divide the mother's house between the sons, which would have meant that the wives of the sons would have been on top of each other and always fighting. The birth of a daughter allows them to justify overriding the principle of equal inheritance for all children by the principle of providing houses first and foremost for daughters. This too is perceived by some on Kalymnos as a "tradition," one that people seem to be challenging more and more in word and action. But those who still uphold it do not stress its traditionality, but its rationale – a rationale which must be seen within the parameters of the current situation on Kalymnos whereby daughters continue to need houses if they are to be attractive as marriage partners. This view of tradition as inherently non-rational echoes Hobsbawm's (1983: 4) argument that "objects or practices are liberated for full symbolic and ritual use when no longer fettered by practical use." However, the cross-cultural applicability of such a view must be a matter for comparative research.

If, then, certain practices provoke a longing for the "old years," others are vigorously debated, and others are universally condemned. But it is clear that "custom" or "tradition" is not what was set in stone in ancient times, but what must be debated and reinvented in the continual process of identity-construction in the present. I have perhaps created this view of "tradition" because I did not focus on items perceived as unambiguously traditional, but on dynamite, dowry and inheritance practices, and other gendered stories which fall ambiguously in the gaps between "local history," "tradition" and "custom" and "the old days," whether positively or negatively valued.

Other authors working in Greece who have focussed more directly on expressive "tradition" have given a rather different picture, one which is apparent in the anthropological literature, particularly that on tourism.[31] In Poppi's schematization (1992: 130), tradition and custom are viewed negatively in places in the midst of trying to "modernize." These places may then revalue "tradition" when it becomes a product for tourist consumption and provides the cash not for infrastructural "modernization" but for the acquisition of consumer goods. Some suggest that this leads to the crude packaging of "invented tradition," as Skiada (1990: 289) argues has occurred on Olymbos:

> The debate is whether "tradition", as local people call it, should be preserved and how. On the one hand, Olymbitian youths and local tourist developers fight against conservatism and facilitate the process of modernization. On the other hand, elder Olymbitians, the emigrants, and some outsiders, namely, tourists, and researchers/lovers of ethnic folk arts, mourn the loss of the local folk tradition. Each of the above social groups has different reasons for fighting or facilitating the process of rapid change which follows urban patterns and includes technological improvements and have various ways of pursuing their interests.

Others argue that tradition is being destroyed by an all-consuming and consumerist modernity. Buck-Morss (1987), for example, makes a complex and convincing case for the economic and symbolic inequalities produced by Western tourism in Greece that result in the devaluation of local ways. This opinion is echoed by many Kalymnians. But Buck-Morss' formulation is weighted too heavily on the side of the powers of the center and of capital, to transform the very consciousness of those living at the "periphery." She claims (1987: 228-9) that:

> In Mirtos only a few village families actually make their living off the tourists, and the number has risen by just six or seven in the last five years . . . But as a symbolically powerful agent in the appropriation of tradition, the new tourism's presence is monumental . . . The tourists, as travelling players, enact an allegory of consumer modernity for a village audience, whose response is . . . mimetic.

Yet in spite of the ambivalent attitudes recorded in these chapters, and in spite of the view of "tradition" as the non-rational and non-logical, few Kalymnians fear that "tradition" is on the verge of disappearing or being hopelessly corrupted. Whether they point to the use among the young of the distinct Kalymnian dialect, their attendance at church and religious rituals, their own hospitality to me and my family, or the deafening displays of dynamite at Easter time, they feel that "tradition" is holding its own. It does so precisely because, at least up until now, it is not a relic from the past to be preserved like a monument, but ironically it retains its vitality through the very debates over its significance. Its relevance, its applicability to different practices – to changing gender relations, to the relationship of Kalymnos to the power of outside authorities – is debated and re-created, along with "modernity," in the words and actions of the present.

Notes

1. See Friedl 1962; Campbell 1964; Herzfeld 1985. Casselbery and Valvanes (1975), working in one of Kalymnos' smaller villages, argue that residence patterns are better described as natovicinal and matridomestic, indicating that husband and wife generally come from the same village. They also note a fairly equal frequency of couples living in the same house as the woman's mother, in an attached house, and in a house nearby. This conformed to my observations for the neighborhood in which I lived, although I did not collect sufficient data to state this quantitatively.

2. While Kalymnians referred to the "abolition" (κατάργηση) of the dowry, what was abolished in the revision of the Greek family law by the socialist PASOK government was *obligatory* dowries. Dowry itself was not made illegal. For a full discussion of the relevant changes see Pollis (1992).

3. On the shifting associations of the word "dowry" see Estevez-Weber 1983; Herzfeld 1980.

4. According to folklorist Themelina Kapella the "traditional" dowry of rich families on Kalymnos included "gold sovereigns, a house weighted down like a boat, fields, orchards, and a store in the town square" (1987: 17; my translation).

5. Note that in this example power imbalances in the past are seen to have favored men. The contradictions in these images of male and female power are discussed in a later section on past "matriarchy" below.

6. See Pollis 1992; Stamiris 1986.

7. Walker 1989; see also Allen 1986; Estevez-Weber 1983; Salamone and Stanton 1986; Stamiris 1986: 104; and for a foreshadowing of this see Friedl 1962: 64–8.

8. Parents increasingly do provide houses for sons. Not only because of foreign wives, but because of the growth of the ideology of equal inheritance (see discussion below). But in the majority of cases these houses built for sons are summer houses rather than primary domiciles, and they are built, generally speaking, subsequent to the building of houses for daughters, or at least subsequent to the knowledge that parents will be able to provide for daughters in cases in which the son is substantially older than the daughter.

9. See Kenna's (1976) discussion of the symbolic association of women's tending of houses, fields and graves.

10. Of course the existence of "primitive" matriarchy has been a topic in anthropological thought (and social thought more generally) tracing back to the writings of Bachofen and Engels. For a review of the issue see Gronborg 1979; Leacock 1981. The matriarchy thesis has specific Greek (Minoan Crete) references as well (see Eisler 1987), a fact which some Kalymnians made reference to.

11. See Cowan 1996.

12. This practice, noted by a number of Kalymnian women, has been extensively documented in Athens by Estevez-Weber (1983).

13. Bernard, however, claims that significant planning for future sponge expeditions went on in the coffee shops. Furthermore, a man could do significant damage to his family finances by reckless spending on entertainment, putting additional burdens on his wife (see Bernard 1976a: 305).

14. A view that accords with Rogers' (1975) description of gender relations in a French peasant context.

15. Tanner 1974; Sutton 1984. As Sutton (1984: 2) writes of the assumptions of earlier approaches: "Women's power was something that required explanation; men's did not. Nor did women's lack of power call for explanation. The biases of that period led to explaining the seeming anomaly as resulting from men's inability to exercise the authority requisite to their roles due to their relative 'powerlessness' in the economic and political structure."

16. Though he makes little attempt to explain this (see 1976a: 308–9). One wonders how much of his view of gender relations is based on the idealized statements of the sponge-fishermen themselves, with whom he conducted his primary research. This is suggested in passages such as the following, which echo Campbell's work among the patrilocal Sarakatsani: "A Kalymnian woman must understand that a man's **philotimo** [honor] is at stake every time he deals with women. The side of family life which faces on public display must demonstrate the husband's control of the situation. A woman's own **philotimo** depends to a large extent on her not doing anything to harm her husband's **philotimo** . . . A man's honor depends on the shame **possessed** by his wife, sisters, and mother. If a woman does not possess shame, she brings dishonor on her family, specifically on the men of the family. The dishonor throws open to public questioning the men's authority to control social, political and economic life" (1976a: 306).

17. In legendary instances this system is said to have led to one dowry

providing for five weddings. See Kapella 1987: 21. Also see Zairi 1992 for a full discussion of the practice of writing a part of the dowry to the groom.

18. Most of his data refer to the first half of the twentieth century.

19. Kapella (1987: 20; my translation) describes it thus: "To the responsibilities of the father fell the house and the cash, whether he was rich or poor, though he provided more or less accordingly. It was a concern for the father from the moment she was born and he put his head in his hands [a gesture of pain]. Daughter meant house."

20. As noted above, this may in part reflect a response to a practical necessity: the growing number of Kalymnian men marrying non-Kalymnian and non-Greek women.

21. Since the laws of Greece provide for equal inheritance for all children. Bernard (1976b: 296) also reports a case in which a girl successfully sued her two married sisters for one third of their dowries so that she would be able to put together her own dowry and marry.

22. The impact of these legal changes on Kalymnian inheritance practices is a subject of my ongoing research on the island.

23. Vernier (1987) distinguishes between a number of different inheritance strategies on these islands, based on the degree to which other children beyond the first daughter are considered as potential inheritors.

24. See Frangopoulou 1988; also Vernier 1987: 384.

25. While this ability to defy state authority has been well-documented by Herzfeld in Crete (1985; 1991), local historians have also shown how Kalymnian leaders were able to manoeuvre their way through the Ottoman bureaucracy in protecting the "privileged" status of Kalymnos under Ottoman rule (see Frangopoulos 1952: vol. 1; Sakellaridis 1986a).

26. The "European" system means simply that parents are not responsible for providing for their daughters in order for them to be married. This was also referred to as the "American" and "Australian" system. In one case I was told that a Kalymnian man who had moved to Australia was berated by the Kalymnian community in Australia when he built a house for his daughter before her marriage. He was told that Greeks had finally got rid of this burdensome custom, and he should not be bringing it back.

27. For a nuanced discussion of the way changes in dowry practices by the aspiring middle classes in nineteenth century Athens came to equate marriageable women with commodities, see Sant Cassia 1992: 94 ff.

28. Loizos (1994) pays particular attention to the ways that different fieldwork situations may have influenced the image of gender relations that the ethnographer then describes as prototypical for the community. Working in Turkey, Kandiyoti (1994), in the same volume, gives a suggestive account of different versions of masculinity and femininity that may be constructed at different stages in the life-cycle, and in different intra-family relations (i.e. son–mother, son–father, brother–sister), as well as in different institutional contexts. See also du Boulay's (1986) discussion of "Eve" and "Mary" images of womanhood in Greece.

29. "Αρχίνηξε" is Kalymnian dialect.

30. Local historians refer to dowry not as a "custom" but as an "institution" (θεσμός). See, e.g. Zairi 1992: 162–3.

31. On Greece see Buck-Morss 1987; Cowan 1992; Seremetakis 1994. A review of anthropological approaches to tourism can be found in Graburn 1995.

Analogic Thinking as History

So very much having passed before our eyes
that our eyes in the end saw nothing . . .

having known this fate of ours so well
wandering around among broken stones, three or six thousand years
searching in collapsed buildings that might have been our homes
trying to remember dates and heroic deeds:
will we be able?

having been bound and scattered
having struggled, as they said, with non-existent difficulties
lost, then finding again a road full of blind regiments
sinking in marshes and in the lake of Marathon
will we be able to die properly?

George Seferis, *Mythistorema #22*

Eat, in order to remember.

Kalymnian woman, 1989

Introduction

In the preceding chapters we saw that both the content and the value
of "tradition" and "custom" were subject to frequent debate in the
present. But "history," which we saw in the guise of "local history,"
left less room for interpretation of its form or significance. This we
saw most clearly in the case of the Rock War, which was debated as
"tradition," as the actions of women in defense of Orthodoxy, but
was formalized and not challenged as "history" as the actions of men
in the name of the Greek nation. In the next three chapters we will
explore indigenous notions of "history" as another way of categorizing
the past and bringing it to bear on the present. We will see that while
the content of history, like the content of tradition, can be rigorously
debated, the meaning or significance of the term is not. In this
chapter I examine the ways Kalymnians talk about what they define
as "history," relying as much as possible on "local voices" to give a

sense of the texture of such discussions. In previous chapters I concentrated on gender, generation and other social cleavages in understanding the different discourses of tradition. In these next chapters I argue that such social differentiations are less relevant for understanding history which has a more hegemonic status than tradition on Kalymnos. By this I mean that the basic assumptions underlying history's significance or relevance cut across social divisions and are rarely challenged. These assumptions are the focus of my concern here.

I will begin the chapter with a discussion of some of the uses of the word "history" itself, and examine in detail the way that these uses are refracted in different domains of experience. Discussions of history reinforce each other at the political, religious, local and personal levels, and in doing so gain some of the "self-evidence" referred to above. For as Foster, discussing national identity, puts it: "the centrality of history . . . inheres in the relationship between historical consciousness and 'everyday life' the everyday historical memory that informs a subject's sense of what is 'normal, appropriate or possible'" (1991: 241). In this sense, notions of history are hegemonic on Kalymnos, since they are directly tied to unquestioned assumptions about Kalymnian and Greek identity: "It is historical memory – a particular if often unarticulated concept of the past – that above all defines the nation as a collective subject and generates 'a sense that "we" are the achievement of history'" (ibid.: 241). Through the examination of certain underlying assumptions about interconnectedness, and the explicit use of metaphor and analogy, Kalymnians move rhetorically between these different levels of experience, and in doing so they make history make sense in the present. The body of this chapter will show how these historical tropes are applied to different themes and events through the exegesis of a long conversation on the meaning of "history" between myself and a Kalymnian woman. In the conclusion to the chapter I will offer an interpretation of how these attitudes towards history affect Kalymnians' sense of historical continuity and what implications this might have for an anthropological understanding of this issue.

In the following two chapters I will examine some of the implications of these general remarks on historical attitudes for the way Kalymnians interpret certain events occurring in the present, in particular the war in ex-Yugoslavia and the question of the naming of former Yugoslav Macedonia. At the same time I will illustrate the way that the past is brought into the present as a dynamic force, as a lens of understanding which affects the Kalymnian view of the present in a culturally specific way.

The Domains of Experience and some Movements Between Them

History & Histories

Since one of the main arguments of this chapter is that Kalymnians think of different domains of experience – national, religious, local – as transparent to each other, let me begin not with History (ιστορία) on the grand scale, but with the "histories" (ιστορίες) that infuse everyday life. At the local level, "histories" are disputes, quarrels or acts of shame (sexual infidelities, stealing) that alter the normal pattern of daily life in predictable ways.[1] As an act of mischievousness or boredom one might "make histories," in other words, cause an argument with someone as a way of breaking up the daily routine. But the ideal is for a family to pass the day without such "histories," or without histories becoming outside knowledge. At a neighbor's house one may inquire "what happened?" as a way of uncovering the "histories" of others. In one's own house, by contrast, activities are performed ideally because they "pass the day" uneventfully (περνάνε την ημέρα). For a family to "have history" inevitably means that they have stains on their name owing to past sexual, social or financial misconduct. To quote a popular saying on Cyprus: "Happy the girl who has no history" (Walker 1989: 4).

The above suggests a male bias to the use of "histories," that histories are in general more harmful to women than men. On Kalymnos this may be more true in theory than in practice. I was told about the histories of men as much as of women. While women's "histories" tended toward the sexual more than men's, it was not uncommon for men to be held guilty for a "history" of sexual crimes (e.g. adultery). It should also be noted that what is defined as an "event," a "scandal" that breaks up the routine of everyday life, has some variability, particularly across generations. Pre-marital involvements are certainly losing their air of "event" among the younger generation, and certain segments of the older generation. As one man told me: ten years ago, you used to hear all about the wild behavior of a young woman in the neighborhood. Today she may still be doing the same thing, but her exploits are no longer subject for gossip. Other people mentioned similar examples: how it used to be shocking for a woman to sit in a coffee shop, or to ride a motorcycle. Now such things have lost their status as events for growing sections of the population.

Although I discuss gender here, it is not a key category in my analysis below. One could argue that just as women are more likely to be present in "histories," they are correspondingly more likely to be absent in "History," as I suggested in my discussion of the exceptional nature of the Rock War. In spite of this, I found that when it came to national rather than local history, women and men on Kalymnos discuss events in similar ways.[2]

For Kalymnos as an island to "have history" need not necessarily be negative. But it does mean that a routine has been broken: that Kalymnians acted in some way to inscribe themselves in larger events by resisting (or collaborating with) the Italian Occupation of the island, by becoming saints,[3] or by possessing the markers of religious devotion in the form of chapels and the magical stories which surround their construction (see Dubisch 1995). At the local island, national and religious levels therefore, "history" and "histories" describe disruptive events. But they are not simply new or unusual events. Rather they are events that fit particular patterns and reveal the perceived truth of an individual, an island or a people.

This brief discussion is not meant to exhaust the meanings of "history" or "histories." As we will see there are more complex and sometimes divergent uses of the term. In particular I want to note that a key use of the term, the idea of history as property, is not mentioned in this chapter. I do treat it at length, however, in my discussion of names and "heritage" (κληρονομιά) in Chapter 8.

The Culture of Politics

Kalymnians often decry the "histories" – local and national – that keep them from succeeding individually and collectively. They claim that they (as Kalymnians and Greeks in general) spend too much time arguing politics rather than looking after their own affairs. Kalymnians believe that people in the US lack interest in politics. They perceive this as linked to the fact that Americans don't try to "eat" their neighbors, and look on their neighbors' successes not as causes for envy, but for emulation. This lack of interest in national and personal politics is seen by some Kalymnians as one of the characteristics that make "America" admirable, and that has allowed the US to thrive. By contrast, just as a Kalymnian will supposedly try and undermine his neighbor at every turn (to "make histories"), when there is a national election on Kalymnos life stops and people from opposing political parties do not speak to each other for weeks. Store owners complain that around election time they must hide their politics so as not to lose customers.

It is important here to describe the role played by national party politics in Kalymnian life, if some of the meanings of "History" are to be tackled. National politics are ubiquitous on Kalymnos and to judge from the media, in Greek culture as a whole. A popular TV show satirizes national politicians by portraying them as different animals. A sitcom makes joking reference to splits in the Communist Party in Greece. Greece's leading tabloid newspaper focusses almost exclusive

attention on the alleged scandals of politicians.[4] Thus I was only
slightly surprised when I witnessed a five-year-old boy playing around
by marching back and forth in mock military form, rhythmically
intoning, "Pa-pan-dre-ou-Mit-so-ta-kis-Pa-pan-dre-ou-mit-so-ta-kis," –
the names of the leaders of the two principal political parties in Greece
in 1992. Interviews and feature articles in all kinds of popular magazines most commonly focus on politicians. Even when interviews
are with musicians, actors or artists the subject of politics, political
inclinations and evaluations of popular political leaders, inevitably
arises.

   In their ubiquity I would argue that politics and politicians serve a
similar function in Greece to that of popular culture and "stars" in
the United States. Politics and politicians form a storehouse of references for conversations in the present. The names of political figures
become identified with certain kinds of behavior and thenceforth can
be used as labels for that behavior. If you are known for your rakish
behavior, you may be referred to as Papandreou, who had taken a
young wife while in his seventies. In a similar manner, Prime Minister
Mitsotakis became identified with oppressive behavior during his
tenure. Depending on your political leanings, if you wanted to say
that someone was acting oppressively on Kalymnos, you might call
him "Mitsotakis." To jokingly refer to someone as a thief, you could
call him "Koskotas," after the president of the Bank of Crete whose
involvement in embezzlement scandals contributed to the downfall
of the socialist PASOK government in 1989. Names can be changed
into verbs, as in a newspaper interview with comic actor/director
Lakis Lazopoulos (Diotsos 1992). When mentioning that his political
loyalties could not easily be swayed, Lazopoulos said: "I won't Theo-
dorakize," i.e. do a Theodorakis (δεν θα Θεοδωρακίζω) after composer–
politician Mikis Theodorakis who had recently switched from being a
socialist MP to become a minister in the conservative government.
These are a few examples of the shared set of references which form
the collective common sense that makes for an imagined community
of all Greeks.

Metaphors Everywhere

When making these often joking references to macro-politics, Kalymnians tie their local experience to national events, thus anchoring
the imagined community in daily practice. In his recent study of the
workings of bureaucracy, Herzfeld has argued that the nation-state
subordinates local identities to the collective good. But in doing so, it
cannot quite displace these local identities, "it must draw upon them
for symbolic nourishment, for they provide the language that
the people best understand" (Herzfeld 1992b: 35). Herzfeld traces

metaphors of kinship and "blood" to the roots of Western nation-alism and the discipline of anthropology which arose from this context (ibid.: 40–4). In these chapters I give an in-depth, synchronic explication of what is surely not only a local Greek phenomenon. If all nations rely on metaphors of kinship and local experience, relatively newer nations such as Greece may be more explicit about such connections than older nations which have learned to hide these "symbolic roots" in rational, bureaucratic jargon (ibid.: Chapters 1 and 2). At the same time this explicitness means that ordinary Greeks may be able to achieve greater awareness of the workings of national and international politics than their counterparts in Western Europe and the United States. Despite being physically isolated on the "peri-pheries" of Greece and Europe, Kalymnians debate, decry and try to understand the larger system that encompasses them. Their mode of understanding the present, through appeals to history, is the subject of this and the following chapters.

Let us return to Kalymnian political references. If these are meta-phors, or in Fernandez's formulation the predication of pronouns on an inchoate subject, it is interesting that the source and target domains of these metaphors seem interchangeable. Fernandez has argued that the source domain of a metaphor is commonly something with which people have considerable experience; it is through this experience that they can unravel more experience-distant domains. Thus for Fang, heavily involved in forest exploitation, the metaphor of breaking and cutting has particular salience (1986: 15).

Examples of explanations of politics through local experience are abundant. They are evident in repeated claims that Greece is surrounded by "bad neighbors." As one woman put it, "why can't countries get along. Just as it is better for us as neighbors to be civil, to greet each other and help each other when in need." This woman ran a small neighborhood vegetable stand, and had to deal with neighbors and possible conflicts on a day-to-day basis if she was to have a clientele; thus this analogy no doubt had a particular salience for her. In another example, a store owner discussing the invasion of Cyprus told me that if Cyprus and Greece had played along with the US, things wouldn't have turned out so disastrously. When I protested that the US had acted unjustly to promote its own interests, he replied, "If someone powerful comes and demands a cut of my store, what do I do? I give it to him. Better not to have to give it to him. But better still not to lose the store."

But if metaphors predicating an understanding of larger politics on familiar experience come easily to Kalymnians, what is striking is that one encounters the reverse – metaphors that explain local experience in terms of larger politics – with equal frequency. A man who had to stay with friends while his house was being repaired told me, "I feel like an Albanian refugee." A woman complaining about her father's dictatorial manner said, "he thinks men should act toward women like the Turkish invasion of Cyprus." A woman notes that attempts to secretly meet one's boyfriend are "like Watergate." Through all of these claims to metaphoric equivalence, Kalymnians insist on the mutual comprehensibility of local and international experience. As Fernandez (1986: 205) describes the process:

> Metaphoric predication produces exceptionally wide classification and "symbolically coerces into a unitary conceptual framework" that whose designation was previously quite separate in our experience. The experience is of the collapse of separation into relatedness. It is, as it is called, the "shock of recognizing" a wider integrity of things.

For Kalymnians, however, this recognition is no "shock." These metaphors are so common in Kalymnian discourse because it is an accepted fact that families and governments work in the same ways. However, their repetition suggests that Kalymnians continue to find something revealing or compelling in them. Numerous people explicitly stated that the family is the "cell" of society, that if Greeks took care of their own house, the society would flourish. While such formulations have a certain conservative ring to them in the US political context, on Kalymnos I found that these beliefs crossed political and gender lines. They could have patriarchal purposes, as was the case when one married man in his forties told me: "The family is just like a government. Each member looks after the other members, but I am the head of it. My wife plays an important role in this government, because she must run things when I am away." But a woman in her fifties, commenting that women run things in the family, observed, "the family needs proper management (διαχείριση) if it is to run properly, just like the government."

This predication of relatedness also extends into the religious domain. Religion and politics are linked symbolically at almost all public ceremonies, with the mayor and the (Metropolitan) bishop both in attendance at holidays such as the celebration of the Greek War of Independence and the Annunciation on 25 March, and also at holidays with no immediate church/state connection such as Ohi Day (28 October) when the Greek Prime Minister Metaxas rejected an Italian ultimatum and launched Greece into war with Italy. Or the Epiphany – the baptism of Christ – (6 January) when I watched on television the Prime Minister standing side by side with the Archbishop of Greece (Seraphim) and cutting the cord that drops the cross into the sea (representing Christ's baptism).

The only major holiday which does not demonstrate this convergence of church and state is the recently instituted commemoration of the Polytechnic student uprising of 1973 against the Greek military Junta. This holiday is celebrated in schools with re-enactments and songs. At the high school celebration I attended this student struggle was implicitly linked to student movements in general: blackboards were covered with peace signs and slogans in English including "Make Love, Not War." This was followed by a student march and public deposition of wreaths in the main square of Kalymnos harbor. There was no church presence at this ceremony, a fact explained, as one person told me, by the cozy relationship between the Greek Church and the Junta during the dictatorship years. Significantly, this holiday was celebrated and remembered by many middle-class, educated Kalymnians. But my less-educated informants, even those who were left-wing, did not observe this holiday, and a number of them confused the events of the Polytechnic uprising with the Turkish invasion of Cyprus in 1974.[5]

The linking of church, state and family goes beyond such obvious symbolic confluences, which with different emphases and in different combinations, can be found in most Western states. Once again, it is through metaphor and analogy that these domains are brought together and conflated on Kalymnos. Thus, when telling me biblical stories, a woman analogized Pontius Pilate to the present Prime Minister. Saint Peter, she said, was like the then Defense Minister Varvitsiotis. And Christ, coming through town telling people the good word was like the socialist party PASOK passing through Kalymnos saying, "we promise this, we'll do that" (as a PASOK supporter she said this without irony). While some of these analogies were perhaps intended for my understanding as a non-Orthodox Christian, it is still striking how easily she found correspondences in the political domain. Similarly, many Kalymnians analogize Orthodox saints to political connections: just as these connections allow you to get in a word with the politicians who hold power, the saints allow you to do so with God.[6] The saints are also thought of in terms of local and kinship metaphors: "worship" of them I was told numerous times, is no different from the commemoration of respected ancestors. Just as you put pictures of your parents and grandparents up in your home, so you do with chosen saints. Indeed, old black and white photographs vie for space with the gleaming blue, red and yellow colors of icons on the mantles of most Kalymnian homes.[7]

These metaphoric equivalences could be interpreted as a reflection of the patronage and personalized politics which allegedly characterize Greece's "underdeveloped" political condition. However, they can be viewed in a more complex fashion: as part of a dialectical process whereby village Greeks make claims to an officially validated history while simultaneously making larger events comprehensible by reducing them to local terms.[8] On Kalymnos these equivalences assert the mutual comprehensibility of different domains of experience. The Kalymnian man's comment that he felt like an Albanian refugee does not make a claim to official history – it suggests jokingly an ability to empathize with another's basically similar experience. By the same token, claims that "my husband is a Papadopoulos" (leader of the Greek Junta), or that "my father acts towards women like the Turkish invasion of Cyprus" are not employing experience-distant concepts, since embedded in these statements, even with their hyperbole, is the belief that oppressors are fundamentally the same.

This has considerable implications for the way people view history on Kalymnos. If politics provides a grab-bag of horizontal references to make sense of everyday life, history – conceived largely as the history of the acts of leading political and religious figures – provides the vertical references that expand upon and confirm Kalymnian understanding of the present. One example of this is provided by a Kalymnian man in his twenties, with left-wing leanings, describing the plight of former socialist Minister of the Economy Tsovolas (tried and convicted during the Koskotas scandal mentioned above). He claimed that Tsovolas was a radical supporter of the people – he had risen up from a poor background – whom the right-wing felt that they had to get rid of. Thus, Tsovolas was like Socrates: a "democrat" who was disposed of by the right-wingers of his time, just as every right-wing government oppresses the democrats and tries to fool the people.

Such comparisons are appropriated from the length of Greek history, and for some Kalymnians, from world history too. A Kalymnian communist party member described all the world's struggles as versions of the struggle between capitalism and communism. Thus the guerrillas in the Philippines could learn from the experience of the Greek communists after the Second World War, and not accept false peace treaties with their government. For Kalymnians no event stands on its own, but must always be understood in the wider context of similar events drawn from other times and other places.

It is important to note that the communist cited above would certainly reject the equation of religion and politics. Rejection of the link between church and state can certainly be more commonly found at the level of popular rather than state discourse. Some Kalymnians are interested in religion to the exclusion of politics, and vice versa. There are those who decry both religion and politics as the corrupt manipulations of the power-hungry. Others may reject the more suffocating aspects of the family or local values. What is interesting, as I illustrate below, is that even those who reject certain parts of this equation, do not reject the underlying assumptions about how these domains operate. A religious narrative about the past may be dismissed by a Kalymnian non-believer, but the structure of the narrative will be applied by this person to understand personal, national, or in the case of the communist, class history.

In the next section I expand on these points by illustrating some of the themes and tropes used in talking about the past. In order to give flesh and substance to the abstract claims I've been making, I will present the transcripts of a conversation about history I had with a Kalymnian woman, followed by my commentary.

Maria: The Lessons of History

Background

Maria is in her sixties, married with three children, eight grandchildren and a semi-invalid husband. Maria's formal education stopped in fifth grade, when her father took her out of school so she could care for her sick mother, despite the advice of her teacher, who said she was an excellent student. She taught herself to read mostly through following the liturgies in church and reading business documents. She prides herself on this ability to navigate documents, as well as her skill in running the business affairs of her family and representing the family in public, even before her husband became ill. She avidly follows the daily news through television and radio, and is therefore able to converse on the latest political events. She does not restrict herself to events in Greece, but is equally up-to-date on events in Europe and the United States, and would often fill me in on the latest developments of the socialist party in France, racial attacks in Germany, or the presidential elections in the United States.

I do not wish to suggest that Maria represents every Kalymnian. At certain points I will juxtapose other voices to articulate views divergent from Maria's, although I believe that even these divergent views share the same underlying assumptions. I choose to focus on one extended conversation in order to follow the coherence of one Kalymnian's thoughts and to tease out the world view implicit in it. However, in choosing to present what I believe to be largely shared assumptions, I run the risk of portraying the Kalymnians as overly nationalistic. I have suggested elsewhere in this book some of the explicit and implicit ways in which Kalymnians challenge nationalist presumptions, and regard them as the creation of politicians. Similarly, if I were to focus on Kalymnian recountings of the Italian Occupation, I could find numerous examples of memories which challenge the "official" story of Kalymnian resistance to outside rule. To recapitulate my point made above, even those on Kalymnos who implicitly or explicitly challenge the content of national history, do not challenge its form, and it is the form that I wish to concentrate on here.

This conversation took place while Maria was taking a break from preparing lunch (she shares duties with her daughter for feeding her husband, her daughter's family and often her son's family). I use the word conversation in the sense that Maria was directing her comments to me, and some of her argument seemed geared to the fact that she knew I was an atheist, since we had discussed these matters before. Maria spoke, however, with very few interruptions from me, except an occasional request for clarification. In a sense her statements seemed directed beyond me to a general audience, as it was clear that she had given considerable thought to these matters.

I did not set the theme for Maria before I began taping. Instead I said that I would turn on the tape-recorder while I read her a passage from a book of local folklore about the nameday of local Kalymnian Saint Panteleimonas, and asked if she could help me understand it. Quickly Maria moves the conversation in other directions, and we never return to the book.

The Great Exemplars

Maria: We give thanks for the suffering of Saint Panteleimonas: his suffering, beating, torture, killing, happened in order to make us strong. Because we draw meaning (αντλούμε νόημα) from the lessons of the saints.

David: For life today?

Maria: For life today. They are the ones who gave us the lights, just as you go to University and are taught by your professors, we were taught by them . . . They taught us with their self-sacrifice – [giving example] an eighteen-year-old boy doesn't get upset to have his life taken . . . for God, because it is worth it. Thus the saints become teachers of the world for us. We draw meaning, we are inspired by them . . . In church they read the names of all the martyrs . . . and I keep track and count, and they name hundreds of people who sacrificed themselves for Christ. It's true . . . not a falsification: the idolaters, the rabbis will take my head and I'll become an example for my generation: these are the great men of that period. And they have remained in the [history of] the Church. How? Just as Karamanlis [current president and former prime minister of Greece] will die but remain in history, and many will be taught by his achievements. The new generation of politicians that will come, will say, "you don't know how we will solve this problem? Remember what Karamanlis back then said during the Cyprus crisis? *This* is what he said, and Greece was saved."[†] We today

---

[†] A reference to the Turkish invasion of Cyprus in 1974 which led to the fall of the Greek Junta. Karamanlis, who was in exile at the time in Paris, was called back to Greece by a rump dictatorship to deal with the Cyprus crisis. It

imitate them [the Saints] for religion . . . Now people are not put on the cross, there are no more idolaters, it is our *nation*, we no longer become martyrs, as we did with Turkey for 400 years.[†] [Giving an example of martyrdom]: They tell you "say sorry" [deny your religion]. "No, God is great!" "I'll kill you!" "Go ahead, my generation will witness it, and they will rise high." If I give in, say it's not true, God doesn't exist, the child will see it and learn from his father that God doesn't exist. The nation is lost. These people [the Saints] sacrificed themselves and became examples, and our reli–eeh–our nation is based on these people. Politically we copy Plastiras, Sophocles Venizelos, Eleftherios Venizelos,[††] now we will copy Karamanlis for certain things that he managed well for the nation. They remain in the history of the nation, and these [saints] remain in the history of the church. We have examples now, prototypes, and on these we base ourselves.

Here we find a clear statement of the way exemplars from the past are selected, the actions of great figures that can guide people in facing the crises of the present. Here this idea is expressed in explicitly nationalist terms. Other Kalymnians compared Greece and Turkey as countries with long histories, which can learn from their mistakes, in contrast to the United States, a country with little history. This is a view expressed in the media. For example, a magazine article claims that Thucydides is recommended reading at US military academies for the insights he sheds on the cold war: "[post-cold war] analysts are now looking to the past to interpret the present and understand the future. The disadvantage of this method is that today's world rulers don't have a past at their disposal. Thus they must look to the nations who have it [history], even if they themselves have forgotten it. Thucydides becomes modern again!" (Yiannopoulos and Pantelis 1992; my translation). Implicitly it is Greece which has forgotten its own history. On Kalymnos it is a commonly held view that Greece has failed to make good use of its own history, to take advantage of it properly, to learn from it, and to promote it internationally. This is perceived to be particularly true in relation to the "Macedonian Question" discussed in Chapter 8. People on Kalymnos and in the news

---

is widely believed that his negotiations were crucial in stopping the Turkish army from taking even more of the island.

[†] A reference to the Ottoman Empire, which is commonly referred to as the "400 years of slavery."

[††] A listing of three of the leading republican politicians in Greece in this century. It is interesting that she counterposes them here to Karamanlis, who is a leader of the Conservative party.

media commented that Greece couldn't expect other countries to appreciate its position on the issue, since Greece's own younger generation was ignorant of the history of Macedonia. The same observation is made by Maria when she says that if these prototypes are lost and if people no longer stand up for their religion, then children will learn from their parents that God doesn't exist, and the nation will be lost. Maria picks up this theme later when she discusses how the younger generation has turned toward European models: "They don't want the Greek Universities, they have turned in that direction, [towards Europe] in a few years, for this reason the end of the world will come. From my son's generation, they have stopped believing in the examples that I believe in, and if you tell him he says: 'mother, you are stupid!'"

As I argue above, there is a complete isomorphism between the religious and the political domains in this discourse.[9] They are recognized as separate domains, but as Maria states, "politically, we imitate Plastiras . . ." there is a constant slipping back and forth from one to the other, even a confusion of the two: "our reli–eeh–our nation is based on these people." The family is also involved as the agent of transmission, or in the case of her son, failure to transmit the past, a theme that is further assessed in the next section of Maria's discussion.

Constructing a "Historical" Narrative

This next excerpt comes after Maria has been discussing religious themes. In particular, she compares the miracles of Orthodox Christianity to western science – the latter may be able to send men to the moon, but it cannot produce miracles, make the dumb speak or the paralyzed walk. Her defense of Orthodoxy is partly directed to my atheism. As she repeatedly says, these are facts and we have documents to prove it. "These aren't the fantasies of poor women: kings, ministers, they all come to see these miracles, are they all idiots, David?" From here, she continues the blending of religion, politics and family in her discussion of key "moments" in Greek history.

Maria: I'm not persuaded easily. But for certain documents that I see the nation accepts, the ministry teaches in its books . . . In '21 didn't people see the Virgin Mary in the sky – since there are people still alive from '21, as history tells us.[†] These are recent

---

[†] This reference to '21 is initially confusing, since "21" usually refers to 1821 and the Greek War of Independence. However from the context it is clear Maria must be referring to 1921, which would mark the Greek campaign into Asia Minor. As I will discuss below, this reference makes sense in terms of her larger theme of "sacrifice" for the nation.

things, when we're talking about 100 years. Understand? These things have been taught to our children from our parents. My own grandmother lived this event . . . In '74,[†] with the Cyprus crisis, when there was war and the army was running to the border, people of all different ages gathered, not soldiers . . . and were running all together to save the fatherland, especially since it was the Turks, with whom we have bitter experience, since they ruled us for so many years. And immediately in front, at the train stations, there was the icon of the Virgin . . . and behind it the people. Facts, serious facts. Our forefathers lived them and [unclear: possibly "transferred them directly to the race"].

David: They saw the icon in the sky?

Maria: They saw the icon in '21 . . . In the middle of the day you could see it. Not just you, everyone . . . And now during every difficult moment the icon of the Virgin goes first and afterwards goes the army. This generation believes because it is still only the second generation – it's not yet the third generation – we've just entered the third generation now from '21. Understand. There are still Macedonian fighters up there – seven or eight people who are in the parades.[††] . . . It's been transferred from our grandfathers to our fathers, to us. I can't not believe my parent about that which he heard and saw from his father. This isn't something over the centuries – it's recent . . . The Virgin is our protector . . . We raise the icon at difficult moments and it's something moving that makes your hair stand on end. We believe this, David . . .

Didn't I tell you about Constantine the Great – that isn't recent, it's very old. '21 is recent. [She tells the story of Constantine leading his armies into battle and seeing the sign in the sky from God: "in this [sign], vanquish!" (εν τούτω νίκα)]. These aren't recent events, but they remain in history, and the people who come after teach it and believe it, it can't be erased from the books . . . The state and the leaders don't want to lead us, the new generation, astray. On the contrary, they have changed many things, have modernized them many times.[†††] New books enter into history because there was the War of 1940, which was yesterday, which I remember myself.

[†] She actually says '47, but from the context it is clear that this is a slip of the tongue, as she is clearly referring to the events of 1974.

[††] A reference to the Balkan Wars prior to the First World War in which the Greeks won what is now Greek Macedonia.

[†††] Suggesting that the history books have been updated to accommodate recent events.

It entered into history with the way that we fought the Italians and the Germans. These things remain from generation to generation. The little children who didn't live '40, just as I didn't live '21 but I believe it, now when we tell little stories at home, [giving example]: "Grandma, tell me something!" "I'll tell you Petro [her grandson], one time . . . [tells story of how her family was turned away from an air-raid shelter during a German bombing, and then minutes later the shelter was blown up] . . . These now I transmit as tales to the children and they will keep it and tell it: "you know, my grandmother told me, when Germany was here –" Thus tradition is transmitted from generation to generation, the sufferings that the nation has undergone. I was taught what happened in '21, I teach what happened in '40, they [the children] will live other events which will intervene certainly, and thus tradition lives on, from generation to generation, and thus has lived the history of the Church . . .

Here we see Greek history tied together as key events in a narrative of self-sacrifice for the Church and for the nation. Maria's choice of 1921 as a key "event" is idiosyncratic. Usually 1922 is referred to since this marks the "Great Catastrophe" when, after the failed Greek campaign into Asia Minor, hundreds of thousands of Greeks were slaughtered and fled their homes on the coast of Asia Minor to become refugees in Greece (see Clogg 1992 for details). However, the reference to 1921 fits Maria's narrative in two senses. It parallels the events of 1974 in two ways. First, in terms of the raising of the icon, which links the two events together (even if in the first case the icon appeared in the sky and in the second it was raised by the army, the act of raising it, according to Maria, was meant as a reminder of the appearance of the icon at an earlier "difficult moment of history.") Even the appearance of the icon in 1921 is not viewed by Maria as a unique event, but as a reflection of what happened in pre-Byzantine times with folk hero Constantine the Great and the appearance of a sign of victory in the sky. Second, in both cases Greeks had gathered together to fight the Turks. Even if this fight was in vain in 1921 and 1974, people had been willing to sacrifice themselves and become exemplars for the nation. Thus, these actions also parallel the acts of the Saints (Maria's principal political–religious comparison), who were willing to give their lives not to defeat the Turks, but to uphold their religion, in the faith that future generations would remember them. This connects to her complaint that more and more people, such as her son, are no longer willing to sacrifice themselves for the nation, but worry about their personal welfare first and foremost. Thus, Maria's choice of 1921 rather than 1821 as a key event makes sense – in the earlier year Greeks sacrificed themselves but were victorious.

The Generational Connection

Maria's choice of 1921 also fits with her generational theme: she knows that the events of '21 are true because her grandmother lived them, and she cannot doubt that which she has been told by an ancestor who was an eye-witness. In the same way she will transmit the history which she has lived to her children and grandchildren. History is thus personalized: the new generation of politicians will look back and say "Remember how Karamanlis solved this problem?"; so the next generation of Maria's family will say: "You know, my grandmother told me that when Germany was here . . . " Thus Maria's sufferings during the Second World War become metonymic of the sufferings of the nation and of the Church. To paraphrase one Kalymnian woman in her early twenties:

> It is very important to know the history of the place you come from because only through understanding all the things that our parents suffered and survived can we gain the strength to face the future and appreciate what our parents have created – both their strengths and their faults.

This same generational connection establishes continuity between the recent and the ancient past. Just as Maria transmits what she was taught from her grandparents and her parents to her own grandchildren, the ancient events were lived by "our forefathers" (οι παππούδες μας). As Maria, discussing Constantine the Great's miraculous vision, puts it: "These aren't recent events, but they remain in history, and the people who come after (ο επόμενος λαός) teach it and believe it, it can't be erased from the books."

These events are familiarized in another way. They are not abstract dates, but rather are referred to as familiar markers: '21, '40 and '74, rather than 1921, etc. As such, the mention of the dates themselves becomes evocative of emotion and association. This is indicated by a tendency in Kalymnos (and in the media) to use dates and periods of history as familiar references in everyday speech which stand metonymically or symbolically for a larger content. Thus the leaders of the Greek dictatorship are commonly referred to as the 21st of Aprilers, marking the date of their seizure of power.[10] The leading terrorist group in Greece named itself "17th of November," thus evoking the attack by the Greek Junta on a student resistance movement in 1973 which killed over 100 students. On Kalymnos I heard people refer to right-wing neighbors not as "Junta supporters" but simply as "He is very Junta" (είναι πολύ Χούντα) thus using a whole period of history, or at least an association with the leaders of the 1967 to 1974 dictatorship, to characterize the neighbor's proclivities. In a similar manner, a man referred to an old woman of unsavory character as a "whore, not from

'12, from '21," (πουτάνα όχι του δώδεκα, του εικοσιένα; in this case
referring to 1821) mean that she is a very old whore.[11]

In all these tropological uses of dates, as with the uses of names
discussed above, history is brought into local experience, and the
two are used mutually to illuminate each other. Historical dates and
historical figures are part of the storehouse of references whereby
Kalymnians negotiate events great and small, at the same time their
constant usage makes history something familiar, not distanced from
the average person.

History As Pattern

It may be useful here to summarize what I have been suggesting about
the category "history" in Kalymnian thought. By way of contrast, if
we look at US popular culture, "making history" means doing something that has never been done before: setting a record for the most
home runs, the hottest day, the most consecutive terms in office (and
simultaneously consigning the former record-holder to "history," i.e.
to oblivion and forgetfulness). On Kalymnos, history refers to unusual
events which can nevertheless be incorporated into a pattern. Thus,
the Greek Revolution was an act of resistance equaling the bravery of
past battles against all odds, such as Thermopylae, that set a pattern
for future acts over the next 170 years. It was also a return of Greece
to the stage of world "history," an awakening from a historical slumber
of 400 years, a dark period where essentially nothing "happened"
except the passing of time.[12] A Kalymnian man in his sixties, discussing
how the younger generation knows only prosperity and material
increase, told me: "the younger generation thinks that every day is
the same, that every day is getting better and better, they will have to
live through a war to understand." It is interesting here that modernization, i.e. things getting "better and better" is not associated with
"history" but with flat uneventfulness, while "history" means the
disruption of routine, an event that bursts on the scene, often bringing
destruction in its wake. Of course "events" themselves are not objective
facts, but are culturally defined as such. Ricoeur (1981: 167) has argued
that an "event" requires a narrative in which to fit. Similarly, it is the
construction of narratives around themes or patterns, as shown above,
that makes for the selection of certain events as significant.

This sense of history as pattern also helps to illuminate Collard's
(1989) discussion of historical consciousness in a mainland Greek
village. Collard is surprised by the absence of discussion about what
she sees as a key period in the village's history: the years prior to the
Greek Civil War, when local self-government had been considerably
developed. This period, because of its association with communism,
was still taboo when Collard conducted her fieldwork in 1979. Collard

came to realize that villagers were actually talking about this period in oblique fashion in their discussions of Ottoman rule as a time of village autonomy, "when government didn't sit on our heads" (1989: 97). Although it was beyond "living memory" the Ottoman period had come to stand in for this "taboo" period in discussions of the theme of local autonomy. If it is seen in the context of my discussion of history as repeating pattern, it is not surprising that one period could easily substitute for another, taboo period. As noticed above in Maria's tracing of the theme of "sacrifice" across Greek history, such substitution need not involve periods of time directly experienced by the narrator. Indeed, their distance from the narrator probably increases their plasticity in this regard.

This sense of history as pattern is different from the pattern suggested by "custom" as defined in the previous chapter. Custom is repeated action, but of an expected variety: tied to the predictability of the calendar or of life cycle rituals. Custom is not disruptive, though it is set apart from everyday life insofar as it is anticipated as a break from the everyday routine. Easter is a prime example of this, as are certain saints' days, especially if they involve an outing to a chapel in the mountains (as is the case with Saint Yiorgos, Prophet Elias and numerous others). "Tradition" (παράδοση) is a more elusive term, which can overlap both custom and history. As discussed in Chapter 5, tradition can often be used interchangeably with custom. However, when distinguished, tradition is perceived as that which characterizes the people who claim the tradition: it is our tradition to resist outside intervention, we are a resistant people. But as we will see below, "history" also has this quality of being characteristic of a people, and thus it may occasionally slip into the domain of tradition. This shading between history and tradition is captured in a speech by a local school-teacher given at the celebration of Greek Independence day in 1992. As he put it:

> The seal of 1821 is the spiritual outbreak, the power that makes man pass the boundaries of nature and enter into the space of history. What were the invisible and inexhaustible powers that preserved unextinguished, the flame of Hellenism in the black years of slavery? . . . It was above all Greek tradition. This tradition is the treasure house that protects through the centuries our undying spirit, our undying heart . . . It made the blind Homer show men who had the eyes to see the secret beauty of the world . . . It made Alexander the Great keep Homer under his pillow, and made him live his thirty-year life like a superb myth that lasts for centuries . . . It made Kolokotronis [Greek revolutionary leader] wear a headdress like an ancient Greek.

Once again "history" is the event, 1821, which erupts on the scene, disrupting the flat sameness of the years of Turkish rule. But it is not any random event, it is a fulfillment of "tradition" an acting out of the essence of what the Greek people are, as shown through the myriad events that make up their "history."

As Herzfeld (1992c) has argued, there are certain shared themes and tropes employed in politico-historical discussions in Greece, and disagreement focusses not on the rules per se, but on the deployment of events in these discussions. Some of the themes mentioned by Herzfeld include the idea that Greece's problems are the result of betrayal from outside, in addition to betrayal from within. In each case debates do not center on whether "betrayal" itself is a legitimate representation of events, but rather on the question: who is doing the betraying? Similarly, I believe that assumptions about pattern in history and intergenerational continuity can be regarded as rules which are not disputed by Kalymnians, even though the events to which they refer may be disputed. For example, the young woman cited above in discussion of the importance of remembering the sufferings of one's parents is a social rebel and an admitted atheist. She would certainly reject Maria's historico-religious examples as fantasy. But she accepts the basic premises about history, suffering and generational continuity. Similarly, here follows the statement of Skevos, a man in his early thirties, an educated computer specialist who disdains both politics and religion, believing all political ideologies to be phony, and much Christian belief to be childish. After I had made lunch for him, he began discussing the generation gap in material possessions, and how the younger generation doesn't have to work for things like the older generation did, who lived through wars and other deprivations. He admitted that he was caught between the younger and older generations, "with one foot in the shit of each." I turned on the tape recorder and asked him to reflect on the significance of history.

Skevos: I think it's very significant for someone to know about the existence of his, I don't want to use the word "race," because that's nonsense, but categories of people – no, that's worse. Types of people. How his type has functioned . . .

David: Cultures . . .

Skevos: Bravo, yes. The Romans, for example, as soon as they heard about the existence of a people somewhere, wanted to go and conquer them. The Chinese went and organized different lands . . . [Compares the Toltec, a "completely metaphysical" people with the Japanese who lived "with sword in hand."] You see the differences! All this is a piece of what we call history.

Skevos differs from Maria in expressing a more critical view of history. He does not trust the received wisdom of school texts and wants to research history for himself – a reflection of his education. Nevertheless, his basic view of the significance of history is the same as

Maria's: history reveals the underlying character of a people. It is worth noting his discomfort with different words: race, category, type, which also reflects a more educated background. Skevos suggests that from the individual events of history you can read the patterns of different peoples, just as Maria used the pattern of "sacrifice" to string together a narrative of exemplary events for the Greek nation. When I suggest that Skevos' critical attitude towards history is more educated, it is because I believe that such attitudes are now taught at schools on Kalymnos. In conversations with six teachers at a local junior high school I received two responses to the following question: "What do you want your students to learn about Greek history from your classes?" Half the teachers responded that they wanted to impart a more critical view of history itself, the ability to see different points of view about history and evaluate different sources. They also said they wanted to teach students to seek causes for events, in particular the underlying economic interests driving history. And half the teachers said that they wanted the students to see that history is relevant to their lives today because it repeats itself and the Greeks have remained unchanged over the course of their history. If the latter view comes closer to capturing the ideas that motivate Maria's narrative, both views imply a reading of history as pattern, a concept I believe is shared by most Kalymnians.

Overcoming "The Enemy Within"

In this next excerpt from my discussion with Maria, she lays out another major "theme" or "pattern" uniting Greek history: the recurring figure of internal dissent which has caused Greece's failure to thrive. This theme is touched on at the start of this chapter when I discuss the Kalymnian view of their own "politicization" and the problem with "histories," i.e. quarrels that keep them apart. Maria is restating her point that certain events – Christ's Crucifixion, the appearance of the icon in the sky in 1921, the war of 1940 – remain in history and are taught in the books of the church and the nation, when I interrupt her.

David: But Andreas changed the history of the war of '40.[†]
Maria: Andreas couldn't change that history because there are people still living from back then, the Macedonian fighters whom you see in parades, how can you change it?
David: But about the history of EAM/ELAS.

[†] My reference is to the rehabilitation of the wartime communist resistance which had been blacklisted during all post-war administrations until the election of Socialist prime minister Andreas Papandreou in 1981. Part of this rehabilitation involved the revision of school textbooks to reflect the critical

Maria: EAM was recognized by Andreas, and he has made them pat-
riots (εθνικόφρονες), he's made them pensioners . . . those who
returned after we beat the Germans, returning, we killed each
other. [Giving example]: "I fought more, I . . ." That's the bad
of the Greeks, that we don't thrive and become greater – before
we return [from battle] we make plans: "What did [your] division do, my division was better. Let's make our own party,
let's call it EAM, and let's take the reigns, take command of
the nation." And they were stealing from the front, the cunning
ones, weapons, clothes, to be ready when they entered into
Athens . . . to fight, and if need be to kill EAM in order for
ELAS to win out . . . So these are the faults of the Greeks. Come
back, tie things up, value the people who were lost, if someone
was more powerful and managed to kill more Germans give
him a place that he deserves. It's not for you to want to become
king and to kill your brother . . . Understand it. That's why we
don't move forward. We beat the Germans, everyone glorious,
me more, you less, whatever anyone could, now lets find a
proper person to lead the nation. Instead we want forty parties.
That's why we don't advance, even though we have all the
basics.

Maria continues giving a few local examples. The reader need not
follow all the details, lodged as they are in local and national politics.
The point to be noticed is Maria's attitude towards these "historical
figures" who may be in the opposite political camp. One example
concerns the statue of Kalymnian Skevos Zervos, best known for his
agitation in support of Dodecanese unification with Greece during
the years of the Italian Occupation (see Doumanis 1997). When PASOK
came to power they removed his statue from the harbor of Kalymnos
because he had been a supporter of the King. As Maria notes: "All for

---

leadership provided by the Greek communists (known as EAM-ELAS) in
resistance efforts against the German occupation. Note that later in her
discussion Maria seemingly confuses EAM and ELAS, which are acronyms for
the military and political wings of the communist resistance respectively, and
assigns them to opposing political parties. It is possible that she is referring to
the splits among the communist leadership at the time. More likely, I believe,
is that she is making a general point about Greek infighting, and thus historical
exactitude has become unimportant in this context. Note also the common
usage of Papandreou's first name, another device by which Kalymnians localize
and familiarize the national; although this works both ways as it is also
motivated by Papandreou's explicit cultivation of a populist image.

the parties . . . [he was] very patriotic, it doesn't matter what party he was, he was a Kalymnian who offered a great deal to the world." What is striking here is that Maria is a very loyal and vocal supporter of the Socialist party PASOK, and its leader Andreas Papandreou. Another time when her husband and I were talking about Skevos Zervos and she entered the room her immediate reaction was: "Oh yes, Zervos, a king-supporter." Her criticism of Papandreou and PASOK seems unusual, insofar as it is always the dissent of the *other* party that threatens national unity. In a similar way, I was surprised by Maria's genealogy of great leaders. It fits with the normal liberal genealogy: Venizelos, Plastiras, but instead of the usual choice of George Papandreou, Maria substitutes the conservative Karamanlis; in spite of her critical attitude towards Karamanlis that she expresses on issues such as the Macedonian Question. Maria's change in her assessment of these conservative politicians whom she normally criticizes must be seen in the context of her overall argument. Since Maria is making a case for the disastrous effects of party politics on the course of Greek history, she solidifies her argument by proving her own ability to overcome such divisions and to put aside her party preferences in the interest of the unity of the Greek people. This is what many Kalymnians mean when they talk about "learning from history."

Living "History" and Explaining its Misfortunes

Maria is wrestling with one of the key issues in modern Greek consciousness: if we accept the proposition, as most Kalymnians do, that each "people" has a continuity expressed through its history, how can we explain Greece's former greatness and current marginality. As Maria puts it:

> What have we sunk to now – to become the servants of the Europeans. The French, the Europeans say that they come to Greece to be taught and inspired. We didn't take care to civilize ourselves . . . Now we'll enter the EU like lice, to find bread. If we had done it however, civilized, to get along with other peoples – just like in America, where all different peoples from all over the world became one company and have risen to the skies. We are condemned for our egoism, for our ideologies.

Here internal dissent is the culprit, and a historical narrative is constructed which focusses on the Civil War.[13] Once again these larger historical events are seen as operating on the same principles as local "histories." It is egoism, the bane of Greek village life that condemns neighbors to squabble and sabotage each other, which is responsible for the failure of Greeks as a nation to work together and to thrive. Here Maria contrasts the Greeks with the Jews, who are seen to have done well as a "nation" because they do not have this egoism, and are always willing to help fellow Jews in need. A second narrative, constructed around the theme of "betrayal from outside," is at other times invoked to explain Greece's current plight. This narrative involves different events such as the role of Greece's allies in the Asia Minor disaster of 1922 or the invasion of Cyprus. These themes are agreed-upon devices with which to structure historical narratives, even if the events to which they refer (e.g. "who is the betrayer") are disputed. Through such narratives history is "telescoped," "not, however, in the sense of some structural amnesia that simply leaves out intervening generations but through a principle of identification between seemingly similar events" (Herzfeld 1992c: 73).[14] Through an examination of Maria's discourse I have attempted to show the means by which such similarities are constructed. They are based on a perceived isomorphism between the political, the religious, and the local domains of action. An isomorphism is illustrated by the fact that the same themes or figures Maria used to construct a politico-religious history are often used in the construction of personal histories. One woman tells her story as a series of sacrifices by her in order to benefit often ungrateful relatives. Another woman's story is one of "betrayal from outside" on the part of a sister-in-law determined to wreck her marriage. Personal stories are almost always constructed around such themes, and just like the national histories discussed above, events are not just "telescoped," but remembered and described in great detail as "proof" of the particular theme: sacrifice, struggle or betrayal. These themes are not only intended to create coherent narratives of the past, but to read and interpret current events in the present, both at local and national levels.

For Kalymnians, then, national history is a collection of such stories organized around different themes. The stories themselves are multiple and rich enough to support different themes in different contexts, as noted above. In the same way, personal histories can have shifting themes. Based on one day's actions, a neighbor may be constructed according to one theme (for example, ingratitude) and stories will be mobilized to support this view. Another day, if good relations are re-established with the neighbor, another theme will be substituted (basic generosity) and the neighbor's "history" reorganized accordingly. This is not to say that Kalymnians view each other in one-dimensional terms. These different interpretations co-exist and are mobilized at different times. But in more reflective moments, one neighbor's assessment of another will often admit to their strengths as well as their faults. What is important here is the sense that one's actions and those of others are constantly being "historicized," i.e. added to the themes that will be perceived as defining of one's life. Thus one is always on the lookout for one's neighbor's escapades, their potential "histories." By the same token, one's own good deeds must have attention brought to them, so that they will be remembered. And thus the frequent injunction when I was invited to people's houses "eat, in order to remember."

People's generosity must be remembered if it is to be part of their own "history." Similarly, a Kalymnian may give food or money to a poor person, again with the injunction to "remember my dead father." In this present act the person who performs it is remembered as generous, and the memory of the person's father may be rectified (it is in the same spirit that you feed people at a μνημόσυνο, a ceremony dedicated to the memory of a deceased ancestor). Analogously, people caught stealing from their neighbor's fruit tree can use the excuse that, "I saw the fruit and thought of your dead parent [who previously owned the field]. Thus I had to have it." This excuse – calling on the person's links to his/her ancestors through inheritance of property – is seen as an acceptable rationale for such behavior.

Koester (1989: 14) makes a similar point about memory in linking reputation and history in Iceland. As he puts it, reputation was about past actions, but also determined present actions: "Icelanders, recognizing that acts and events were formed into stories, acted in storymaking ways." It is this sense that history matters in the present that runs through Maria's discourse, and that I will clarify in my conclusion.

History Now

> A Kalymnian man Panayiotis, aged thirty-five, and a French woman Joelle, aged twenty-five – who teaches English on Kalymnos – were having an argument in English at a bar. They began discussing the recent wave of immigrants to France. Panayiotis said that most of these immigrants were coming from France's colonies, so the French government was responsible for creating the situation, it couldn't just get rid of them now. They were just coming to get their due. Joelle responded that these immigrants had come to France on tourist visas and stayed, thus they were in France illegally and should be sent back. They've been independent since the 1950s and thus weren't French responsibility any more. Panayiotis closed the conversation by saying: you think you can just erase all that because you gave them independence? That doesn't change what France did.

I report this multi-national conversation because it epitomizes the sense that Kalymnians have of their own historical consciousness, and others' lack of it. Here, it is the sense of historical debt that is brought to the fore. In other situations, other themes will predominate. But running across different themes is the sense of a link between past and present, that the past is relevant to an understanding of the present. This feeling of relevance was expressed to me by a Kalymnian man, Manolis, in his twenties, who told me that he had shown a tourist an ancient pot and asked him if he felt anything.[15] The tourist had said no. Manolis continued, "Whereas when I go to a museum and see these things, my hair stands up on end!" I confessed to Manolis that while I understood what he was saying intellectually, like the tourist, I also could not feel it. He responded, "Imagine if your grandfather had made this object." Manolis' response was apposite in a number of ways. First, he had taken up the profession of his great-grandmother – bee-keeping – and had preserved many of the objects that she had used for bee-keeping.[16] Manolis also was eager to show me a book by the ancient Greek writer Strabo, which discusses Kalymnian honey as the best in all of Greece. He clearly felt linked to that ancient history. Now his suggestion to me that I imagine that my grandfather made the pot made sense. I could imagine feeling moved by holding something very old that my grandfather had created. For Manolis, there was no disconnection between the two experiences: his relation to his ancestor and his relation to Kalymnians in the ancient past who were bee-keepers. As Maria stated it, ancestors provide the link between the generations which promises the continuity of history. Perhaps there is nothing surprising in the idea that claims of descent from a common ancestor are a crucial means of forming group identities. But what is at stake here is not an actual common ancestor, since Kalymnian genealogies (like genealogies in most of Greece) are remarkably shallow: they trace back a maximum of three, more commonly two, generations except in unusual cases. Rather, descent provides an analogy for the way history is transmitted from past to present. Your relationship to your grandparent is a metaphor for your connection to ancient history (an idea I expand on in Chapter 8).

Manolis' challenge to me was to imagine a relationship to an ancient object as if it had been made by my grandfather. If I could imagine the latter relationship, I could extrapolate to the former. The fact was that I could imagine what I might feel if my grandfather had made the object. Within my own cultural upbringing it is perfectly "natural" and "reasonable" to feel connected to one's grandfather. And yet, given that kinship is as much a cultural system as any other aspect of culture, as an anthropologist I realize that there is nothing "natural" about my connection to my grandfather. To return to the macro-level, much recent analysis has focussed on the invention of tradition and history. Work on nationalism, from Gellner to Anderson, has posited a radical discontinuity between the national identities that arose in Europe in the late eighteenth and early nineteenth centuries and those which had come before. In the case of Greece, this insight has produced a spate of work that intends to demonstrate the "invention" of Greek national identity by the appropriation of an ancient past as filtered through the imagination of late eighteenth-century Western Europe.[17]

But the fact of invention is often used to suggest that these representations are somehow false, mystificatory or worse.[18] Perhaps this is why
they appeal to a Greek Marxist (Garganas 1992: 7) attempting to
debunk Greece's present-day claims to ancient Macedonia:

> The efforts of the bourgeoisie to extend present nations backward in
> time to show their historical continuity from the earliest of ancient
> times are laughable. The formation of nations and the development of
> national consciousness are social processes tied to the development of
> the bourgeoisie and of the capitalist mode of production. To transfer
> these concepts into previous historical periods of pre-capitalist modes
> of production is just myth-making, furthering the interests of the current
> bourgeoisie.

Here another "truer" history is substituted for the falsifications of
nationalism. However, this history involves the same type of claims
to continuity that Maria and Manolis make, whether they set the
critical period for the development of national identity at 200 or 2,000
years ago. If we take analyses of the invention of tradition to their
logical outcome, as Handler and Linnekin (1984: 281) did, we realize
that any claim to intergenerational continuity, whether it be one
generation or twenty, is an "invention," which reflects the needs of
the present:

> In the limiting case we may unreflectively perform some action exactly
> as we learned it from our parents; yet the performance is never com-
> pletely isomorphic with past performances and, more important, our
> understanding of the performance is a present-tense understanding,
> generated from the context and meanings of the present.

Any other claims to a connection between past and present must be
seen as "inventions" in the same way that Maria's and Manolis' juxta-
positions of different events are "inventions." It is one thing to
dismiss particular claims to continuity on the grounds that they justify
repressive regimes or understandings. But what I am questioning is
the current trend to dismiss claims to continuity simply on the formal
grounds that 3,000 years of continuity is "laughable." I am suggesting
that there is nothing structurally different about a claim to continuity
of thirty years or of 3,000 years. This is because most such claims
are not claims of exact identity; they recognize both similarity and
difference. I am not simply trying to make the point here that all
history is invention. Rather, I am questioning the process by which
some attitudes towards history are dismissed as non-rational, while
others based on similar principles are upheld.

This will become clear in the next two chapters, in which I juxtapose
Kalymnian understandings of the current events in the Balkans with
those promulgated by the Western media and my own understandings.

In the next chapter I use several arguments I had with Kalymnians over the war in ex-Yugoslavia as a chance to see some of the principles I have laid out in this chapter "in action," and to examine some of the surprises they provoked for me as I tried to come to terms with this war and the question, "What should 'the West' be doing?" In this chapter I let the Kalymnians speak for themselves as much as possible, on an issue for which Greece has received vilification and incomprehension in the Western media – its (supposed) support of Serbia. In the following chapter I examine the question of the naming of the so-called "Former Yugoslav Republic of Macedonia," and examine why this issue has stirred emotions on Kalymnos. Here I do not focus on explicit Kalymnian arguments, but rather attempt to reveal some of the underlying cultural assumptions that allow the "Battle for the Name" to make sense to Kalymnians, and by contrast fail to make sense to much of the West. In both of these chapters I will be building on the basic premiss I've established above: that we can understand the significance of the past by examining how and why it becomes relevant for discussions of current events, as it was for Panayiotis, but was not for Joelle.

Notes

1. Herzfeld has described a basic split in Greek usage between history, or "history in general" as "an instrument of the state's ideology, and "histories" of social disharmony" (1987: 41–6). My Kalymnian material would tend to confirm such a distinction. Here, however, I am interested in looking at what the two terms have in common as well as their differences.

2. This seems contra the analyses by Caraveli (1986), Goltsis-Rosier (1993) and Seremetakis (1991), although only Goltsis-Rosier discusses explicit narrative practices, the other two focussing on ritual and non-discursive historical consciousness. As I suggested in the last chapter, the fact that women and men share a sense of being historical actors on Kalymnos is tied to the very different residence and inheritance patterns compared to the patrifocal communities of these other analyses which require women to develop their own, separate "poetics."

3. Such was the case with St. Savvas, whose sainthood was confirmed during the course of my stay on the island.

4. I'm referring here to Αυρνιανή (Avrianí), which as a supporter of the socialist party, focusses on the scandals of the Right. Avrianí does have its counterparts in the right-wing press as well.

5. There is some justification for the association of the two events, as both were blunders which led to the downfall of the military Junta.

6. The obverse of this is that "priests" and "politicians" are often declaimed in the same breath as crooks only interested in looking out for their own interest. On saints as patrons see Campbell (1964: 342–6).

7. One school principal who was a religious scholar captured both of these connections in discussing the role of saints in people's lives:

The saints . . . are not our saviors. God is our savior. But because they achieved their own saving, and they love us and are close to God, we believe that they have the power to pray for us. Just as you would ask your father, your mother, your friend, your relative to pray to some greater power, to intervene to help you. We pray to their icons, we give honor not to the wood or the color, but to the person who is represented, to that holy person. Not the material, but the person. Just as I honor my father or my mother, and I have photographs of them, and so when I see them I long for them and I kiss their image. The love I have inside of me for them pulls me, and the material element that I have before me, the image, draws me and I kiss it. I don't kiss the paper nor do I honor the paper, but my mother and father.

8. Herzfeld 1992a: 118. On Greek "underdevelopment" see Mouzelis 1992; Woodhouse 1990.

9. Cf. Dubisch's (1995) analysis of the convergence of nationalist and religious discourses in people's pilgrimages to and perceptions of the shrine of Tinos. She also notes the use of similar metaphors and themes in discussing different religious and historical events, an issue taken up further below.

10. In his short story "The Most Tragic Mistake," Kalymnian writer Yiannis Aigaios (1992: 19) writes "The conversation had centered on [pre-Second World War dictator] Metaxas . . . Following this the school principal compared the 4th of August [date of Metaxas's seizure of power] with the 21st of April, since the teacher had lived through the Metaxas dictatorship as a student in Athens . . . And he claimed that the 4th of August was less tyrannical than the 21st of April, that the 4th of Augusters [leaders of the Metaxas dictatorship] had some moral principles in contrast to the Aprilers, who were simply vulgar." The term "4th of Augusters" is more common than "21st of Aprilers."

11. A reference to 1912, a date associated with the Balkan wars and Greek territorial gains in Macedonia and Thrace. The reference to "'21" in this statement is to 1821, not 1921.

12. As a school teacher, Panayiotis Giamaios, put it in his speech at the main church of Kalymnos on Greek Independence day: "After nearly four hundred years [of Turkish rule] Greece once again found its place in world history with a great political and military act: the Revolution of 1821."

13. For a "literate" parallel, see Sakellarios who constructs a narrative of connection between the Pelloponesian war, the fall of Constantinople and

the Asia Minor disaster as three great tragedies which can be laid at the doorstep of national divisions (1977: 30). Similarly, Sakellarios uses his discussion of the "miraculous" events of the Rock War for a meditation on the "many examples in the life of a people of its protection by God" (ibid.: 91). He goes on to give several examples of miraculous interventions in Greek history, but is also concerned to make the general point, like the man who compared Socrates to Tsovolas, that the powerful throughout history try and exploit and take advantage of the powerless.

14. Cf. White's (1978) "kinds of stories." In referring to "themes" and "kinds" I am touching on a debate that has gone on in folklore on the classification of folktales. Ben-Amos has criticized approaches that examine folktales in terms of "themes" or "kinds" because their selection involves "personal, cultural or theoretical subjective judgements which defy analytical objectivity" (Ben-Amos 1976: 219). This is particularly the case, Ben-Amos argues, in cross-cultural classifications. While noting the debate over these terms, for my purposes the term "themes" is meant not as a classificatory device, but rather to suggest certain regularities in present-day Kalymnian representations of the past, the ontological status of which is beyond the scope of this book. For a similar approach to historical narratives in anthropology see Borneman 1992.

15. The λαήνες which are brought up by sponge-divers and which decorate many Kalymnian homes.

16. With reference to my discussion of Kalymnian matrifocality in Chapter 5, it is interesting to note that descent may still be patrilateral when Kalymnians speak in the abstract, but in practice it is often matrilateral.

17. See Danforth 1984; Just 1989; Herzfeld 1982a; Kitromilidis 1990.

18. A point argued by Friedman 1992; 1996.

Dana Summers, The Orlando (Fla.) Sentinel, The Washington Post Writers Group

The "Great Powers" grind up Yugoslavia (Mitroporlos 1993).

seven

A Historical War:
Local Conversations with
Global Implication

The Great Powers play games at our expense.

Local saying

Introduction

In this chapter I further my discussion of Kalymnians' attitudes
towards history by showing how history becomes relevant to their
understanding of current world events. I contrast this with the surprise
their views provoked in me and the challenge they presented to my
own understanding of these events. I then unpack these views along
the lines laid out in the previous chapter: in terms of the historical
themes on which they are based, and their resonances in local views
of interpersonal relations, character and human motivation. I begin
this chapter with the larger events, as depicted in two cartoons from
the editorial pages of two newspapers, one in the United States and
one in Greece. The first, printed in *USA Today* (August 1992), shows a
frowning Hitler. Instead of his trademark mustache, the word "Serbia"
has been imprinted across his lip. As this cartoon was printed during
the height of reports of Serbian "concentration camps" in Bosnia, the
intent is clear. For Americans, Hitler represents the arch-villain of our
century, to whom current bad guys are inevitably compared (as
Saddam Hussein was by George Bush). The Serbs are simply the latest
"bad guys," the latest "Hitler." However, a Kalymnian seeing this
cartoon might read it differently and assume that it was a historical
reference to the Second World War and Hitler's butchery of the Serbs.
For a Kalymnian to compare present-day Serbs to Hitler would be as
incongruous as comparing Greek revolutionary leaders to Turkish
pashas. In my discussions with Kalymnians and readings of the Greek
national press it became clear that Serbian resistance to the Nazis is
perceived as rivaled only by that of the Greeks and both were seen as

playing a critical role in delaying the Nazi attack on Russia and changing the course of the Second World War.

My second cartoon, taken from the leading Greek Sunday newspaper *To Vima* (Mitropoulos 1993), would make perfect sense to Kalymnians, but might cause puzzlement to US readers if it appeared in *USA Today*. It shows a fat man with a top-hat representing the Western "Great Powers," passing Yugoslavia through a meat grinder and getting ready to eat it on a plate. This cartoon succinctly sums up a view of the war commonly held on Kalymnos: that the West had a major responsibility for the war in Yugoslavia, and any further intervention on their part would have made matters worse. During the course of my fieldwork a number of Kalymnians labored to convince me of the truth of such a view.

Thoughts about the Serbs and the disintegration of Yugoslavia might seem an odd topic for consideration in a book about a small Greek island off the coast of Asia Minor. However, although Kalymnos is geographically isolated from the centers of power, it has not been politically isolated from the rest of the world. In the twentieth century alone it has undergone occupations by the Ottoman empire, the Italians, the Germans and the British. Ignorance about world events is a luxury many Kalymnians feel they cannot afford, much less ignorance about what is going on in a neighboring Balkan country.[1] For many Kalymnians, Yugoslavia is not distant at all. They were well-informed about an issue which took second place only to the Macedonian controversy in the Greek press. This included the national newspapers bought at the main news agency, where men would stand around discussing and disputing the day's events; televised news broadcasts, a focus-point for many Kalymnian families in the evening after dinner; on radio broadcasts, playing constantly during the day as women cooked their meals or as shopkeepers without many customers tuned in; and even in church handouts, a source of news for some of the older women who took less interest in the daily events as portrayed in more secular venues. Not all Kalymnians keep up with world events, but the majority do.

History and Global Positioning

In focussing on the views of the war in Yugoslavia as promoted in the Greek media and expressed by Kalymnians I hope to present a view of international events coming not from the centers of power and information, but from a country on the peripheries of Europe, and from an island on the peripheries of Greece. The 1990s have seen a growing anthropological concern with the ways in which encompassing global, national and regional systems and processes are dialectically affecting and mediated by local meanings. The "local" and the "global" have become catchwords for processes we are keen to understand:

how meanings and structures interrelate at the most intimate and the most far-flung levels. Anthropologists from different camps are analyzing the ways in which identities and boundaries are being re-drawn by the dramatic increases in transnational migrations of peoples, capital, commodities and media. Such transnational flows have brought "relatively distant social worlds, events and relations within the experience of one's immediate world."[2] In this and the next chapter I concentrate on the latter process in order to show the different ways that international events are encompassed and translated by explicit and implicit local structures of meaning. In this chapter I focus primarily on explicit discussions. In doing so I heed Tsing's call for "complex global conversations." Tsing writes about the processes by which a people (the Meratus Dayaks of Southern Kalimantan) are marginalized "as their perspectives are cast to the side or excluded" (1993: 5), and the ways in which they engage with this marginality. Like the Meratus Dayaks, the Kalymnians "share with anyone who might read this . . . a world of expanding capitalisms, ever-militarizing nation-states, and contested cultural politics" (1993: xi). The Meratus Dayaks are marginal to state and international concerns, but this does not make them archaic survivors, "forced to catch up with the twentieth century" (ibid.: 7). Similarly, the Kalymnians may be "peripheral," but this does not make them backward, nor does their concern for history make them part of the past. As Tsing describes, peripherality has never meant isolation. Rather, "Mobility over a diversified landscape fosters a proliferating appreciation of differences; Meratus note minute distinctions of taste, language, and style between themselves and their neighbors" (ibid.: 61). This description could have been written for Kalymnian seafarers and migrants. The fact that Kalymnos seems, at times, even to its inhabitants blissfully free of the troubles plaguing us in the New World Order has not dulled the islanders' commitment to understand and manipulate as best as they can the world around them.[3]

In this chapter I engage both myself, an anthropologist from the United States with left-wing, internationalist political viewpoints, and some of my Kalymnian interlocutors, with their very different historical experiences, in conversation. For as Tsing notes "a starting point for careful participation in these conversations is the recognition that theories cannot be abstracted from global positioning" (1993: 31). Similarly, Marcus has extolled "imaginatively constructed . . . socially situated conversations." These conversations on current issues of international concern will "alter in often striking ways the manner in which contemporary society and culture have been otherwise assimilated in the theories, concepts and analytic frames of more conventional academic writing" (Marcus 1993: 1). This resonates with Tsing's description of a cultural dialogue which "requires turning one's back on the analytic distinction between theory and ethnography, in which the former looks out confidently from the particularized and unself-conscious world of the latter" (1993: 31).

By placing Kalymnian theories about world affairs side-by-side with what we would recognize as academic ones, I am suggesting that we must see our own formulations of history as symbolic systems, just as we do those of "other" cultures. This can be done most usefully not by abstracting theories for competition in a free marketplace of ideas, but by paying constant attention to the way theories are embedded in global positioning.

Global positioning and local experiences are crucial to comprehending Kalymnian understandings of the war in Yugoslavia. For the Kalymnian view of the "great powers" is formed from experiences at the hands of these great powers.[4] At the same time, the ways in which Kalymnians discuss their relationship to the great powers must be understood in the context of local practices and experiences. It should be clear that when I discuss "Kalymnian" views and discourses that these terms are always in the plural. I may generalize about common opinions on Kalymnos (as well as in the Western media), but I also note significant divergences of opinion. Furthermore when I make references to "Greek", "Serbian" or "Croatian" character they always refer to the discourses of local or global actors, and I do not accept these terms as analytic categories for the purposes of my own study. As always, I am trying to understand how these categories are used by, and make sense to, local actors.

Interpretations of the war in Yugoslavia in the Western media have stressed two aspects. The mainstream press has, for the most part, promoted the notion of ethnic sentiments kept in check during the years of communist rule which have now emerged from "historical deep freeze." As one *Chicago Tribune* headline reads: "Serbs' baffling defiance has ancient roots." The article goes on to note that the Bosnian Serbs "are poetic in their defiance, unbending in their ties to the land, tearful in their accounts of 1,000 years of history" (Myers 1994). To paraphrase one US senator discussing the arms embargo against Bosnia: "This is a tragedy that doesn't go back two or three years, but 600 years. And very few of us can understand it." The senator himself confirmed this statement two sentences later when he referred to Bosnia as Croatia. The implications are clear: the current war is an "irrational" product of "ancient hatreds" and an obsession with the past that makes little sense to citizens of the "modern" West. The Western media do not ignore history, but they categorize concern with it not only as irrational, but as irrelevant to the business of international power relations. This is why the supposed Serb invocation of history is both "poetic" and "baffling." By contrast I found that the "historical" appeals of Kalymnians in their attempts to explain the war were not forays into the irrational. Nor was history seen as irrelevant. Far from it, their appeals to history were inextricably tied, in different ways, to their understanding of international geo-politics in the present.

While in my own readings of the Western media I had discounted statements about Balkan tribalism, I was affected by the media focus on Serb atrocities. Since I had limited prior knowledge of Yugoslavia, my view of the war there had been formed largely when I was in the field (from January 1992 to August 1993), through reading Western and Greek media accounts. Other than the mainstream US and British newspapers and magazines available on Kalymnos, I had access to clippings from the left-wing press (*The Nation, Z Magazine, Mother Jones*) sent by friends and family, and which I collected on a brief visit to the US in January 1993. I also was reading an account of the history and current situation in Yugoslavia by British journalist Mark Thompson (1992). What struck me was the basic similarity of perspective on this issue in the mainstream and alternative press during 1992 and 1993. Here, apparently, was no Gulf War, cheer-led by one side and denounced by the other. While one could differentiate accounts in terms of levels of complexity, there was very little disagreement over who were the victims – the Bosnia Muslims and the Croats – and who were the perpetrators of this war – the Serbs.[5] For example, a book put out by the editors of *The New Republic* (Mouzavizadeh 1996) includes a timeline of the war up until the Dayton Agreement. This timeline makes no mention of the expulsion of over 100,000 Serbs from their homes in the Krajina by Croatian troops in June of 1995. As Balkan historian Stevan Pavlowitch (1994: 215) describes it:

> It was difficult for television to focus viewers' attention on incomprehensible horrors without clearly distinguishing between "good" and "bad." Reporters, like viewers, were ignorant, and their task would have been arduous if they had seen more than one side. If a culprit, and only one, had to be identified, it had to be the Serbian side.

Leading feminists were decrying the mass rapes that the Serbs were said to be using as official policy. Anti-imperialists such as Chomsky and Said were advocating that the world community take action to stop Serb aggression. When I read that the Serbs had inherited one of the largest armies in the world while the Bosnian Muslims were barely equipped, this also gained my sympathy for the Bosnian cause.

Local Reflections on an International Crisis

The Return of Religious Fundamentalism?

I may have known little about Yugoslavia prior to arriving in the field. But I had read what I considered to be reliable sources, and registered shock and horror over reports of "ethnic cleansing," mass rapes and concentration camps. I was surprised to find that my Kalymnian friends overwhelmingly did not share my views. While I tended not to directly challenge peoples' opinions as part of my fieldwork, I felt a certain outrage at what I perceived as Kalymnian lack of sympathy with the horrors of war perpetrated by the Serbs. Was this a case of what Huntington has labelled the new "Clash of Civilizations," in which nation-states and their ideologies cede their ability to mobilize mass sentiments to "civilizations" (by which he generally means world religions)?[6] Were the Greeks supporting their "Orthodox Brethren" without concern for right or wrong, but purely out of perceived self-interest? There seemed to be some evidence for this view. It was certainly not difficult to find articles in the respected Greek press by clergymen calling for support of the Serbs in their "holy, religious war" against the Muslims, and claiming that "in Bosnia the Serbs are fighting for altar and hearth, with the cross in one hand and a weapon in the other." Even the voice of the "respectable" left, the Euro-communist newspaper *Avgí*, ran articles reporting on the destruction of Serbian churches and religious monuments by Croats during the current war, while in the same issue an opinion piece explained the advantages for Greece of having common borders with Serbia through the carving up of Yugoslav Macedonia.[7]

On Kalymnos some expressed sentiments along these lines, iden-tifying the Bosnian Muslims with the Turks. Some asserted that the Muslims in Bosnia were indeed Turks left over from the days of Ottoman rule, rather than, as I had read, Slavs who had converted to Islam in the fifteenth century. Others, even some who were quite critical of Orthodoxy or were atheists themselves, stressed the role of the Pope in a conspiracy to aid the Catholic Croats and the Muslims in order to undermine Serbian Orthodoxy. In this interpretation the Serbs were continuing the battle both against the Muslim East from the days of the Ottoman Empire, and the catholic, papist West from the Middle Ages. It would be impossible for most Greeks to conceptualize as unjustified any attack by Greece on Turkey, given the history of Ottoman rule of Greece. Likewise the Serbs are conceptualized as avenging old debts of past oppression. In the Greek press much was made of the fact that Greeks and Serbs were "traditional allies" who had not fought in over 600 years (Eikonomidis 1993).

I think two points should be made about such views. First, that this argument was as much about Greece's relevance to international affairs in the present as it was about the history of the last 1,000 years. This is also true of my own understandings of the Yugoslav war, as Kalymnians often pointed out to me. Let me begin by placing Kalymnian views in the context of Kalymnos' and Greece's "global positioning." The implicit view in much of these Kalymnian discussions was explicitly stated to me by one Kalymnian man in his twenties. To paraphrase:

> The next war is going to be a religious war. All major wars have started in the Balkans, and mainly between Greece and Turkey. Because we are at the crossroads of Christianity and Islam. But the Pope and the Catholics have supported the Muslims and undermined Orthodoxy time and again. Which is a mistake, since we're all Christians.

Such a view could have been abstracted from the above-mentioned theories of Samuel Huntington. However, I believe that it must be seen rather differently – as a plea for the relevance of Greece to the New World Order. Kalymnians have become well aware of the renewed importance of Turkey to the Western alliance in the wake of the Gulf War and the formation of new sovereign Muslim states from the former Soviet Union.[8] While Turkey's stock has consequently risen, Greece's strategic value as NATO's Balkan outpost has diminished partly as a result of the fall of the communist governments of Eastern Europe. This leaves Greece with very little bargaining power on issues such as Cyprus and Turkish violations of Greek waters. Some Greeks believe that a perceived Muslim threat to Europe is Greece's only hope for continued geo-political relevance to the Western alliance. This opinion was especially strong during my fieldwork in 1992–1993, a time when some voices in western European were suggesting that Greece should no longer be part of the European Community (see Verney 1996).

The second point about these views is that they cannot be abstracted from the more complex arguments about the war in Yugoslavia either in the Greek press or as expressed by Kalymnians. The fact that both the Serbs and the Greeks fought the Ottoman Empire is only one part in a series of historical parallels that makes Greeks sympathetic to the Serbian point of view. Furthermore, the call for religious solidarity does not necessarily represent a mainstream opinion within the Greek church or the Greek public. It was decried by the leading figure of the Orthodox Church, Patriarch Bartholomew, in his speech to the European Parliament (18 April 1994). It has been increasingly criticized in the press as the attempt of certain religious fanatics to impose their views on the Greek public.[9] Although the religious dimension cannot be neglected, to simplify Greece's support of Serbia down to religious affinities misses the more complex discourses about the Yugoslav war which I encountered on Kalymnos.[10]

The Role of the "Great Powers"

Let us examine some of these local arguments in greater detail, and start by taking the religious bull by its horns. One Sunday returning

from church, Katina brought home a pamphlet distributed by
the Kalymnian Orthodox Christian bookstore and signed "Orthodox
Christian Brotherhood Lidia" (1993). The pamphlet, titled "Learn
Justice," interestingly enough does not focus on the common Orthodoxy of Greeks and Serbs. Instead it is an attack on the hypocrisy of
the world powers who claim to be sending "humanitarian aid" to the
victims of war. It proclaims:

> They [the West] decided on the dissolution of Yugoslavia. They fomented
> ethnic sentiment and uprisings. They led them to the "slaughter" of
> war. They are the most guilty for the bloodshed. And now the shameless
> ones, in order to mislead international public opinion, shed tears because
> humanitarian aid is not reaching the embattled (εμπολέμους). What
> hypocrisy! The guilty ones take interest in humanitarian aid but not in
> the arming of the warring sides which happened in order to promote
> their interests and to create spheres of influence.

In shifting the blame from the Serbs to an international community
(imagined as united), this pamphlet confirms what every Kalymnian
knows: that the great powers (also referred to on Kalymnos as τα
μεγάλα συμφέροντα, i.e. the "great interests") are never concerned with
humanitarian aid, but with promoting their own interests.[11] Nor is
their view of "interest" simplistic: as many Kalymnians remarked, not
only were state interests being promoted in the war in Yugoslavia (or
previously in the Gulf War), but also the interests of arms
manufacturers. One Kalymnian teacher told me that he had seen a
program on TV in the early 1980s ("during the early years of PASOK,
when they let things like this get on TV"), saying that the arms
manufacturers would have to create a new Vietnam in order to
continue their high profits, and that a likely location was the Balkans.
This understanding of world affairs is so ingrained in Kalymnians that
I have had ten-year-old children explain to me that the US goes to
war in order to benefit weapons manufacturers.

That the actions of the great powers or interests are nefarious, is
not a conclusion arrived at by the Greek press or Kalymnians simply
through analysis of the present situation. It is a perceived "pattern"
based on which past events are strung into historical narratives in
the manner discussed in the last chapter. To give a sense of this, I
return to the pamphlet, which after criticizing the West's one-sided
interpretation which portrays the Orthodox Serbs as evil and the
Roman-Catholic Croats as "angels," goes on to draw the following
analogy:

> The facts in Serbia call to mind the drama of the Cypriot people. These
> great hypocrites (μεγαλόσχημοι) pushed the barbarians to invade the
> great Greek island (Μεγαλόνησον) of Cyprus, and the occupying forces

remain there from 1974 to the present, defying international law and threatening the entire island with seizure. On the one hand the hordes of Attila spread misery and catastrophe and the Turkish air force without resistance bombarded the unarmed population, while on the other hand the powerful of the earth were indifferent. And the only thing that interested them was to send humanitarian aid . . . O Hypocrites! Until when will you continue to play this shameless game? Who do you think you're fooling? The peoples [of the world] have minds and logical thoughts and mouths to shout loud: "Learn justice!"

The Inhabitants of the Earth

The shaming of the great powers with which this pamphlet ends is similar to the response of one older Kalymnian man who, after hearing a news broadcast announcing NATO's intentions to enforce the Vance-Owen Plan[12] (if it was approved by the Serbs – this was April 1993), exclaimed "In front of the whole world!" (μπροστά στον κόσμο). In other words: "isn't the West ashamed to be announcing its intentions so openly." The thrust of this expression is that it is usually applied to local "histories," where it is the height of folly and hubris to announce one's dirty deals "in front of the world," i.e. the local community. It is the equivalent of saying that you have no fear of what people think of you. The metaphoric reference to "the world" in local discourse takes on an ironic literality when used in the context of a news broadcast about an issue upon which the eyes of the world are focussed.

Historical Parallels

The contrast drawn in the pamphlet between great-power interest in Yugoslavia and indifference in Cyprus featured prominently in the discussions of several Kalymnians. It was a clear reminder of the selectivity of great-power concern, and of the way they may promote wars for their own advantage and then offer a bandage (i.e. "human-itarian aid") to the survivors. The notion of paired examples is used by Herman and Chomsky in their book *Manufacturing Consent* (1988) to make this point about selectivity and self-interest on the part of the US government and the US media. They focus on the media's different treatment of similar acts of genocide which occurred in the late 1970s in Cambodia and East Timor, in the former case carried out by a communist "enemy" of the US and in the latter by an anti-communist "friend" actually receiving military supplies and training from the US. This use of paired examples is clearly popular in Greece. But rather than restrict it to events taking place in the same timeframe, as Herman and Chomsky do, it is regarded as equally relevant and valid to draw on examples from history, from twenty years or 200 years ago. Thus an article in the leading Sunday paper *To Vima* (Ploritis 1994) responds to EU condemnation of the Greek blockade of Macedonia by citing another blockade (the famed "Don Pacifico incident") that was carried out against Greece by England in 1850 on the pretext of protecting the property of a British citizen in Athens.[13] This blockade, described in considerable detail, sets the pattern for similar blockades by the great powers against Greece over the last 150 years. As the author notes:

> Why do we remember all these old histories? But because these "past events" should not be at all passed over and forgotten. In other words: blockades, bombardment . . . are **just and holy** when conducted by the **"powerful**," but **unjust and criminal** when dared (even to a degree) by the **weak** [emphasis in original].

These acts are referred to as "protection of nationals" in the Don Pacifico incident in 1850, or "protection of UN forces" at Goradze (Bosnia) today; whereas Greece's actions are referred to as "breaking of EU law" and "strangling a tiny state. Injustices which are **never** practiced by the powerful." Here the author appeals to a local discourse on how the rich and powerful (both Greek and non-Greek) can always get away with things which the poor cannot. This belief is evident on Kalymnos in discussions of tax-evasion and other more serious crimes, and it is often used as a justification for illegal activities by those who define themselves as "not powerful."

Interference by the great powers as they look after their interests has been a feature of the Greek experience since the inception of the modern Greek state.[14] This history is traced through Cyprus, the Greek Junta, the Civil War, the Asia Minor catastrophe all the way back to the sacking of Byzantium by the Crusaders in 1204. It is a view of the past that some Greek intellectuals (for example, Dimou 1976; Mouzelis 1993) treat as an aspect of Greek "fear of responsibility" (ευθυνοφοβία) by which their own mistakes are displaced onto foreign interference (ο ξένος δάκτυλος), the meddling of "outsiders." But this interpretation does not explain the fact that great-power meddling is analyzed and decried not just when it involves Greece. The communist and the mainstream Greek press both give coverage and analysis to the political and economic interests and games of the West in Africa, Asia and elsewhere around the world.[15] A Kalymnian example is provided by Sakellarios (1977: 31) who in describing the beginning of the Italian Occupation of the Dodecanese, links Greek experience to that of other "small peoples:"

> Unfortunately self-interest (το συμφέρον), the hypocrisy of the powerful, the disappointment and exasperation of the small, formed then and still forms the image of the ethical collapse of the world. The millions

of Greeks, Armenians and other small peoples who were pulled up from their hearths and slaughtered proclaims through the centuries the works of the barbarians and the spiritual and ethical lack (πόρωσιν) of the supposedly civilized peoples who make up the Great Christian Family.

Furthermore, whatever one's view of "fear of responsibility," this interpretation of history provides a way of reading present events which focusses on certain aspects of the "story" ignored or neglected in the Western press, including the normally vigilant left-wing. Since the Euro-American press to which I had access had not covered the issue of possible Western interest in the area, I interpreted the Greek and Kalymnian position as a willful misreading of events. As I told one of my Kalymnian friends: "On almost all issues concerning foreign policy, the left and mainstream press in the US have different positions. But on this they are in agreement that the Serbs are at fault." His response was, "Doesn't that make you suspicious?" I would normally take seriously a charge of great-power profiteering if it appeared in what I consider to be the reliable left-wing press. However, because these allegations came only from the Greek press and Kalymnians, and were based on a reading of history rather than specific knowledge of the present, I largely discounted them. I later saw them gain credibility – several years into the war the interest of Germany and the United States in Yugoslavia began to be carefully detailed in certain small publications.[16] Few Kalymnians would be surprised to read the following report of US secretary of defense Perry's trip to South-Eastern Europe in July 1994 (BBC 1994):

> Perry stated that his country will increase its presence in the area, regardless of the outcome of negotiations [on Bosnia] . . . While visiting US troops deployed in Macedonia, Perry said this country is "key to the stability in the region." [He] also considered possibilities of holding joint military maneuvers with Bulgaria, Romania, Albania and Greece. Perry continued his talks with the government in Athens on possible opening of two more NATO bases in Greece, and Turkey is also interested in such a base on its territory . . . As it is now, NATO is likely to remain present in the Balkans in the several years to come.

The fact that US policy is motivated by its attempts to establish spheres of economic and political interest, or to re-establish its predominance as world leader in contra-distinction to Germany or the European Union, went virtually unremarked, even in the left-wing press. For Kalymnians and for the Greek media more generally, it simply confirms the lessons that history has taught them.

Given the thrust of my argument here, Greece's complicity with NATO's designs on Southern Europe may on the surface seem contradictory. But the fact that Greeks decry the abuses of the great powers does not entail that they are unaware of the need to co-operate strategically with them. Just as the Kalymnian store owner cited in Chapter 6 tackled the dilemma of powerlessness by noting that it's better to give up a cut in your store than to lose it all, Greeks may dislike their bargains with the powerful, but recognize that some bargains are necessary in order to survive. Sympathy for the Serbs then, results in part from the belief that like the Greeks, they are victims of great-power machinations. This is summed up in the popular expression: "they play games at our expense" (μας παίζουν παιχνίδια).

Memory and (Failed) Reciprocity

Another way that the Kalymnians relate past to present, which has implications for their view of the war in Yugoslavia, is through notions of historical debt and its betrayal. Greeks are well aware of how often the promises made to Greece by the great powers have been betrayed. This awareness is commonly voiced in the context of the West's failure to appreciate Greek resistance to the Nazis in the Second World War. When EU members such as Denmark or Holland criticize Greece's actions in relation to the Macedonia issue, or the alleged failure of Greece to uphold the blockade against Serbia, Greek commentators respond with the query: what was Denmark doing when the Nazi tanks were rolling into their country? Did they put up three weeks of resistance (after repulsing Mussolini's army) thus delaying Hitler's attack on Russia? (Politis 1993). The current Western criticisms of Greek positions on Macedonia and Yugoslavia are seen as a betrayal of the historical debt owed to Greece for its sacrifice for "Europe" in the Second World War. However, this debt can reach back much further than the Second World War. One journalist responds to the Danish foreign minister's criticism (over Macedonia) that Greeks should "behave like Europeans, not like Balkaners," with the query: "Does the Danish minister forget that the word 'Europe' and all it symbolizes came from ancient Greece . . . [while] Denmark's heroes are pirates who pillaged their neighbors" (Lampsas 1992). When I asked one Kalymnian man in his thirties about the notion that Greece didn't have to obey EU rules because of what they had done in the Second World War, he concurred, explaining: "We got screwed for Europe, and it doesn't make any difference that fifty years have gone by."

To understand this statement, we must put it in the context of Kalymnian views of debt and obligation. As Herzfeld has argued, Cretan exchange relations are always about setting up long-term reciprocity. The foreigner, who wants to make immediate payments for services, "short circuit[s] the temporal play that is locally the means of creating active friendships" (1991: 84). My own attempts at reciprocal gifts while I was on Kalymnos were often refused or accepted with reluctance. Gifts that I brought on my return from a visit to the US were more acceptable. But for the most part it was assumed that repayment would come over the long haul, when I was a professor and had established myself in my career. Despite this, I found out that detailed accounts were already being kept. One family whom I had got to know in 1980 remembered, thirteen years after the fact, that I had written them a postcard after I had left Kalymnos. This postcard was interpreted as a recognition of my obligation for their hospitality, and I was compared favorably to other Americans who had not sent postcards.

Herzfeld has suggested that one of the meanings of the term "honor" (φιλότιμο) is "the ability to recognize one's social 'obligations' (υποχρεώσεις)' (1987b: 80). Since, as Hirschon (1992: 45) has argued, there is a widespread belief in the undesirability of being under obligation or indebted to others, this seems to guarantee that social relations will often culminate in feelings of betrayal. Personal narratives on Kalymnos often involve the recountings of injustices and betrayals of just this kind perpetrated against the narrator. These include the failure to fulfill social obligations, to repay and recognize past generosities, with neighbors, godparenting relations, but more particularly within families, where failure to reciprocate is seen as the worst sort of betrayal, since perpetrated so directly against "one's own" (see Herzfeld 1992c: 74). Such debts often pass through generations, with children either redeeming or repeating the wrongs perpetrated against the narrator. As Skiada cites one of her Karpathian informants: "'In Olymbos it is a matter of time before one's secret becomes public knowledge. Nobody ever escapes from something wrong he/she *or an ancestor of his/hers* did; people always remember and act accordingly'" (Skiada 1990: 85; emphasis mine).

Unusual circumstances provide further justification for feelings of betrayal. A sister who insisted that her mother's inheritance be divided equally between herself and her brothers, instead of claiming it all for herself, thirty years later, feels that they never repaid the debt. As she puts it:

> I dowered all my brothers. I gave to all of them, to all. I, who didn't see [receive] from them, as the Kalymnian tradition goes, a little dowry, despite having three brothers. Three brothers I had, and the Kalymnian tradition was for the brothers to dower their sister, especially for me, since I was the only sister. But I never saw a thing from them.

Her ironic use of the verb "to dower," never normally applied to a man, with reference to her brothers suggests the extent of her unpaid sacrifice, since she had reversed the normal gender roles. But the feeling itself is common: an act of generosity in the past has been snubbed and continues to be snubbed in each subsequent interaction as the debt goes unrecognized. Each time one of her brothers came to Kalymnos for a visit, it was a new opportunity for the woman to confirm that they still failed to fulfill their obligations, and to retell her story.

Kalymnians have long memories not only for failed reciprocity, but for specific acts of malice. To paraphrase one Kalymnian man, who stereotyped the British and the Greeks in the following manner: "The English get drunk and get into fights. But when the fight is over they buy each other drinks. A Greek won't forget, but will spend years plotting his revenge." One woman explained to me that in fights with your neighbors all church teaching goes out the window. Even if the church tells you to love your neighbors and forgive them, you can't let people slander you and sit there and not say anything, or people will think you are an idiot. So you raise your head high (σηκώνεις το κεφάλι) and defend yourself. This woman commented on a specific case of a ninety-year-old neighbor who had slandered her family twenty years previously, but had recently begged forgiveness of them during the Easter ceremony. The woman saw this as a calculated move, since if you ask forgiveness you will be saved.[17] She also noted that when she was ninety years old perhaps she would be able to forgive and forget old wounds, but until then she could not.

It is striking that several weeks later this woman used very similar language to discuss the war in Yugoslavia. As she told me, during a civil war civilized behavior is forgotten, and all you think about is destroying your enemy.[18] She also said that the killing happening now would not be forgotten any time soon, since you would long remember seeing your family killed in front of you, just as Kalymnians have memories of the Turks. Her husband then added: "It's just like the Americans with the Vietnamese. Now they will never be able to get along." I remarked that Americans forget these things, and they responded: "That's good, but we cannot, though this doesn't mean that we can't travel back and forth to Turkey or to Germany for business and get along fine." This last comment suggested another parallel: that you might continue to be cordial to your neighbors, do business with or lavish hospitality on them, while at the same time not forgetting the wrongs that they had committed against you. A Kalymnian shepherd in his seventies who had been listening in on the conversation, added his own gloss: "The Serbs are just like us, they are tough, they fight with knives and don't forget what you've done to them. The Greeks are bad. They will kill you to avenge the death of their grandparents. However much time goes by, they don't forget."[19] Here this shepherd utilizes another prevalent historical theme to draw parallels between Serbs and Greeks: the Greeks have fought best when they are in desperate circumstances – from the Battle of

Marathon to the Battle of Crete (1940).[20] From the Greek perspective
the Serbs are historically "underdogs" because, like the Greeks, they
fought against Hitler when many other European nations did not.
They are underdogs in the current war because they have the world
community united against them.

Character, Continuity and "Myth"

In the context of these beliefs about the workings of local/national
relations, we can comprehend the "debt" owed to Greece and Serbia
by the West, and also the justifications that Kalymnians ascribe to
Serbia in its struggle with the Croats. Many Kalymnians know that
the Croats formed the pro-Nazi fascist *Ustashe* which slaughtered
thousands of Serbs during the Second World War. As one man in his
thirties insisted: "the Croats were worse fascists than the Nazis." For
Kalymnians it is therefore absurd to talk about the Serbs as the
"fascists" in this war, as suggested in the cartoon from *USA Today* with
which I began this chapter. It is very difficult for Kalymnians to
conceptualize such a reversal, since, as argued in Chapter 6, they
believe that history reveals the underlying character of a people. Given
the role of Germany in supporting current Croatian independence as
well as the embracing of fascist symbols and rhetoric by the new
president of Croatia,[21] the Kalymnians feel vindicated in their
interpretation. And the Serbs would be "idiots" to ignore these signs
and to allow history to repeat itself at their expense. It is the same
belief in underlying character revealed through history which makes
it possible to argue the relevance of "paired examples" as discussed
above. The great powers always have and always will act in an
exploitative manner to protect their economic interests. Thus it is
just as relevant to talk about British naval blockades from 1850 as it is
to decry British and American perfidy over the invasion of Cyprus.

   Once again this view of nations or "peoples" is mirrored at the local
level in the belief that individual "character" cannot change, and is
in fact inherited. Kalymnians would refer to the actions of a person's
parents or grandparents as proof of their inherited bad character. "Shit-
family" (σκατοφαμίλια) or "shit-race" (σκατόρατσα) are common terms
in denouncing an entire kin-group with the same bad traits. When I
posed the question of whether someone's character can change, most
older Kalymnians were adamant that it could not, but some insisted
that although a person can hide their true character it will eventually
come out. Younger Kalymnians were more divided on the question,
one man argued that a strong desire was all that was needed to affect
change in an individual, but for a whole nation to escape its history
was much more difficult.

   If these views on national and local character resemble pre-Second

World War racialist thinking in the social sciences, this coincidence is perhaps not fortuitous. Analogously, Bakalaki (1994) has illustrated a "curious" convergence between Western-influenced nineteenth-century educated Greek views of gender roles and the beliefs described as part of "Greek village culture" by anthropologists since the 1960s. If, as I have suggested in these last two chapters, local views are influenced by and influencing of national ones it is no surprise that such influences go beyond the borders of Greece. As I argued in Chapter 2, Kalymnians are, and probably always have been, construct-ing their identity in relation and in opposition to many "others." My goal here is to describe as richly as possible the current constellation of concepts used to make sense of the past, while making no claims about their "authenticity" or "essential Greekness."

In raising these issues of history read as continuity and repetition, both at the level of individuals and "peoples," it seems necessary to clarify how this fits into anthropological discussions of "history" and "myth." That is, why do I resist categorizing this Kalymnian activity of imposing "timeless" themes on the past as "myth-making"?

The notion that there exist "cold" societies which think of the past in terms of myth, as opposed to "hot" societies which think in terms of history, has been roundly rejected in anthropology. However, many continue to use the categories "history" and "myth" to describe different aspects of society, or different modes of consciousness within a society. Thus, Hill contrasts the "mythic consciousness" that is concerned with structure and social reproduction with the "historical consciousness" that is concerned with change. He argues that in every society "mythic and historical modes of consciousness complement, rather than oppose one another" (Hill 1988: 9). Similarly, Hanson argues that for the Maori the "space from 'cold' to 'hot' may be divided into as many as five distinct degrees of dynamism or levels of historical consciousness . . . and that it is possible to identify most or even all of them in single societies, depending on the sorts of experience being ordered"(1983: 287).[22]

The notion that "myth" is about social reproduction and "history" about change is a rather vexed one, even if we accept that the two "modes of consciousness" coexist. As Sahlins (1985: 53) has argued, structures can reproduce themselves whether they are "inscri[bed] in habitus," or "objectifi[ed] as mythopoetics." Appeals to the past need not be appeals to stasis, as Valeri (1990: 155) puts it: "one can find in the past arguments for change, not simply for changelessness." The analogic, or "paradigmatic" use of the past, as Valeri (ibid.: 161) argues, does not necessarily imply some ideal of societal reproduction,

but simply . . . the ideas of comparability of all human actions *qua* actions . . . Since the relationship between past and present is analogical

and not merely replicative, the past need not exactly replicate the present
to function as its precedent ... the perception of difference plays in
fact a great role in th[e] comparison.

This is what we saw in Maria's discussion of "examplars" in Chapter
6. To express this differently: to see events as unique and without a
sense of historical depth, is to be unable to see possibilities for change.
To deny, for example, the relationship between French colonialism
and the post-colonial situation between France and Algeria, as Panayiotis argued in the last chapter, is to serve the status quo.

However, my task is not to decide whether Kalymnian attitudes are
conducive or obstructive to "change," difficult as this would be to
define. Rather, I have tried to suggest how certain views of the past
are utilized in the interpretation of present events in a distinctive way.
Thus more relevant to my task is White's argument that whenever
the historian attempts to explain events, she necessarily enters the
realm of repetition and coherence, in other words, myth (1978: 56–
7).[23] In interpreting the war in Yugoslavia then, both the Kalymnians
and the Western media employ interpretive structures (myths), which
are based on past experience.[24] The only difference between them
seems to be that the Kalymnians (and the Greek press) are relatively
more explicit about their interpretive structures than the Western
media.

"Un-civil" Wars

Despite their view of the historical role of the Serbs and Croats,
Kalymnians did not necessarily see the Serbs as "right" in this war.
Instead, as many people insisted, this war had to be considered as a
civil war – everyone was at fault and atrocities were committed by all
sides.[25] In this context they called for a policy of non-intervention.
What they objected to was the notion that the Serbs were the bad
ones and the Croats and the Muslims had their hands clean. This
position was understood and formulated in the Greek press from the
start of the war, but it only began to gain credence in the West, at
least as far as the Croats were concerned, several years into the war.

In emphasizing that the war in Yugoslavia was a civil war in which
atrocities were being committed on both sides, Kalymnians were
employing current understandings of the Greek civil war. As one man
put it: "Both sides were at fault, but because the right-wing won,
everything was thrown onto the communists and their names were
blackened." He saw this as parallel to what the world was doing to
the Serbs. Similarly, the sense that these wars leave lasting scars is a
reflection on the civil war experience. In 1989, forty years after the
civil war, the brief formation of a coalition government between the
Communists and the Conservative party caused an uproar in which I

heard many Kalymnians asking: "How could the Communists sit down at the same table as those responsible for the Civil War?" Others saw it as a long overdue "healing" of the wounds that had divided people ever since the war. But the Greek Civil War is not only spoken of in terms of right-wingers and communists. Even on Kalymnos, which did not participate directly in the war, people referred to the terrible experience of "brothers in the same house killing each other."[26] Disputes or "histories" within the domestic unit are more dangerous because they are ideally more repressed so as to preserve the family's unity against outsiders. The same logic renders civil war, when it does erupt, the most bloody form of conflict and the one that leaves the longest scars.[27]

It is important to note that Kalymnians do not see this concern with the memory of past injustice as a good thing. The man who stereotyped the brawling British saw their ability to forget their arguments as a positive trait. Indeed, a number of people, including a junior high-school principal, with whom I spoke about how much history was learned by the younger generation, expressed the sentiment that maybe it was time to forget history in order that people could live together in peace. For this reason many people looked positively on the United States as a place without long memory. Just as in the United States "people don't try to 'eat' [i.e. exploit] their neighbors," the American people are seen to have progressed because of the country's stability. But this is precisely why I was told that I, as an American, could not understand the war in Yugoslavia. As one man in his thirties explained it to me:

> [Yugoslavia] was always a soup. It was never quiet. Never! . . . There was always someone passing through trying to conquer the area . . . They were always going at each other. Why do I use you for comparison? Because America, outside of its civil war, never had anything like that . . . You had things quiet, that's why you progressed . . . Exactly for that reason, after so many years of stability you can't understand the uncertainty and fear of someone who knows that his father was saved from the Asia Minor disaster by chance. That person, when he hears that the Turks want to take the Dodecanese, jumps up. Not like someone who looks at it from outside. Since without a moment's hesitation, [they don't try] to sit down and talk about their problems. Right away they grab their guns and start a war, they don't even consider that there might be another way. That's why the older generation has to die off, not just give up power, because that type of politician never gives up power, they must die (ψοφίσουν) and then we'll see what we can do.

Note what begins as a discussion of the war in Yugoslavia quickly shifts to the Greek catastrophe in Asia Minor, and the fear of Turkish designs on the island chain that includes Kalymnos, thereby suggesting a pan-Balkan experience. My informant contrasts this experience with my own as an American, thus "globally positioning" me as unable to understand the "history" that motivates action here. In this statement we can see the ambiguous legacy of the past for a young Kalymnian. It is a past which he respects, since his parents and grandparents have suffered it. It is one that he "understands" (καταλαβαίνει), a word which implies you have lived and experienced something, which continues to have a hold on you. At the same time he sees it as something that holds people back. This same sentiment is expressed in relation to the Greek civil war: the older generation is blinkered by the past, it cannot forget and transcend those divisions; this must be done by the younger generation. In saying that they must "die off" he uses the verb ψοφώ, which normally refers to the death of animals, thereby suggesting that living with such fears is no better than living like an animal.[28] The younger generation on Kalymnos is more likely to express the belief that character can change, and they are also much less likely to refer to the sins of ancestors in their judgement of a person. Thus they hold out the hope of freeing themselves from the burden of a long memory.

Conclusion

In this chapter I have used material from the Greek mass media available on Kalymnos as well as the explicit discourses of Kalymnians in order to present the dominant positions I encountered concerning the war in Yugoslavia. As I have tried to suggest, these positions rely heavily on interpretations of the past at the same time that they are often shrewd readings of present global power arrangements. I believe I have shown that these readings are not primarily motivated by religious allegiances; they rely on numerous perceived analogies between the national, the religious and the local. More significant are attitudes towards the great powers, (the US, the Europeans, the Pope) and the ways in which they time and again "play games" at the expense of the "smaller peoples." These attitudes towards the powerful can be traced through Greek and world history, and find resonances at the local level particularly with regard to issues of debt and betrayal and attitudes towards memory and forgetting. In addition, "debt" and "betrayal" work as historical themes that are traced across time in order to construct narratives to explain present experience. They are able to do so because of local views of character, which consign continuity of action and essence to individuals, families and "peoples." I argued that this view of the past, which some might see as "static," should not be thought of as "myth" any more than more "dynamic" views are. To consign Kalymnian thinking about past and present to the realm of "myth" would suggest that it is based more in the "symbolic" and "non-rational" than in the "practical" and the "rational."[29] But, as I have shown with regard to custom and tradition, Kalymnians are deeply concerned to assert what they consider to be the rational, pragmatic bases for their actions. And contrary to our expectations of myth, the historical themes I have delineated here do not blind the Kalymnians to present realities. On the contrary, in the case of great-power interest in Yugoslavia and the revival of Croatian fascist rhetoric and symbols, these "myths" revealed truths about the situation well before they were recognized in the dominant discourses of Western media (insofar as they have been recognized at all).

The issue of "rationality" returns in the following chapter, as I examine another burning issue of concern in Kalymnos and Greece: the naming of the Former Yugoslav Republic of Macedonia, and the seemingly "irrational" passions this issue has evoked in Greece. In my assessment of the controversy over "the name" I will further examine another key issue in understanding historical consciousness: the linking of intergenerational continuity and historical continuity. Once again I will situate this in the context of perceived parallels between the national, the religious and the local. In this instance, rather than focussing on the explicit arguments used to defend the Greek position, I will suggest that certain customary practices, which have no clearly articulated relationship to national issues, form an implicit background against which current struggles over Macedonia are read and understood.

Notes

1. That this has long held true for Greece more generally is indicated by Clogg's comment about nineteenth-century Greece: "Foreign travellers were frequently astonished to come across Greeks in the most unlikely of places with a lively and informed knowledge of world affairs, even if they were prone to believe that the whole of international politics revolved around Greece" (1986: 85).

2. Munn 1990: 1; see also, Glick-Schiller, Basch and Szanton-Blanc 1995; Hannerz 1989; Kearney 1995; Schneider and Rapp 1995.

3. This was brought home to me in late January of 1996 when Greece and Turkey came to the brink of war over the possession of the Greek island of Imia, a few miles from Kalymnos. Kalymnians with whom I spoke by telephone expressed both their fear and their anger over the perception that their fate was in the hands of the powerful once again.

4. The term "great powers" has a specific meaning, referring to the nineteenth-century powers England, Russia and France who were so crucial in determining the early course of the Greek nation. But it also is used more generally to refer to the powerful countries of the West and the United States.

5. One exception to this was Glenny (1993), whose book, first published in 1992, as well as his BBC reports throughout the war, gave a more nuanced account of the causes and perpetrators of the war, as well as the one-sidedness of press coverage. It is interesting that the accounts of two Croatian–American anthropologists (Mestrovic 1995; Olujic 1995) claim that the responsibility of Serbia for atrocities was *downplayed* by the West as an excuse for not intervening in the war. Perhaps this reflects their focus on Western diplomats and policy-makers, rather than on media accounts *per se.*

6. As Huntington (1993: 22) writes:

It is my hypothesis that the fundamental source of conflict in this new world will not be primarily ideological or primarily economic. The great divisions among humankind and the dominating source of conflict will be cultural. Nation states will remain the most powerful actors in world affairs, but the principal conflicts of global politics will occur between nations and groups of different civilizations. The clash of civilizations will dominate global politics.

Huntington identifies the key present-day civilizations, "objectively" defined based on religion, language, culture and history, as "Western, Confucian, Japanese, Islamic, Hindu, Slavic-Orthodox, Latin American and possibly African" (ibid.: 25).

7. The quote is from Hristodoulos 1993. On the left see Mavroidi 1992; Apostolopoulos 1992.

8. During the Gulf War US President Bush described Turkey as "America's staunchest ally" (see Brown 1991; Evert 1991).

9. See Someritis 1994; Psychogios 1994.

10. Such a view of religious affinities also ignores the animosity between Greece and other "Orthodox Brethren," such as the Bulgarians, and, most currently, the Yugoslav Macedonians (see Gavrilis 1997).

11. Cf. Hirschon's (1989: 29-30) discussion of the views of Asia Minor refugees in Piraeus, who blamed the 1922 catastrophe not on their Turkish neighbors, but on the meddling of the "Great Powers."

12. The now defunct plan developed by Lord Owen and Cyrus Vance by which Bosnia-Herzegovina would be divided into ten self-administered cantons while still remaining in a federated state.

13. Clogg (1986: 79) sees this as part of a pattern of great power intervention in Greek affairs which "reached almost absurd proportions as in the Don Pacifico incident, the high-water mark of Palmerstonian gun-boat diplomacy."

14. See Couloumbis, Petropoulos and Psomiadis 1976; Katris 1971; Coufoudakis 1987; on intervention in Cyprus see Hitchens 1984.

15. See e.g. "Who is killing Africa?" (*To Vima* 1994a) for an analysis of the political and economic role of Europe, the United States and the Soviet Union in the crises in Rwanda, Somalia and elsewhere. Also see *To Vima's* special report on Rwanda (1994b) subtitled "the games of European colonists sowed hatred and division between Hutus and Tutsis." This report includes a special inset on "The dirty games of Paris" in arming and training the Hutus.

16. See Pavlowitch 1994.

17. Orthodox doctrine holds that once you admit your sin and ask forgiveness of someone the sin can no longer burden you, whereas the other person can be burdened with it if they don't forgive you.

18. See my discussion of the war as a "civil war" below.

19. Cf. interesting parallels in Denich's (1995) description of the deeply rooted militarization of male culture in post-war Yugoslavia.

20. This explicit analogy is made in a letter to the newspaper *Kathimerini* (Tatakis 1993), in which the writer compares the plight of the Serbs to that of Greek Revolutionary war hero Makriyiannis fighting the Ottoman Empire against overwhelming odds.

21. See Denich 1994; Hayden 1996.

22. See also Peel 1984 and 1989; Pina-Cabral 1989.

23. Ironically, White makes extensive reference in his argument to Levi-Strauss, the supposed originator of this dichotomy which has so long bedeviled anthropological thinking.

24. Herzfeld (1992a: 93) collapses the same supposed distinction between "literate" and "rural" histories in his discussion of newspapers and historical interpretation in a Cretan village. As he puts it:

There is no **a priori** reason to suppose that any of the groups studied by anthropologists deny or ignore the specificity of historical events. On the other hand, they do apparently stereotype events. So, for that matter, do scholars, notably in the convention of periodization . . . [pace] literate prejudice [which] often attributes to scholarly historians an emphasis on the uniqueness and specificity of events, while representing peasants as 'reducing' events to anonymous formulae.

25. I have no sympathy for those who absurdly attempt to deny Serb atrocities, nor did I hear such a position argued for on Kalymnos. For a critical review of such attempts at denial, see Alterman 1997.

26. The Dodecanese were under British protectorate from the end of the Second World War until 1948, and did not enter into the Greek Civil War.

27. In discussing the war in Bosnia Glenny (1993: 172) gives a slightly different take on the significance of "civil war":

The Bosnian Serbs, Croats and Moslems have been adorned with many different cultural uniforms over the centuries by which they identify one another as the enemy when conflict breaks out. Despite this, underneath the dress they can see themselves reflected – it is the awful recognition that these primitive beasts on the other side of the barricade are their brothers which has led to the violence assuming such ghastly proportions in Bosnia. The only way that fighters can deal with this realization is to exterminate the opposite community

28. ψωφώ also implies an unattended, untended death of a stray or wild animal, and thus has particularly disparaging connotations here (I owe this insight to Neni Panourgia).

29. My quotation marks here should indicate that I am not opposing the symbolic and the rational as categories of analysis, but rather as categories found in the discourse of Kalymnians and in the Western media.

A message to the tourists Kos, 8192.

eight

History Revealed, Custom Concealed: Names as Heritage and as Inheritance

> You are celebrating the 500th anniversary of the discovery of America.
> Well, we are 1,500 years in front of you, and we don't need any outsiders
> telling us whether Macedonia is Greek or not.
>
> (Kalymnian woman, February 1992)

Introduction: Considering Nationalism

Since the breakup of Yugoslavia, the naming of the new independent nation on Greece's northern border has become a *cause célèbre*. Greece attempted to deny the Former Yugoslav Republic of Macedonia (FYROM) the right to choose for itself the name "Macedonia," or any derivative including that name (for example, New Macedonia, Slavo-Macedonia). This resulted in Greece becoming isolated from its allies, and being vilified in the Western press.

In this chapter I return to the question of intergenerational and historical continuity. I examine how it is established, not just in explicit discourses, but in everyday practices on Kalymnos. In Chapter 7 I looked at explicit Kalymnian uses of the category "history" in understanding international events. I will look here at the underside of history. I suggest some of the ways that the category of "custom," which tends to be devalued in explicit Kalymnian discussions of current events, provides an unarticulated background against which the actual understanding of historical continuity makes sense to Kalymnians. In a sense, then, I turn Kalymnians views of the past against themselves. Kalymnians attempt to deconstruct Western forgetting of the past in the case of Western involvement in power-relations in places like the Balkans. Similarly, I question the Kalymnian banishment of a certain type of devalued past, represented by "custom" in their own understanding of another international controversy. At

173

the same time I recognize the real world politics that Kalymnian forgetting reflects here. To admit the role of custom – in this case kinship and naming practices – in their thinking about an issue of concern to nation-states, would, given the parameters of international discourse, confirm their status as backward, under-developed and non-modern.

This chapter is also framed in opposition to state and international discourses of rational action, where "mystical" understandings of "the past" or "custom" are often ruled out of bounds in "serious" discussions of politics or economics. But rationality is in the eye of the beholder. Terdiman (1993), for example, has extended Marx's insights to suggest that reification, the forgetting of the pasts that make up the present, is a *par excellence* characteristic of the West since the Industrial Revolution. It is therefore the task of the analyst to uncover the hidden pasts behind claims to rational action made by nation-states, market forces and other political actors. In addition, one must always keep in full view the unequal playing field on which discussions between Greece and its Western allies of "history" and "custom" occur.

The importance of uncovering the hidden past that may lie behind even explicit discussions of "history," is paralleled by the need to uncover certain key aspects neglected by recent anthropological theorizing about nationalism. Specifically, I shall look at the way local-level kinship ideologies and practices feed into feelings of nationalism. A number of recent studies of nationalism and nationalist ideologies have tended to move away from the top–down emphases inherited from writers such as Gellner, Hobsbawm and Ranger, and, to a lesser extent, Anderson. Many recognize that it is no longer sufficient to study State processes such as schooling, the mass media, national traditions, rituals and ideologies, in order to debunk and denaturalize their nationalist assumptions. It is also necessary to show how these ideologies often achieve their appeal by accommodating themselves to local-level discourses, and by mobilizing already existing cultural ideas.[1]

Despite this renewed interest in the articulation of the local and the national, anthropologists have tended to ignore the significant contribution that anthropological theory could make to such studies through its interest in kinship ideologies and practices. One would think that kinship would be germane to elucidating the local bases of nationalist appeals. Yet studies of kinship ideologies and practices have only recently been considered in the analysis of nationalism. Even a recent *Annual Review of Anthropology* article (Peletz 1995) which reflects such trends in its desire to prove that "kinship is not dead," and to "bring kinship studies into the 1990s," mentions nationalism only in passing, and provides no references on the subject – and this in an article calling for the "repatriation" of kinship studies in anthropology.

The general decline of interest in kinship that occurred in the 1970s and 1980s can be related to the theoretical shift from concern with local societies to that of nation-states and global processes. Kinship has traditionally been understood as the key organizational principle of pre-state societies. Its significance in the study of modern nation-states has been underplayed, particularly since, as Herzfeld puts it, "The absence of kinship seems to be one of the defining characteristics of the West's view of itself" (1992a: 68). Kinship, in these contexts, remains as mere metaphor, while nation-states are now run along the principles of "rational bureaucracy." Thus, the recent and salutary anthropological move to reject the isolated field community and to study wider or non-territorialized communities and processes, has unfortunately led to a questioning of the usefulness of many of anthropology's categories and methods.[2] But kinship is not a phenomenon restricted to isolated villages. As Herzfeld argues, nation-states' claim to run on bureaucratic principles is simply a trick to remove kinship principles from critical inspection, and to "deflect attention away from so embarrassing a dependence of the "rational" upon the "symbolic" (1992a: 148). The study of kinship, whether regarded as practice or metaphor, can therefore once again be crucial for understanding national discourse and its local ramifications.[3]

In this chapter I am arguing for a double remembering: of the significance of other pasts in the understanding of "history" on Kalymnos, and of the significance of traditional subjects such as kinship in anthropological analyses of wider discourses and processes.

The "Macedonian Question": Media Reflections

I came to the above questions through my attempt to decipher the issue that dominated the Greek political scene, the Greek media and the discussions of ordinary people during the period of my fieldwork on Kalymnos, Greece (from January 1992 to September 1993). That issue was the "Macedonian Question" (το Μακεδονικό), i.e. the dispute over the name of the new country on Greece's northern border. With its evocations of Alexander the Great, it seemed relevant to my interest in the past in the present, and yet for a long time I was unsure as to how. In my attempts to comprehend this issue that I heard about everyday, I received little help from the Western or the Greek press, nor, for interesting reasons I explore below, from the explicit statements of my informants. Instead I heard a surface discourse, a discourse that hid some of its key assumptions about local systems of kinship, inheritance and naming behind the patina of acceptable international speech.

Disputes over the borders and populations of the geographic region Macedonia have broken out before, during the Balkan wars at the beginning of this century,[4] and during the Greek Civil War following the Second World War.[5] But since the 1940s Greek academics and politicians had by and large assumed the border issue to be settled. However, when what was formerly the territory of Yugoslavia recognized as "Macedonia" declared its independence from Yugoslavia in late 1991, Greece once more took an intense interest in its northern borders. The ramifications of the handling of the "new" Macedonian Question within Greece were huge: they led to the dismissal by prime minister Mitsotakis of his exterior minister, Samaras in April of 1992. Samaras soon went on to form his own party, "Political Spring," largely on the impetus of his uncompromising, ultra-nationalist views on this issue. The Macedonian Question was also a major factor precipitating the downfall of the Conservative government and the return to power of the Socialist party in late 1993. Greece's blockade of FYROM during 1994 and early 1995 led European Community leaders to seek to bring Greece before the European Court. Some unofficial voices even suggested that this debacle was an opportunity for the EU to be rid of one of its more irritating and economically unproductive members. As a *Guardian* headline concisely put it: "The European Community is Fed Up with Greece's stand on the Macedonian question and its Economy."[6]

At the time of writing (autumn 1997), Greece and FYROM are still involved in negotiations sponsored by the UN, though their positions have moved closer together. Greece has lifted its blockade in exchange for FYROM altering the official symbol on its flag and an article of its constitution (see below). The question of the name is still outstanding. While Greece's official position seems to have shifted towards a compromise on the "name," FYROM's official position remains that they will accept no other name than "the Republic of Macedonia."[7]

Commentary on this issue in the international media and newspapers of the US and Western Europe has either ridiculed or been openly hostile to the Greek position. Greece's behavior is attributed to the current outbreak of "Balkan tribalism," in which "ethnic hatreds" are seen as the endemic result of the cultural otherness of a Balkan region, which is portrayed as the dark half of the more "civilized" and "rational" Western European states.[8] Tribalism and ethnic hatreds both suggest irrational ties to kinship and locality that are inappropriate when conducting the business of nations. Greece, from this perspective, has been acting irrationally in blocking the legitimate nation-building activities of another country. And if ordinary Greeks were depicted at all it was as blindly following their leaders. A "Voice of America" (1994) broadcast gives a flavor of these views:

> Salonika [Thessaloniki, Capitol of Greek Macedonia] is a Balkan city with a veneer of Western affluence. The streets are choked with cars.

The shops are brimming with the best the West has to offer. But the people – their temperament, lifestyles and diet – tend to be more Balkan . . . As far as Greeks are concerned, the Former Yugoslav Republic that calls itself Macedonia has no right to use the name or symbol of Macedonia because, they insist, Macedonia is Greek. This is not something one can discuss rationally with local residents. The message is made very clearly on posters and stickers, and in speeches and chants at frequent mass rallies.

In this typical piece, Greeks are accused of an irrational concern for history, one that is a reflection and result of their non-Western, "Balkan" identity which is only loosely cloaked by a veneer of Westernization. There is also a certain ingratitude implied on the part of the Greeks: despite enjoying the best of what the West has to offer, the Greeks persist in their hysterical obstructions.[9]

The Greek government, by contrast, based its position on the claim that in using the name "Macedonia" FYROM was declaring its future expansionist aims on the neighboring Greek province of Macedonia; it is claimed that these aims are inscribed in FYROM's constitution.[10] As exterior minister Andonis Samaras wrote to his fellow EU exterior ministers in August 1991: "The Greeks believe that the Macedonian name is part of their own historical heritage and should not be used to identify, in an ethnic sense, another nation."[11] Two of the leading crusaders on the issue in Greece put it thus: "if Skopje retains the name of Macedonia, the Macedonian Question will be perpetuated. There can be no Macedonian Question without the name of Macedonia" (Martis and Papathemelis 1992). Note that Skopje refers to the capital of FYROM – this is a pejorative reference meant to reduce the country to its capital city. It parallels the Greek reference to FYROM as a "statelet" (κρατίδιο) rather than a full state. The fact that FYROM is a country much smaller than Greece, with an almost non-existent army does not reassure many Greeks. They believe that just as the struggle over possession of Macedonia can be traced back to the turn of the century, such struggles over Macedonia will no doubt go on long into the future.[12]

The second rallying point of the Greek position has been the assertion that FYROM "falsified" or "appropriated" Greek history by claiming descent from the ancient Macedonia of Alexander the Great. This falsification has extended to the use of certain symbols associated with the ancient Macedonian kings, such as the Star of Vergina which, until recent negotiations, adorned FYROM's flag (see Brown 1994). Some extreme FYROM nationalists (those associated with the VMRO-DPMNE party) claim to be directly descended from ancient Macedonians and Alexander the Great. Others, such as president Kiro Gligorov, claim that the current population of Macedonia descends from the Slavic peoples who settled in Macedonia in the seventh century AD, thus forming the biological basis of the present-day Macedonian nation. A third position claims that present-day Macedonians are a result of the mixture of the invading Slav population and the indigenous "ancient" Macedonians.

Greece's claims to the ownership of ancient Macedonian history have been particularly ridiculed; newspapers such as the *New York Times* (1994a) have referred to Greece's position as "hysteria over history." One unidentified Western diplomat was cited in the *New York Times* (1995) describing Greece's position as "totally irrational." It is ironic that in their focus on the issue on "history," the Greeks felt they were on solid ground. In choosing the ground of "history," the Greeks believed they were speaking a language understood by European nation-states, since they had been told by those same European powers that Greece was the cradle of Western civilization. This transpired to be an ineffective strategy for the Greeks. Indeed, a number of Western commentators criticized Greece for not knowing its own history well enough. In an article in *Time* entitled "Greece's Defense Just Seems Silly," Strobe Talbot (1992; emphasis in original) writes with considerable irony: "The situation has all the makings of a **tragedy**, which Aristotle, another great Macedonian, who was Alexander's teacher, defined as the result of **foolish pride**." Talbot suggests that modern Greeks need to make a more careful study of ancient Greek philosophy, as Westerners like himself have. This again suggests that Greece is not a fully mature player on the international scene. If "history" was an uneven terrain for Greece to present its case to the West,[13] it was all the more so for significant local factors. In particular, certain aspects of local kinship ideology played a role in motivating Greek opinion over the specific issue of "The Name." These local factors had to remain hidden from public discourse because of their very association with custom and thus backwardness both for the Greeks and for the West.

Anthropological Input

A number of anthropologists have recently begun to address the Macedonian issue. Karakasidou has laid out how the Greek government's long-standing denial of the existence of a "Slavo-Macedonian" minority within its borders has politicized culture: "redefining the once largely personal social issues of ethnic identity, language, religion and ethnic ascription into the realm of national concerns" (1993b: 5). Karakasidou details the role of state institutions – schools, churches, marketplaces and the military – in attempts to inculcate Greek national consciousness and practices in a population that did not previously think of itself in such terms. She also suggests some of the ways that women were both "targets and agents" of national inculcation by the Greek state (Karakasidou 1997). Danforth (1995: chapter 3) argues that a distinct Macedonian national consciousness arose in the first half of the twentieth century as a reaction against the nationalizing projects of Greece, Bulgaria and Serbia. Elsewhere Karakasidou has argued that Greek intellectuals have served the role of "cultural warriors" by protecting the purity of Greek national heritage with regards to Macedonia. She notes that "intellectual discourse changes dramatically when national matters are at stake" (1994: 45), and suggests that from 1992 to 1993 there was a virulent campaign by the Greek state and some leading intellectuals to squelch any public dissent on the Macedonia issue.

Karakasidou and Danforth have provided analyses of the origins of the current crises. They have both done this through an examination of issues such as the instability of the Balkan region during the twentieth century, government acculturation programs and forced population movements. These factors are all reasons for the continuing border disputes between Greece and its neighbors. Similarly, political scientists and historians of Greece invoke current transnational politico-economic causes to account for the instability of Greece and other Balkan countries that makes them particularly receptive to nationalist ideology at this historical moment.[14] All these authors draw to a greater or lesser extent on studies about the invention of tradition. They regard the de-reification and historicization of the national identities and nationalist ideologies which they believe are the cause of the current controversy, as of utmost importance. Danforth describes this view directly: "The anthropology of nationalism must dereify the nation; it must deconstruct national cultures and identities" (1993: 8). In his book Danforth (1995) goes beyond this: he attempts to give a sense of the life histories and views of ordinary people caught up on opposite sides of the issue, or caught in between. Through his presentation of the voices of migrants to Australia from the region of Macedonia (Greek and Yugoslav), Danforth gives a sense of the choices involved in the decision to identify with one or another nationalist project, or to reject them all.

Although these explanations are important and valuable, they miss one piece of the Macedonian puzzle that troubled me as I conducted my fieldwork: that is, why were my Kalymnian informants, who were normally so critical of their government even over issues such as the Turkish threat to Greece, so taken up by the Macedonia issue? Why on this issue in particular did they appear to be parroting official positions? Danforth helps us understand how those who have lived the history of border struggles attempt to interpret their situations. However, his and other works failed to help me understand why Greeks far from Macedonia seemed so taken up by this issue, and in particular, why the question of the name seemed to strike home.

It wasn't until I began to examine the kinship, inheritance and baptismal naming systems on Kalymnos that some local light was cast on this international issue. Genealogies were not part of my original project, which I imagined would focus on narratives of local history and remembrances of the Second World War. Indeed, kinship was not a major part of my graduate training, and I didn't include it as part of my project design. When I embarked on my fieldwork, I felt that kinship as a domain of study had been well covered by the classical ethnographies of Greece. What could I possibly add to these? I also felt that kinship was no longer on the agenda of current anthropology. It was only at the insistence of my advisors, half-way through my fieldwork, that I began to undertake the collection of genealogies. It was through such genealogies that the relationship of family naming and inheritance patterns to issues of continuity with the past – conceived as a "national heritage," – became evident.

The View from the Island

As I argued with regards to Yugoslavia, Kalymnians are often clear-headed and incisive in seeing to the heart of international power politics. I was therefore initially mystified by their focus on what appeared to be a trivial issue. When I began conducting fieldwork on Kalymnos in February of 1992, the Macedonian question had become a leading topic of day-to-day discussion, displacing Cyprus, Turkish threats on the Aegean, and other issues of Greece's relations with its neighbors. This seemed particularly strange on an island such as Kalymnos – distant from Greek Macedonia, but located only three miles off the coast of Turkey – where one might expect the Turkish threat to the Aegean to be a more primary concern.[15] Although Turkey was not absent from discussions, Macedonia took center stage. It featured in everyday conversation as well as in student rallies, the speeches of local and visiting national politicians, clerics and school-teachers on holidays such as Independence Day and Ohi Day.[16]

Was the furor over this issue a creation of the media, politicians or public opinion? Clearly the Macedonian question had stirred up public sentiment, demonstrated as much by mass rallies in Athens and Thessaloniki as by the interest expressed by ordinary Kalymnians in their daily discussions. Unlike many other issues that were in the news during my stay on Kalymnos, most Kalymnians did not feel that politicians were simply manufacturing this issue for their own purposes. It had struck a chord with public opinion, and although some politicians were able to exploit this, they did not create it.[17]

On Kalymnos it was felt that politicians had mismanaged the effort to articulate the Greek position abroad. This was remarked upon to me by an older couple while watching a television show (Logo Timis, 3 December 1992) about a Greek-American who had developed a database program containing all the works of the "great thinkers" of the West. The interviewer quickly turned the issue to how this would assist Greece on the Macedonia issue, and the computer scientist obliged by saying that through his program people would be able to see how the work of Aristotle, a pre-eminent "Macedonian," fit within the corpus of Greek thought. He complained, however, that the Greek government had given him no support for his project despite repeated requests and its obvious benefits for Greece. The Kalymnian couple latched onto this point, and told me what useless bastards (μαλάκες)[18] were in the Greek government who let opportunities like this get away.

This is the first suggestion I had of the significance of history as property. The interviewer on this TV show commented that Greece was missing an opportunity to "sell that which it already has," i.e. its history (perhaps in contrast to the agricultural and other products that it must produce and sell to the EU). In my discussion with the couple I protested that ideas were not agricultural fields, while they insisted that this was exactly what they were, property.[19] This connection between family inheritance and national heritage – "ideas as fields"[20] – first suggested to me a connection between local and national naming practices, between the way Kalymnians saw the Battle for the Name and the significance of naming practices on Kalymnos in general. It motivated me to explore in greater depth the Kalymnian naming system and naming strategies. This enabled me to understand how the giving of baptismal names was critical to their understanding of spiritual and material continuity.

Names, Big and Small

I sat with Popi at her kitchen table with a tape-recorder as she recounted to me her version of a recent family dispute between her mother and her brother's wife. Popi often quarreled with her sister-in-law, and was particularly critical of her foreign ways. She shared the following family story with me as her honorary brother, partly since relations with her own brother were strained. A transliteration of the tape follows:

> For Sevasti it was bad enough that her son had married a non-Greek woman. But now that Jane, the foreigner, had given birth to a second son, she was being obstinate about the name. It's true that the mother has the right to give the name of the second son, but Jane was not going to name it after her own father, as a Kalymnian woman would. Rather, she wanted to choose a name that sounded good, a name that would be unrelated, useless to either of their families. Sevasti wanted the child named after her own father, Haralambos, since she herself

hadn't had a second son to whom she could transfer this name. She begged her son Mihalis to persuade Jane, but he said, "I promised her that she would choose the name of the second child. If you pressure her we will have problems. Keep quiet, and I'll bring her around slowly." One day, as Jane was still debating her foreign names, Mihalis started calling the baby, "Haralambos, my sweet, my joy" [Haralambos literally means shining joy]. Jane said, "Hey! What are you doing! You want that name, don't you?" Mihalis said, "No, no! It's just that it's a happy name." Jane said OK, that they could call the baby Haralambos until she could come up with another name. Thus, when the baby turned forty days and had to be taken to church to be blessed by the priest according to Greek custom, they had gradually been calling him Haralambos more and more. Sevasti and Jane went to church. The priest asked Sevasti what the child would be named. Sevasti said, "I don't know, ask the mother." Jane got confused, and said, "I haven't decided on a name." The priest said, "Now you must say a name so I can say the blessing for the child. Then when it is baptized you can change the name." Jane said, "Well, I had talked with my husband about Haralambos, but–" "Haralambos is a beautiful name," the priest insisted. So she couldn't think of anything else and the priest didn't have time to wait. She agreed to Haralambos. She went home and had a nervous crisis. Sevasti had won the battle.

My understanding of the significance of the name Macedonia was first stimulated by one Kalymnian man's claim of the reverse: the name's insignificance. In response to news of Russia's recognition of FYROM under the name "Republic of Macedonia" (August 1992) he told me: "I don't care about the name. It's the falsification (πλαστογ– ράφηση) of history that I object to." This comment was striking at the time, but it was only several months later I began to absorb its resonances and its similarity to a statement by a grandmother who had just had a granddaughter named after her: "It's not the name that I'm so excited about. That's silly. It's that a girl in the family solves a lot of problems." In both these cases a denial was used to place a naming practice on a seemingly more rational footing, in the first case by relating it to history or heritage, and in the second to family problems or inheritance. These exchanges indicated to me how names are linked to notions of possession, i.e. ownership through inheritance and through heritage (history).

Unlike naming practices in standard US culture, baptismal names on Kalymnos should not be chosen on the basis of whim or on personal aesthetic criteria. Kalymnians state that babies should receive their names according to a system in which the first male child is given the name of the father's father, the second male child the mother's father. Similarly, the first female child is named after the mother's mother, and the second after the father's mother. Because siblings follow the same system in choosing names for their children, this means that first cousins normally share the same name, having been named after the same grandparent. This naming system has been reported as existing on a number of Aegean islands. It differs from the system of mainland Greece which is more patrilineally biased in that the first daughter is named after the father's rather than the mother's mother. This reflects the greater matrifocality that exists on Kalymnos, as discussed in Chapter 5.

In giving a child the name of its grandparent, "parents were carrying out the sacred duty of *anastassi*, or bringing ancestors back to life."[21] This did not mean that a child was seen as somehow equivalent to the person from whom they took their name, even though some people expressed the view that personal characteristics might be transferred through the name. What names did represent was a means of establishing continuity between past and present, an insurance that even as kin die they are continued in the present. The verb "to continue" is one of the words used to describe the importance of names on Kalymnos. As one Kalymnian told me: "our custom insures that the names continue and are not erased" (τα ονόματα συνεχίζουν, δε σβήνονται). The same informant noted that George born of John, gives birth to John born of George, who gives birth to George, born of John again (the same is true in the female line for first daughters).

The role played by personal names in the establishing of intergenerational continuity is not distinctive to Greece, and can be found in the ethnographic literature throughout the world, among people as different as the Rotinese of Indonesia, the Zuwaya of Libya, the Inuit, and upper middle-class families in the United States, to name just a few.[22] Furthermore, in the Mediterranean ethnographic context, the metaphoric connection of name and honor – that the word for "name" (όνομα) also can be used to mean social standing in the community – also suggests the way names can become indices of the past. The association of the two concepts indicates that a considerable component of present-day status is the family history or lineage that one can claim.[23] Concern with name and naming, then, can be seen cross-culturally as concerned with linking those people who live in the present to the past of the family or lineage. In this chapter, however, I illustrate a particular construction of the relation of naming to property and dispute, and the significance of this for understanding the issue of "national" naming, a connection that is absent from this earlier literature.

There is a considerable affective dimension to naming on Kalymnos. I saw it expressed by grandparents upon seeing their name perpetuated – the sense that they would leave something behind when they died, their particular attachment to the child bearing their name, or a name from their family that they particularly cherished. This emotional connection to names was illustrated in another form by a woman who complained that she and her husband wouldn't tolerate the way their son mistreats them, but for the fact that the son's two children are named after her husband and her own father. As she put it, "he's hung us with the names." This affective dimension is also revealed in the practice of naming a child after a sibling who has died without offspring – a common exception to grandparental naming. A particularly beloved person who dies young may be "resurrected" by the offspring of three or more siblings (sex is irrelevant to such decisions). People who have named children after their siblings talk about how their great pain was eased by the fact that soon after the sibling's death, they could "hear" the name being spoken again.

The emotional dimension of naming is also described by Skiada, working on Karpathos, who notes that grandparents can express their preference by sharing the same bed with their eponymous grandchildren. Grandchildren also claim strong ties. Even Karpathians who have migrated to the US claim that eponymous grandparents continue to influence their major life decisions such as choice of spouse.[24]

Names on Kalymnos far from being about whim or beauty, are crucial ways in which individuals are connected with certain kinds of pasts, and with the future of their family, since they too have the duty to carry on the names. While the past of the family is one sort of connection, names also connect people to a religious past. This is because the great majority of baptismal names are also saints' names. Until recently people did not celebrate on their birthdays, but rather on the day determined to commemorate the saint after whom they were named. Thus everyone named Yiorgos celebrates on the nameday of Saint Yiorgos. The extent to which this tied individuals to the life history of the saint was highly variable. Some Kalymnians told me they felt no greater attachment to their eponymous saint than to any other saint, others recited in great detail the story of their saint's life and martyrdom. One woman was overcome with emotion in telling me "her" story.[25]

The significance of naming is inscribed in the Greek legal code, specifically in the current Greek Family Law. This states that in cases where the parents of a child are divorced, the parent not living with the child must give consent concerning decisions which "will influence the child for his entire life." These include: choice of religion, choice of godparent, major surgical operation and giving of baptismal name. In a case reported in the Greek newspaper *To Vima* (1993) the Greek Supreme Court ruled in favor of a divorced man who protested the name chosen by the child's mother against his wishes.

It is evident that the naming system works to create continuity with various kinds of pasts, both at the level of emotion and family lineages.

However, it is a very particular kind of continuity that is established through naming, one in which the same names are constantly repeated through the generations. Names, then, lose any sense of individuality: "The systematic repetition of a name and its extension to an ever-widening circle of descendants rob it in time of any association with its 'original' persona."[26] When a name is passed from grandparent to grandchild it is that grandparent who is remembered, not the great-great-grandparent from whom the grandparent has taken the name. At the individual level it is a weak form of commemoration – the person commemorated is in fact soon forgotten. But at the genealogical level it is a strong form of commemoration, since names of ancestors are preserved down through the generations. This means that naming is about both short- and long-term continuity. There is the direct relationship between the grandparent or other relative and the child, and the more vague history of the name repeated down through the generations that connects the living person with an unknown ancestor in the distant past. This is also an analogy for the way that continuity with the ancient past is conceived: one's relationship with one's grandparent becomes the prototype for one's relationship with unknown ancestors in the ancient past. Thus naming practices are not merely about establishing continuity within families, but have wider implications in establishing continuities between the present and both a religious and a national past.

Another key feature of naming customs on Kalymnos is their connection to property transmission. Ideally stated, the child who takes the name of a grandparent (or other relative) will inherit the property of that grandparent. This is expressed in the phrase το γονικό στο γονικό, which is roughly translatable as "the parental property goes to the parental heir."[27]

These ideas, however, more accurately describe past reality, when first daughter inheritance was in full force. In past times, when people on these islands were poorer they concentrated on passing on their goods to one or two children and effectively disinheriting the rest. In this way the family property would remain with the single descendent who would be able to make a good marriage and pass on the family names to future generations. In effect, the system of naming justified the inequality in family inheritance.[28] In present times, with increasing wealth, there is the possibility and the desire to provide for all one's children, and first daughter inheritance is described as a "stupidity of the past." Thus, when I conducted fieldwork in the early 1990s there was only a slight favoritism to eponymous children (some examples are given below). But this does not mitigate the fact that at the level of ideology, the connection between names and property persists, and continues to be thought of in terms of family continuity. The importance of naming for family continuity, however, is a pan-Greek phenomenon, although its articulation in conjunction with property transfer is diverse. For example, some connection is reported between naming and property transfer even in areas such as Western Crete, where equal inheritance has long prevailed.[29] This leads me to suspect, though further research is clearly necessary, that the link between names and property would be understood throughout Greece.

For Kalymnians the significance of this link in terms of nationalist consciousness cannot be overstated. It helps us comprehend what has otherwise been a rather abstract discussion. Leontis has recently argued for the importance of "place" or *topos* in modern Greek imaginings of national identity. In discussing the significance of Athens to one Greek demoticist intellectual, Leontis (1995: 79) writes:

> Here the liturgical invocation of the place-name reduces the complex history of Greece's modern capital to the imaginary moment when "Europe received its education" and Neohellenes rediscovered theirs. Athens, once a vibrant city, later a beleaguered village . . . fuses past and present through the immediacy of experience. It becomes one and the same place where ancients and moderns alike observe the same earth, sky, horizon, atmosphere, and sea – tags that unify the topos of Hellenism as they conflate nearly three thousand years of history. The fetishized name of Athens "says it all," reducing to a single breath the distinguished history, cultural contribution, and spiritual continuity of what Psiharis refers to as the national soul.

Leontis elliptically suggests that similar ideas about the connection of past and present in a *topos* animate Greek concern over the Macedonian question.[30] Such abstract conceptions and concerns form an important part of the discourse on the Macedonian question. They can be found both in media discussions and in Kalymnians own discourses, for example, in the claim that "the Name is our soul." These views are part of what the media in Western Europe and the United States have branded the "mystical" character of the Greek position. Nevertheless, such discussions need not be solely interpreted in intellectual, mystical terms. They can also be seen as part of the general process of national identity formation/reproduction in the West, in Greece, or elsewhere. As I mention above in my analysis of heritage/inheritance, names are a significant way in which notions of continuity are connected to ideas of the ownership of a tangible, physical past. Elefantis (1992: 31; my translation), gives a clear picture of what is conceptually at stake in his discussion of Greek nationalism:

> National sentiment is always a claim to or defense of ancestral land (πατρώας γης; also "fatherland") thus it always aims at manufacturing titles of ownership over land, establishing rights far back into the past, so far back that no doubt can be legitimated . . . In order for the

legitimation of rights over land to succeed one must undertake to appropriate the people who used to live on that land, such that the people living there today appear to be direct descendants of these far off ancestors . . . Very simply: it's my father, it's my grandfather, it's my great-grandfather, they're my distant ancestors who are lost in the depths of history and myth; thus it's my field.

For Kalymnians, it is this tangible connection to ancestors and to land, which constitutes a sense of continuity with the past, and is largely embodied in the practices of baptismal naming.

Disputed Names, Disputed Territories

Because naming is linked to intergenerational continuity and property transfer, the selection of a name can become the source of bitter dispute both within and between families. Such disputes take numerous forms on Kalymnos. One would think, given the prescriptive naming system, that disputes would not occur – but there are many exceptions. The increasing number of wives from other parts of Greece and abroad allows for the possibility of greater manipulation and dispute. For example, a mother and father both contribute money and effort to building a house for their son who has married a non-Greek woman. Each one claims in conversation that "I built the house for my son," thereby neglecting the role of their spouse. Each one is eagerly anticipating the birth of this son's first daughter. The woman hopes to convince the son and daughter-in-law (who has said that she doesn't want to name any daughters after her own mother) to name the first daughter after her. The man has made plans to bribe the daughter-in-law the sum of 100,000 drachmas (approximately $500) to give her daughter a name from his family.[31] As he put it, "then my grandchild will give this name to her grandchild, and the name will remain with the property I built." Thus the dispute between husband and wife centers on who will actually be remembered as having left something behind for the future.

Not all disputes involve foreigners. In one case that I recorded (see Figure 1), two fathers-in-law share the name Manolis. When the couple gives birth to a second son, the wife's father therefore feels the right to decide the name because he has not been memorialized by the first naming (it was his name but not, according to the naming rules, he himself whom the child was named after). Thus when the couple announce that they plan to name the second child after the husband's childless brother Nikolas, the wife's father threatens to throw them out of the house. They capitulate to the wife's father's demands, and he chooses the name of his maternal grandfather Nikodimos, largely because it is a name not associated with the husband's family, thereby making it clear to any outsiders that he made the decision.

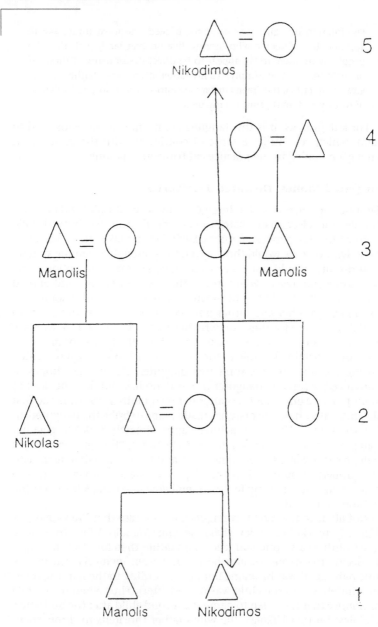

Figure 1. Homonymy: A grandfather asserts his rights.

Similar disputes abound on Kalymnos. In another example, a Kalymnian man was having an argument with his sister over their mother's division of her property. When the sister gave birth to her first daughter and named it after her mother, the brother angrily complained that the little baby had "eaten" his part of the property because now his mother would be more disposed to transfer the property to her grandchild (for the moment to his sister). Later he ironically remarked on his sister's luck in giving birth to a girl at the height of this controversy. The sister responded by ridiculing the brother's jealousy over "a little baby," and implicitly denying that the name would have any impact on her mother's decision. The sister's choice was dictated quite clearly by the naming system, since her first daughter would be given her mother's name except in unusual circumstances. But her denial of benefit from this turn of events is not uncommon. It reflects a strategy of denying interest in gain and stressing selflessness that features in numerous practices other than naming. Names are always supposed to be chosen for the disinterested reason of commemoration, rather than for obviously calculating motives. As Vernier (1984: 53) has described it from material gathered on the island of Karpathos:

> If there were no longer any prospects of an inheritance and the youngest children of large families were given the apparently disinterested names of saints . . . or those of very distant relatives ("just to please them") such a choice was not infrequently part of a strategy for hiding interests . . . it often became clear on analysis that the saint's name was also that of a distant relative. The latter was not infrequently an "American" uncle or aunt, in other words someone who had emigrated, was likely to acquire wealth and might return, and who, it was hoped, would feel some obligation to the person called after him.

Such naming strategies make clear that there is nothing natural, in the sense of reflecting simple biological descent, about the continuity established through inheritance. That ancestors are selected to fit the needs of the present is a phenomenon noted in many cultures, perhaps most notably in Evans-Pritchard's study of Nuer lineages. But if ancestors are chosen to be commemorated according to present strategies, they are still chosen in culturally constructed ways and for culturally constructed reasons. The parallels between the specific use of ancestral names in constructing family continuity, and the use of historical names in constructing national continuity should be apparent. An understanding of these parallels can allow us to elucidate my specific case: the relation between the workings of naming practices on the local level, and the Battle for the Name between Greece and FYROM.

The principal assertion on the Greek side has been that the choice of the name "Macedonia" implies territorial pretensions on the part of FYROM towards Greek Macedonia. When I arrived on Kalymnos in 1992 it was commonly stated in discussions that the "Skopians" were obviously plotting something. The revelation that FYROM nationalists had printed maps showing the "Republic of Macedonia" extending down to the Aegean was simply a confirmation of what most Greeks already knew: that in choosing a name you have some material motives in mind. The constant denials by the government of FYROM of any such territorial pretensions must, for the Kalymnians, seem to be like the strategy of dissimulation and claimed disinterestedness illustrated above, a strategy with which Kalymnians have long familiarity. The fact that at present FYROM, with its tiny army, lacks the ability to carry out any territorial pretensions against Greece, is irrelevant. It resembles the claim by the woman that her brother shouldn't be jealous because "it's just a little baby."

More significantly, naming strategies and their relationship to property are often not short-term affairs, but calculations of future possibilities. The fact that naming strategies work, that the investment in the choice of a name is eventually able to produce, in many cases, the desired outcome of property-transfer, helps explain another puzzle. That is, why did Kalymnians believe that if Greece prevailed diplomatically on the issue of the name it would change anything, or worse, that it would not simply cause the "Skopians" greater resentment and fuel nationalist fervor to make such territorial claims in the future? As indicated in the quotation from Vernier above, the selection of a name does not ensure the transfer of property from the same-named ancestor. However, it does lay the groundwork for a claim that could be made at a future date. The lack of such a name negates this claim, and forces the interested party to seek other means to inherit property from a relative. As one Kalymnian woman explained, the future generations of Skopians will grow up with the name Macedonia, and because of it, think that our Macedonia belongs to them. Another woman made the following analogy in the context of a discussion about Macedonia: as parents must not just think about the present but also about the future of their children, so politicians who are deciding this issue must consider the future as well.

For Greeks living in Greek Macedonia the issue of names and property is still more tangible. In the light of what I have argued about the relationship of property, intergenerational continuity and history, it is not surprising that this has been a major issue in the dispute between Greece and FYROM. As a *New York Times* article reports, the government of FYROM has the names of some 5,000 of their citizens who are demanding the return of land that they lost when they fled Greece in the aftermath of the Civil War. The *Times* article (1994b) cites the following example:

"I had a house, fourteen fields, a couple of vineyards and a chestnut grove," Yatchev said, referring to land just outside Edessa that the Greek government confiscated because his family members fought with the defeated Communist forces in the civil war. "It was my family's property for 300 years, and I want it back." "It belongs to future generations," he said, expressing the almost mystical link to ancestral lands that is still felt strongly by both Greeks and Slavs.

As I've argued, what is portrayed in the Western media as the mystical trait of backward peasants can, in fact, be understood in the light of a complex system of kinship, naming and inheritance. The above material illustrates the direct analogy between local naming practices and the international Battle for the Name – the selection of baptismal names often involves battles. The above example of the couple fighting over the name of their yet-to-be-conceived grand-daughter demonstrates this point. Another example is the one involving Jane and Sevasti. While Jane, the foreigner, felt it was her natural right to name the child – it was, after all, her child – she wanted a name that would appeal to her. For Sevasti, it was important to prevent her grandson from receiving a name irrelevant to both their families, and to take the opportunity to commemorate her own father. It was therefore worth sowing discord within her son's marriage to achieve her aims. Not only discord, but even divorce has been known to result from disputes over naming.[32] It is interesting that Kalymnians condemned such disputes as making too much of names. A number of women who had named their first daughter after their mother-in-law instead of their mother suggested to me that they did this "just to please my mother-in-law," since these names are really not so important.

In attempting to understand this denial of importance of a practice that clearly plays a significant role in the lives of many Kalymnians I return to the claim that, "It's not the name, it's the falsification of history that upsets me." As I've argued throughout, "History" is a valued and validated category in Greek discourse. The reasons for this have been amply documented by numerous anthropologists and historians of modern Greece. They go back to the founding of the modern Greek state in the early nineteenth century, and the role of diaspora Greeks and Western Philhellenes in defining the *raison d'être* of this new state as the restoration of the glories of the Classical Greek past. Because of this, Kalymnians feel they are justified in berating the West for not paying enough attention to "History". There was an injunction posted in English in all tourist locations on Kalymnos in 1992 and 1993 (and in Greece generally): "Macedonia is Greek. Always has been, always will be. Study history!" And it is a glorious history that, as every Kalymnian knows, sets Greece apart from the rest of the world. To paraphrase a comment numerous Kalymnians made to me, "if you go back 2,000 years, people in England and Spain were living in trees. While Greece was the center of Civilization." Or to cite again the epigram with which I began this chapter: "You are celebrating the 500th anniversary of the discovery of America. Well, we are over 1,500 years in front of you, and we don't need any outsiders telling us whether Macedonia is Greek or not."

Naming, by contrast, is only a "custom" (έθιμο). As I argued earlier, the domain of "custom" can in some circumstances be viewed as a justification for present-day practices. Custom was opposed to "folly," for example, by those who wished to legitimate dynamite throwing – albeit a limited and restricted dynamite throwing. However, custom was not seen as a reasonable argument for practices such as dowry or first-daughter inheritance, or for an excessive dynamite throwing that was economically harmful and physically lethal.

Hence custom is viewed by Kalymnians as inherently non-rational. In explicit discourse, custom is only used to legitimate practices which do not play a major role in social life, but are restricted to the realms of ritual and religion. Custom certainly would not be seen as sufficient argument in an international dispute such as the Battle for the Name. Furthermore, customs are part of the domain of folklore and rural or "Eastern backwardness," not of European "modernity." In this way local discourse succumbs to international discourse in obscuring the importance of practices of kinship and naming for understanding national and international disputes.

Even when restricted to local-level practice, an explicit appeal to custom by itself is often insufficient to justify baptismal choices, since the rules themselves provide room for flexibility. An insistence on rigidly following baptismal naming customs, such as naming the first daughter after the mother's mother, is explicitly ridiculed by many Kalymnians especially at times when they wish to be identified as "modern" and "European." Because there is no "rational" reason to uphold a particular naming strategy, to do so makes one appear petty or backwards, while to claim flexibility (at least retrospectively) shows one to be magnanimous. The connection of naming to property might seem to provide a "rational" reason to pursue actively certain naming strategies. However, such strategies are not defined as legitimate insofar as they must be hidden to be effective – in explicit discussion of the abstract custom, there is reason to deny the significance of naming and one's own investment in it. Nevertheless, the same people, when discussing their own family history or commenting on that of others, reveal just how important naming practices remain in daily Kalymnian life and in the establishment of a sense of continuity with the past.[33]

The Resonances of History

In a country that has always been concerned with presenting a "rational" image of itself to outsiders, one can detect many ironies in the Battle for the Name. While international media has labelled Greece's opposition to the name "irrational," Kalymnians in sharing Western assumptions about the irrationality of "custom," were unable to articulate directly their opposition to the name. This distinction can be usefully interpreted in terms of Herzfeld's (1987) discussion of the two competing pasts of modern Greek consciousness: the Romeic or Byzanto-Ottoman past of custom and the Hellenic past of ancient Greek history. As Herzfeld has clearly shown, the Romeic past represents for many Greeks the familiar past of their own experience and that of their parents and grandparents. Yet because of its association with the period of Ottoman rule it is ideologically unacceptable in official contexts, and must be suppressed in discourse directed toward outsiders. As "custom," naming practices are part of the Romeic past which can only be expressed among insiders. Whereas "history," as represented by Alexander the Great in this case, is the standard fare of Greeks' representations of themselves to non-Greek others. Thus in this case, the Kalymnian view, while deeply felt, could not be justified directly through reference to a domain of custom which they felt was irrelevant to international politics. Rather, they resorted to shifting the discussion to other issues that they hoped would be seen as significant, such as "the falsification of history." The relationship of history to everyday life remained unarticulated.

Yet it is precisely local-level practices such as naming that carry a sense of historical connectedness for Kalymnians. Here we see the role played by local practices in naturalizing the connections between history, property and intergenerational continuity, and in making disputes over the past seem inevitable. This is not to deny that appeals to history or to common origins can be effective in and of themselves in mobilizing national sentiment. When placed in a local-level idiom of kinship these appeals become doubly effective, since they draw on the past "not simply to posit a common origin but also to claim substantial identity in the present."[34] The power of this combination helps to explain why Kalymnians can assent to (and even help propel) issues such as "the Battle of the Name," despite the manipulation of the issue by the politicians they are normally so skeptical about.[35]

I have suggested that anthropologists and other social scientists who have examined the Macedonian question, while contributing to our understanding of some of its aspects, have reproduced these same distinctions by concentrating on historical, intellectual and political economic aspects of the issue, and ignoring potential local resonances.

If we focus our analyses on texts, to the exclusion of the social practices which have traditionally been anthropology's bread-and-butter, we risk losing an important opportunity to contextualize the understanding of national and transnational processes in the experiences and practices of ordinary people.[36] This suggests that as anthropologists we must take people's sense of historical continuity seriously, rather than debunking it as the false product of nationalist intellectuals.

In these last two chapters I have employed two localizing strategies to give a sense of how the seemingly abstract, intellectual and nationalistic categories of "history" and "heritage" are incorporated into the everyday discourses of Kalymnians. I have not done so by suggesting that historical consciousness is simply embodied, or symbolically recoded in non-discursive practices, for Kalymnians are extremely articulate commentators on the world beyond the borders of their island. Rather I have suggested how discourses and practices perceived as local (i.e. concerning family, neighbors, local customs), are brought to bear on the world events deemed as significant by the global centers of power. This occurs even in the case of the Macedonian question, where such connections must be denied because of the structures of power in which the terms "history" and "custom" take their meanings. These connections are made possible for Kalymnians, by an analogical mind-set that attempts to connect happenings which might from a Western perspective seem separate either in time, space or the domain of experience (politics, religion, kinship). Thus in Chapters 6 and 7 I showed how Kalymnian historical consciousness entails recognizing "how meanings migrate across domain boundaries, and how specific actions are multiply constituted" (Yanagisako and Delaney 1995: 11). In this chapter I have done my own reading across boundaries in offering a piece in the understanding of the local repercussions of an international controversy. In doing so I have hoped to suggest the continuing relevance of anthropological studies of the margins as well as the centers of power, in order to engage in the full richness of global, socially situated conversations.

Notes

1. See Badone 1992; P. Sahlins 1989; Woost 1993, for a few examples. A criticism of recent anthropological explorations of the culture of nationalism has been that they occlude relevant power relations and rob "agency" from third world countries by suggesting that a cultural system is working itself out

through volitionless actors. Both Scott (1990) and Spencer (1990) have made this criticism of Kapferer's work on Sri Lanka, and it is also an impetus for the ongoing debate between Sahlins and Obyesekere concerning Hawaiian interpretations of the voyage of Captain Cook. We must keep such critiques in mind in what follows. Yet I do not believe we can jettison culture, or "the cultural" from our modes of analyzing political events. That is I still believe one can profitably analyze the *cultural* contexts in which political events occur and are marked out as meaningful in Greece, the US or any other country, without positing those contexts as the "final causes" of these events (Scott 1990: 505).

2. I have in mind here the influence of "cultural studies" on making "texts" the focus of anthropological study, as well as the attack on "fieldwork" epitomized by the work of Llobera (1987). Indicative of the latter emphasis are recent collections on the "anthropology of Europe" such as MacDonald (1992) and Goddard, Llobera and Shore (1994).

3. The relationship of kinship and nationalism has begun to be explored in a number of recent works. For example, a number of feminist anthropologists have drawn on Schneider's critique of Western kinship models to explore the assumptions running through overlapping Western domains of kinship, religion and nationalism which "naturalize" gender inequalities. Thus Yanagisako and Delaney (1995) note that in abandoning the naturalizing assumptions about these different domains, they are not calling for "abandoning the study of the meanings and relations previously confined to those domains." Rather they argue for the need to study the cultural constitution of the domains of "kinship," "religion" "politics" etc., "how meanings migrate across domain boundaries, and how specific actions are multiply constituted" (Yanagisako and Delaney 1995: 11). Delaney (1995), for example, traces the way that the rhetoric of Turkish nationalism was constituted out of local level ideas about procreation, kinship and descent and metaphors of seed and soil which both "made sense" to the population, and had very definite effects on the future shape of the Turkish nation. See also Williams' (1995) broader theoretical statement in the same volume about the importance of analyzing kinship as one among a number of potential interpenetrating classificatory systems (race, caste, ethnicity) that are part of the process of nation-building. For other recent approaches, see Alonso (1994); Borneman (1992); Strathern (1992) and Weismantel (1995).

4. During the Balkan wars prior to the First World War this area was fought over and divided between Serbia, Greece and Bulgaria. Each country attempted to impose national identity on the local, peasant populations, with varying degrees of success. The development of a Macedonian national consciousness seems in part to have been a rejection of these other nationalist projects. For a review of some of the historical issues see Kitromilidis 1990; Poulton 1995 and Wilkinson 1951. For an excellent study of the different factors contributing to the formation of a Macedonian national consciousness in this century, see Brown 1995a.

5. During the Second World War Greece, Yugoslavia and Bulgaria once again fought for the national sentiments of the local population. After the Axis invasion and conquest of Yugoslavia and Greece in 1941 the local population exhibited diverging loyalties toward the partisan movements and the Bulgarian occupiers. On August 2 1944 the Anti-fascist assembly for the national liberation of Macedonia (ASNOM) held a charter meeting, supported by the Yugoslav partisans, which Yugoslav historians have taken as the achievement of statehood by the Macedonian people. After 1991, Macedonian political parties have been polarized on the status of this meeting. The Social Democrats, claiming continuity with Yugoslav Macedonia, continue to celebrate it: VMRO, the more nationalistic wing, denounces it as linked with the project of Serbification and look for more ancient roots (see Brown 1995b). By contrast, for Greek and Bulgarian historians August 2 1944 represents the invention of a new nation. While a complete history of these events still needs to be written, suggestive work has been done by Karakasidou 1993a; Kofos 1964 and Rossos 1991.

6. Cited in Skilakakis 1995: 149. See also Politis 1993; Verney 1996.

7. A concise review of diplomatic wrinkles through 1996 can be found in Veremis 1997.

8. Todorova 1994; for a recent popular example of such stereotyping, see Kaplan 1993.

9. For a fuller account of Western Press coverage of the issue, see Skilakakis 1995: 147–53.

10. Article 49 of the constitution refers to the Macedonian state's interest in the welfare and rights of members of the Macedonian people in neighboring countries. Greece has taken this as a specific reference to the claimed existence of a Slavo-Macedonian minority in Greek Macedonia.

11. Cited in Skilakakis 1995: 260. Skilakakis, a close advisor of then Prime Minister Mitsotakis, argues in his book *In the Name of Macedonia* (1995) that Samaras played the crucial role in mobilizing public opinion to shift attention from the issue of the claims of a Slavo-Macedonian minority in Greece to an almost exclusive focus on the issue of the name.

12. The "Macedonian Fighters" who fought for Greece in the Balkan Wars prior to the Second World War are still an important icon, and the few still surviving take part in national parades on Independence Day (March 25) and other important holidays.

13. The fact that Greek history no longer has the same currency in the West reflects in part the "shifting ground" of multiculturalism in which, as Just notes, "the problem for Greece [is] not to prove that Greek civilization was in fact 'Greek' but to maintain that Greek civilization was in fact 'Civilization.'" (1995: 301; see also Leontis 1995: 223 ff).

14. See Elefantis 1992; Liakos 1993; Mouzelis 1993.

15. I was not on Kalymnos to gauge local reaction during the crisis in early 1996 in which Greece and Turkey came to the brink of war over the uninhabited Greek island of Imia, directly between Kalymnos and Turkey. It is worth noting,

however, that the action of the mayor of Kalymnos in raising the Greek flag
on Imia, which was believed to have exacerbated the confrontation, was
roundly condemned in both Kalymnian newspapers as "irresponsible" and
"dangerous thoughtlessness" (see the issues of *i Kalymnianki* 16 February 1996,
and *i Argo tis Kalymnou* January 1996).

16. The commemoration day of Saints Cyril and Methodius, Byzantine saints
the ownership of whom is disputed between Greece and FYROM, was revived
in schools during my stay on Kalymnos. As one teacher told me, however, it
had been so long since they had publicly commemorated this holiday that
the local priests had to send to Athens for the appropriate liturgy and have it
faxed back to them.

17. See Elefantis 1992: 21; Papadimitropoulos 1993: 81; see also Skilakakis'
(1995: 85–9) account of the popular rallies over the issue in Thessaloniki in
early 1992. A few people on Kalymnos did express the view that the
Macedonian question had been blown out of proportion, to the neglect of
more pressing matters of Greek foreign policy. Those who expressed this view
did not deny, however, that Greece was "right" in its position. The view that
Greece was actually wrong on this issue was extremely rare on Kalymnos. But
I encountered it in surprising places. Of the handful of informants who
expressed this view to me, two were associated with extreme right-wing viewpoints. One, a former Junta supporter, believed that the US and NATO would
protect Greece from any potential military threats, and thus had no problem
with the name Macedonia. Another, also formerly associated with the extreme
right, now based views on a personal reading of the Bible, and a consequent
belief that national distinctions were irrelevant for the true believer. I take
these examples to be a warning against assumptions we might make about
the on-the-ground relationship between political ideologies and sentiments
of nationalism. Indeed, I found that by and large Kalymnians who expressed
"radical" political and social ideas in other spheres, did not have a substantially
different view than that of the mainstream on the Macedonian issue.

18. μαλάκα has the connotation both of jerk-off in the sexual sense, and
jerk in the social sense of someone useless or maladroit. It is roughly equivalent
to the British "wanker."

19. This claim, that the intellectual history of ancient Greece was the tangible
property of modern Greeks, perhaps should not come as a surprise. It is indicated by the fact that the Greek word κληρονομιά means both inheritance
and heritage and is used to refer to the inheritance one receives from relatives
(both in the biological and material sense) and to the national heritage of a
country, such as archaeological objects, traditions or even language. Handler
(1988) describes a similar case for Quebec, in which the word **patrimoine** is
used to refer both to personal and national "inheritance." He has argued that
such a view that sees the objects of the past as the property of the nation is a
feature of nationalist ideologies worldwide, indeed, that "however constituted
or mobilized, and however situated with respect to given political boundaries,
a self-conscious national or ethnic group will claim possession of cultural

properties as both representative and constitutive of cultural identity" (1988: 154). While Handler restricts his analysis, by and large, to objects from the past, is it surprising that modern Greeks, who have been told that their one claim to fame is as ancestors of a culture that provided the West with the ideas of "freedom" and "democracy," would treat such ideas and symbols as equally a part of their national heritage? For a discussion of the way that property and ideas, *topos* and *logos*, have been intertwined in modern Greek thought, see Leontis 1995: 23 ff.

20. Fernandez (1986) has commented on the relationship of material and intellectual "possessions." Indeed, because his recounting of a metaphor of "language as fieldmarker" bears considerable similarity to my discussion of names and property in the rest of this chapter, it is worth quoting at length:

> Anyone who has lived rural life in the **minifundia** landscape of Asturias with its myriad scattered family fields and meadows, with its recurrent family anxieties about the just and equitable inheritance of these fields, and with its folklore and recurrent village rumors about the surreptitious shifting, "inching" ... of these markers in the dead of night in slow aggrandizement of someone else's land will recognize how evocative the metaphor ["language as fieldmarker"] is. It aptly evokes such possessive and proprietorial feelings as are useful to Garcia Arias in his attempt at convincing his Asturian fellow countrymen to protect and revive their patrimony – principally the Asturian language.

> (Fernandez 1986: 130–1).

21. Vernier 1984: 40; 1991: 83 ff. As Vernier describes it, in naming children after their grandparents, parents: "accomplissaient un devoir sacré: celui de faire *anastassi*, c'est-à-dire de ressusciter les ancêtres (on disait que l'âme de l'ancêtre passait dans le corps de celui qui portait son nom) qui leur avaient transmis l'ensemble de leur patrimoine matériel et symbolique" (1991: 83). Kenna notes that grandparents say that namesake children "ensure their physical continuity after death" (1976: 24). And Stewart describes this as "an idea that verges on metempsychosis" (1991: 58).

22. See respectively Fox 1979; Davis 1989; Anawack 1989; Rossi 1965.

23. See Campbell 1964: 300–1; Bourdieu 1966: 220–1; Di Bella 1992.

24. Skiada 1990: 113; see also Tavuchis 1971; Panourgia 1995: 204.

25. The significance of baptismal names can be seen in two other religious aspects. One is the elaboration of the baptism ceremony itself as one of the three major life-cycle ceremonies, and the significance of Godparents. On the baptism ceremony, see Stewart 1991. On Godparents, (who have variable importance in Greece, and on Kalymnos did not generally have an input into the choice of names), see Campbell 1964. A second aspect not discussed here is the commemoration of names associated with All Souls days, in which the priest reads the names of ancestors of each family and asks for their forgiveness. This practice is reflected at the individual level in memorial ceremonies

(μνημόσυνα) and other types of food offerings in which the names of dead ancestors are commemorated (see Panourgia 1995: 134).

26. Herzfeld 1982b: 292. See also Stewart 1991: 58.

27. The implicit meaning of the phrase is "the grandparental bequest is passed to the grandchild." The phrase contains a play on words since γονικό is taken both from γονιός, meaning parent, and γόνος, meaning offspring, or sperm. Thus it should be read as "the bequest of my parent is passed to my offspring." Kenna's informants on the Cycladic island of Anafi claimed that this inheritance system insured that "the same name will be heard on the land" (1976: 25). According to Stewart, on the Cycladic island of Naxos houses and fields are rarely sold because "it is not thought to be the right of any one person to dispose of such objects that are suspended between past and future generations. Those holding them at any given moment are, in a sense, only tending them" (1991: 58).

28. As Vernier (1991: 83–4) notes for Karpathos: "L'idéologie de l'*anastassi* était l'idéologie presque naturellement sécrétée par une société acculée pour survivre à légitimer les droits exorbitants d'une minorité." It should be noted that the case described on Karpathos is different from Kalymnos and other Dodecanese islands in two respects. First on Karpathos both first sons and first daughters inherited from their patrilateral and matrilateral lines respectively. On Kalymnos it was only first daughters who were said to have inherited, perhaps reflecting the greater importance of houses and lesser importance of agriculture on Kalymnos. Secondly, the total disinheritance of subsequent siblings, and their virtual servitude to the first-born children does not seem to have existed on Kalymnos, where some provision was attempted to marry all one's children. Again this may reflect the greater comparative poverty of Karpathos in the nineteenth and early twentieth century in comparison to Kalymnos.

29. Herzfeld 1982b: 292.There is very little information about naming practices in mainland Greece. Bialor who worked in the Peloponnese notes that the occasional uxorilocal groom in a virilocal context may lose his primary naming rights to his wife (1967: 97). Here the link of naming, power and property seems clear, though not commented on by Bialor. Bialor notes there are numerous intra-family disputes over names as well as over inheritance, but says he had insufficient data to comment on the content of these disputes (1967: 106).

30. Leontis describes the sense of threat Greeks feel "that others to the north and west, including the FYROM, are conspiring to divest Neohellenes of their past by arbitrarily interpreting Hellenic history or rendering Hellenism insignificant" (1995: 222).

31. The daughter-in-law, although a foreigner, is recognized to have the power over this decision because 1) as her first daughter, she has the right to choose its name going by the traditional Kalymnian system, and 2) the family recognizes that their son does not dominate the relationship, but easily gives in to his wife (πέφτει εύκολα).

32. Since the husband in this case was not Kalymnian, but from mainland Greece, he wanted to name his first daughter after his own mother, according to the prevailing customs from his area. The wife insisted on the Kalymnian custom of giving the first daughter the name of her mother. Again Vernier provides comparative material from Karpathos. He gives numerous examples of intra-family disputes and alliances and suggests dramatic confrontations over the naming decision, which were settled in a "bid for power" by competing interests in the church on the day of baptism. And he notes the local saying "people can be killed when it is a question of names" (1984: 46). Also see Tavuchis (1971: 159–60).

33. This analysis leaves open the question of the relationship of naming practices to the Macedonian question over the course of this century, as well as potentially changing ideas about naming and continuity itself. The fact that naming practices are seen as "custom" does not mean that we should assume they are static. Clearly the relation between naming and property has undergone shifts and changes in Kalymnos and elsewhere. While historical research on naming practices on Kalymnos remains to be done, it is clear that this custom is undergoing current changes throughout Greece (see, e.g. Hirschon's recent work on nameday celebrations (1995)). And, at least in Athens, there has been considerable flux in baptismal naming practices in this century. Religious names have suffered inroads from a few classical Greek names in the 1930s in certain working-class communities. Similar name shifts are notable in the 1970s and 1980s among leftist intellectuals, who used ancient Greek names associated with democracy in part as a protest against the military Junta (Panourgia 1995: personal communication with author). This suggests that naming practices don't simply form the subtext for the understanding of certain larger events, but they are shaped by these events as well. At this point I can only speculate on what the use of such ancient Greek names implies for the ideas about family continuity which I have explored above. But it would seem fruitful to explore such practices, and to see them in comparison and contrast to other types of "naming," such as changing village names and the "Hellenization" of Slavic names in the region of Greek Macedonia (see Danforth 1995: 160–2) or the current spate of coffee shops being named "Vergina" all across Greece.

34. Brow 1990: 3. See also Valeri's (1990) discussion of syntagmatic and paradigmatic historical structures, and the effectiveness of positing the past as both exemplar and as the result of a temporal chain.

35. This raises the interesting issue of the awareness of national politicians of this connection between local and national naming. At this point I can only speculate on this matter, (and consign it to further study) since politicians would have even more reason than Kalymnians to deny the connection bet-ween "custom" and international politics. Yet I think there is reason to believe that this is the subtext for politicians as it is for villagers, since many of these politicians face similar issues of naming and intergenerational continuity in their own lives. But another factor to be considered is the fact that many of

these politicians come from mainland Greece where the connection of naming and inheritance is less direct and obvious.

36. Danforth does not ignore kinship in his analysis of the Macedonian question. He employs David Schneider's distinction between kinship "by blood" and "by law" in Western ideology to show how Aegean Macedonians in Australia negotiate their ethnic identity and the conundrum of how a woman "can give birth to one Greek and one Macedonian" (1995: 222 ff.). While my material does not contradict Danforth's discussion, it attempts to take it further by rooting the issue in the specifics of Greek kinship/naming/ inheritance practices, rather than in a generalized sense of Western kinship.

Conclusion

"I went to Greece a few years ago and loved it," my American guest, a classicist whom I was meeting for the first time, told me. "But I still can't understand this obsession of the Greeks with antiquity. Why do they stay glued to it, instead of accepting who they are today?" "Who are the Greeks today?" I asked. There was silence . . .

(Panourgia 1995: 29)

So long as the past and the present are outside one another, knowledge of the past is not of much use in the problems of the present. But suppose the past lives on in the present; suppose, though encapsulated in it, and at first sight hidden beneath the present's contradictory and more prominent features, it is still alive and active . . .

(R. G. Collingwood, *An Autobiography*)

Dangerous Histories

This ethnography has sought to capture some of the ways that Kalymnians see the past as alive and active in the present. It is an account of the cultural specificities of historical consciousness, evidenced in distinctive, pluralized discourses in which past events and practices are continually evoked to inform present-day interpretations. A sense of historicity is ever-present. I also emphasize their debates about the significance and value of different aspects of their past, especially in consideration of the world beyond Kalymnos and their position within it. It became clear to me that history for Kalymnians is part of the process by which they define their orientations to this wider world. I show in this book, the different ways that the past is remembered, mobilized or denied, both on home ground and in response to the national and international media.

In such a view, history has the potential to be dangerous to the present. History is dangerous to the present when, in Collingwood's words, it is not cut off, i.e. commodified for tourist consumption, museumified, made an object of nostalgia. Understanding the relevance of the past means more than simply reconstructing the hidden histories of those omitted from dominant national or local historical narratives. It means charting the different modes of a given people's historical consciousness, the different ways that people establish connections between past and present. Kalymnian insistence on engaging the past in everyday life goes beyond the construction of a "politics of identity" at the national, sub-national or personal level. Their "obsession" with the past entails a much broader range of concerns, and stems from their belief that history represents a storehouse of themes and patterns, revealing motivations that constitute important ingredients of the present. Thus in their view it is not sufficient to interpret current events as the random outcome of "free market forces," as has become the fashion in recent years in the US and much of Western Europe (see Carrier 1997).[1]

In the ethnographic context of present-day China, anthropologist Mayfair Yang provides a parallel example of the difference it makes when the past is connected to or cut off from the present. She queries a Chinese official over why she was forbidden to study Chinese ancestor cults, even though similar rituals could be broadcast on national television (1996: 97):

> In the confident paternalistic manner of officials, he replied that the Confucian ceremonies are now separated from any living lineage organization. "It is a historical activity by now. It's all right to 'appreciate' (*xinshang*) and study lineage as a historical phenomenon of the past, but not as a living thing in the present."

As Yang glosses it: "tradition is still visible [for the state], not as a living field of action, but as a neutralized and inert object of contemplation." My findings on Kalymnos concur with this assessment, where some would restrict the consideration of tradition to old costumes and dances, and of history to eulogies for past heroes, but for others it is a "living thing." I would further add that "history," for the centers of power East or West, is "irrational" and "tribalistic" when it is claimed as a resource by those far from these centers. It is acceptable and understandable when it is controlled through state ritual, or sold for tourist consumption. It is also acceptable when it is constructed from above, as in the case of recent attempts by the European Union to forge a common history which is plural rather than conflictual, a "European heritage" supposedly based on shared values of democracy, justice and liberty (see Shore 1995), but which in fact elides the long history of economic and political power imbalances which allow some countries to be considered more "European" while others are identified as "Balkan."[2]

Living in a small country on the margins of Europe appears to entail having one's knowledge dismissed by journalists, Euro-bureaucrats and other opinion-makers, as "backward" and irrelevant to the wider business of constructing "European identity." Or it may simply be ignored. Gourgouris has commented on the complete absence of modern Greece from discussions of the future of Europe, in Western Europe, the United States, and across the political spectrum. He likens modern Greece to the "embarrassing family secret" of Europe (Gourgouris 1992b). This embarrassing secret, I believe – like the silence provoked by Panourgia's question to an American Classical scholar "Who are the Modern Greeks?" – focusses attention on the difficulty posed for westerners by any place which claims a "living history:" of honored names, explosive rituals, or stone-casting, rock-hard women.

Identity and Difference – Local and Global

In her ethnography of the Beng of the Ivory Coast, Alma Gottlieb argues for the centrality of identity and difference as key contradictory principles "at the very core of the social order" (1992: 15). Issues of identity and difference have also preoccupied my analysis. Kalymnians struggle to distinguish themselves, in different ways, from other islanders, neighboring Turks, Athenians, Europeans and Americans. Although 'modernity' often provides the terms of this discourse, I have shown the way Kalymnians give the term their own specific inflection and creative reformulation. "Difference" is explored in their historical narratives, in their use of themes of betrayal and infighting which they believe are distinctively characteristic of Greek experience. In other ways, these historical narratives indicate perceived similarities: between Greeks and Serbs in their sense of themselves as "underdogs," and more subtly, or unconsciously, between Greeks and Yugoslav Macedonians, in their mutual concern for continuity through naming. The feeling of identification and similarity is extended to predicaments of oppressor and oppressed throughout the world, which Kalymnians perceive to be at the heart of unequal power relations. Thus the phrase "they play games at our expense" can expand and contract to include a "they" of local and national politicians or international corporations, and an "our" of Kalymnians, Greeks, or powerless peoples worldwide. The fact that Kalymnians at times stress their own distinctiveness and at times stress human similarities should not, I think, be seen as a logical contradiction. Rather it reflects the context-specific nature of affirming identity, the shifting boundaries of insiderhood and outsiderhood, and the differing perspectives on continuity and change, which must remain a central contribution of anthropological analysis.

Kalymnian views of similarity and difference also help unlock their understandings of historical continuity and change. As with "tradition" and "modernity," dichotomized approaches to continuity and change, "linear" and "cyclical" time, can only impoverish analysis.[3] Kalymnian narratives of the past help free us from these dichotomized views by focussing our attention on the necessary interplay of continuity and change, repetition and difference. This idea is captured by Steven Jay Gould in his book *Time's Arrow, Time's Cycle* (1987) as "repetition with difference," or "time as spiral." In Kalymnian historical consciousness one must always be alert to the common themes that give the past its form as story, while simultaneously focussing on the distinctive aspects of any event which mean it is worth narrating. The power of appeals to the past can be found in the very tension between perceptions of similarity and perceptions of difference.

Issues of change and continuity are prominent in Hannerz's (1996) discussion of "Locals" and "Cosmopolitans" in a transnational world. Hannerz argues that Nigerians who carry dried fish in their clothing on airplanes to London, and bundles of frozen fish-sticks back with them to Lagos, are not Cosmopolitans. The fish-sticks, he notes, are easily assimilated in Nigeria, and "do not alter structures of meaning," thus they reproduce continuity instead of being open to change. No doubt Hannerz would similarly deny the label "Cosmopolitan" to Anne Tyler's "Accidental Tourist," who is forever trying to reproduce a sense of home while abroad. Instead Hannerz defines Cosmopolitanism as "an orientation, a willingness to engage with the Other. It entails an intellectual and esthetic openness toward divergent cultural experiences" (1996: 103). This notion of the globalization of the imagination is what leads some to study the imagined community of the Internet. I am reminded here of the claim of a Kalymnian woman who had never travelled further than Athens that "the whole world has eaten at our table." This phrase captures both a sense that this woman has come to know the world, its events and its peoples, its similarities and differences, through her kitchen table, but also that she has encompassed this world by providing the hospitality which makes world travellers dependent on her cooking.

Yet at the same time the "world" has clearly not uniformly embraced difference, or "intellectual and esthetic openness" as ultimate values. For part of the very process of globalization is not de-territorialization but re-territorialization: the ways that people in the midst of movement and rapid change, are looking for continuity, "*are looking for firm ground under their feet*" (Thomassen 1996: 44; emphasis in original).[4] In attempting to reproduce familiar structures of meaning in a changing world, are Kalymnians consigned to the status of "Locals," or worse, Yokels, as Hannerz's typology might suggest? I would argue against such a conclusion – a concern for identity and roots does not preclude an engagement with difference or a useful perspective on global issues. Thus perhaps the transnational imagination is not only found in airport lounges, border regions or on the Internet. Nor is it merely a matter of an attitude of "openness" toward the other. It is a condition in which peoples living on the peripheries of the peripheries of power feel the need and the competence to understand and comment on issues occurring around the globe. Whether they are reflecting on the ironies of European integration, on the loss of sociability that makes up Western "modernity," or the great power game-playing characteristic of the New World Order, Kalymnians, like other marginal populations, are not simply reproducing their own myths and realities, their own "local structures of meaning" in Hannerz's phrase. They are speaking to the shared realities of our current world. Hence the need for "globally situated conversations."

Everyday Pasts

Kalymnian uses of the past are clearly not always "different" from more familiar ways of knowing, as I observe in my discussion of Kalymnian views of character as embodied in history. Other parallels could also be drawn between, for example, Kalymnian views of "the great exemplars" and the "great men" theories of history popular in the West. However, it is not in the individual pieces that we find the interesting "cultural" differences, to use a term many anthropologists, perhaps unfairly, now seek to avoid.[5] It is in their combination that the many different beliefs and practices of the past take on their richness and their thematic logic. It is the specific way that some of these "similar" beliefs are localized on Kalymnos, translated through metaphor, through ritual, and through other everyday practices into the stuff of people's consciousness that is of interest. And it is only through an understanding of these many different attitudes and practices that we can achieve a sense of why the past seems so relevant in any discussion of politics. It is this cultural difference that caused Panourgia's American friend to perceive Greeks as "obsessed" with the past, and still causes Kalymnians to view Americans as "having their eyes in front" (έχετε τα μάτια μπροστά).

Kalymnian historical consciousness inheres in everyday, sensuous experience, and it is often from this everyday experience that reference to the past takes its power. In arguing this, I concur with Jean and John Comaroff's (1992: 176) definition of consciousness:

> consciousness is best understood as the active process – sometimes implicit, sometimes explicit – in which human actors deploy historically salient cultural categories to construct their self-awareness . . . and it is as crucial to explore the forms in which a people choose to speak and act as it is to examine the content of their messages.

Dynamite throwing is one such active process of historical consciousness by which Kalymnians speak and act. With its rich sensory associations and its close ties to Easter, Greece's central national/ religious holiday, dynamite throwing might seem an ideal object for appropriation by national history. But while island leaders try to restrict dynamite throwing to a limited expression of Kalymnian nationalist sentiment, it has proven to have more explosive implications. Dynamite throwing raises pressing questions about the values of "modernization," a term which provokes many ambivalences for Kalymnians. And the history that it refers to and embodies suggests a willingness on the part of many Kalymnians to go to extremes against any outside interference in their island.

Like dynamite, present-day gender relations became a battleground for different sorts of remembering, forgetting and reclassifying of past events and practices. *Longue durée* practices such as dowry and first daughter inheritance are placed alongside climactic events such as the "Rock War." But memories of these events (apologies for my title) are anything but "cast in stone." It is in light of such past practices, and international discourses on gender relations, that Kalymnian men and women attempt to make sense of their competing present-day visions of "matriarchy" and "patriarchy." Through their discussions and manipulations of such local practices Kalymnians confront the large-scale, worldwide changes affecting their lives. Dynamite and dowry form a commentary, sometimes bitter and sometimes humorous, on those changes and continuities both within and outside of their control.

Even in a country that claims to remember the most painful of its pasts (as Seferis expresses it in his poem *In the Manner of G.S.* "Wherever I travel, Greece wounds me") some pasts will always be ruled as irrelevant, to be forgotten or not included as part of one's current identity. Despite the active historical consciousness of Kalymnians and other Greeks, specific histories have been repressed in Greece, as elsewhere. In the case of the histories of the Greek resistance in the Second World War and the Greek Civil War, considerable recuperation has occurred.[6] For the histories of Greece's minorities, for example, it remains to be seen whether they will become part of public discourse. In the Kalymnian context, I examined the way that the system of first daughter inheritance, important as it may have been in creating the conditions for "matriarchy" on Kalymnos, is not regarded as a useful memory for young women today, who strive to attain ideals of "equality" and greater participation in the "public" domain of island life. The Rock War, with its images of collective female action, may, by contrast, still serve these young women well. But it must first be wrested from the memories of Kalymnian men intent on redefining it in quite different, less threatening terms. The possibility of such a recuperation depends on questions such as whether ordinary women feel they can speak authoritatively about their own experiences, and pass that knowledge on to a younger generation. Another issue is the perceived validity of the memories of "illiterate" women when placed in opposition to authoritative history. In the case of women's experience of the Greek resistance to German occupation, the record is questionable. As Marion Sarafis, widow of communist resistance commander Stefanos Sarafis, observes, "I had been struck by the way knowledge had *not* been passed on, as I saw it in Greek students . . . I had concluded that because of post Civil War persecution, for a whole generation parents had just not talked to their children about past history" (cited in Hart 1996: 285). Yet, one is equally struck by the fact that a recent survey of Greek teenage boys at an evening high school (νυχτερινό σχολείο) found that their most commonly chosen idol was Che Guevara.[7]

In discussing the categories of "history," and "heritage" I argue that gender and age differences do not result in marked differences in the interpretive schemes Kalymnians draw upon. These are largely shared by all, despite the fact that the categories "history" and "histories" do themselves have gender implications. In making this claim, I set myself against recent research claiming to uncover a distinct woman's history in Inner Mani, or a "poetics of womanhood" in mountain Crete.[8] Clearly variations within Greece can account for some of these differences. The prominence of matrilocal residence and matrilineal inheritance on Kalymnos (and other Dodecanese islands) makes women part of the "structure" of kinship relations, rather than peripheral "others" brought into the family group as in the case, described in many earlier ethnographies, where residence is patrilocal. This suggests that an alternative gender-specific "poetics" will be less pronounced where gender inequalities are not so marked. However, the very fact that Kalymnian women have greater relative power and few restrictions on their discourse ironically seems to make it easier for them to embrace the patriarchal discourses of the state. But such conclusions should be treated as tentative for there are issues of methodology here. It is possible that a distinct "poetics of manhood" or "womanhood" is easier to discern when the ethnographic focus is overwhelmingly concentrated on one sex. Further research might pursue this question more systematically through interviews with male and female students in high-school history classes, or through large-scale collections of men's and women's views of some of the significant events of this century: both those that directly affected Kalymnos and those that did not. More historical research is clearly required on Kalymnos and elsewhere in the Aegean to help disentangle questions of the workings of first daughter inheritance, its relationship to seafaring and other forms of male absence, and the complex nature of gender relations during these earlier periods in island history.[9]

"On Kalymnos you meet history."[10] But it is not a history that has been preserved or frozen for the admiration of future generations. It is a living past that seeps into the cracks of the present. I have tried here to show the many ways that the past forms an inextricable part of Kalymnian interpretations of the present. My exploration of the ways Kalymnians historicize the present made me increasingly aware of the very different ways in which the past is treated in the United States. For Kalymnians the past has the potential, described by Walter Benjamin, of being seized "as it flashes up at a moment of danger" (1968: 255). This image sounds as if it were written to describe the sight of dynamite exploding from the mountains of Kalymnos harbor. While in the United States, where one commentator recently claimed that "history is toast,"[11] we ignore the relevance of our explosive pasts at our own risk.

Notes

1. As I have noted throughout it is not my intention to essentialize or "occidentalize" attitudes toward the past in the West. Rather I mean to suggest dominant attitudes found in the international media and Western popular culture for the purpose of heuristic contrast. For an interesting view of "occidentalism" from the perspective of a Cypriot ethnography, see Argyrou (1996: chapter 6).

2. See e.g. Samuel Huntington's (1996) depiction of Christian Orthodoxy as antithetical to Western values. This view is strangely echoed by anthropologists Goddard, Llobera and Shore, who suggest the possibility of drawing cultural correlations between, on the one hand, protestantism, liberalism, and economic development, and on the other, Orthodoxy [Christian], authoritarianism and economic underdevelopment, "with Catholicism somewhere in between" (1994: 25).

3. For too long these categories have been seen in just such binary terms. On the one hand we have presumptions of absolute continuity in primordialist and nationalist understandings of identity, and in structuralist views of reproduction and of history as "cold," "cyclical" and repetitious. On the other hand we have the view of absolute difference and incommensurability, epitomized in "modernist" views of tradition and modernity, such as Gellner (1983) and much recent work that focusses on "debunking" nationalism.

4. See e.g. the essays on transnational migration in Fog Olwig and Hastrup (1997); Sutton and Chaney (1986).

5. See Brightman's (1995) recent discussion of criticisms of the "culture" concept in anthropology. As he argues, these criticisms often operate by for-

"As it flashes up in a moment of danger" – Walter Benjamin.

getting the complex history of "culture" in anthropology, and claiming that the concept locks us into certain understandings belied by a more subtle reading of anthropology's own history.

6. See e.g. Hart 1996.

7. The top idols chosen by boys were respectively Che Guevara, Albert Einstein, Alexander the Great and Nelson Mandela. Girls chose Tom Cruise, Nelson Mandela, Jim Morrison, Melina Mercouri, Marlon Brando, Sharon Stone, Che Guevara and the Greek female Revolutionary War hero Bouboulina (Dede and Sotirhou 1997). Whether these choices reflect an actual concern with the past, or the way politics serves as popular culture in Greece, or both, deserves further study.

8. See respectively Seremetakis 1991 and Herzfeld 1991.

9. Suggestive work in this direction has been begun in articles by Vernier (1987); Dimitriou-Kotsoni (1993) and Papataxiarchis (1995). What is needed now is more large-scale, interdisciplinary studies, along the lines of Sant-Cassia's (1992) work on dowry contracts in nineteenth-century Athens.

10. Nektarios 1986.

11. Safire 1997. William Safire is playing on different metaphors of irrelevance in US popular culture. Irrelevance used to be marked by the expression "that's history." As critic Greil Marcus (1995: 22) explains the phrase:

It means there is no such thing as history, a past of burden and legacy. Once something (a love affair broken off, a fired baseball manager, a war, Jimmy Carter) is "history," it's *over*, and it is understood that it never existed at all.

Safire notes that similar meanings are now more commonly expressed by the phrase "you're toast," or the more recent "you're roadkill," as in a reference to Newt Gingrich as "roadkill on the highway of American politics," as well as the even trendier expression "roadkill on the information superhighway."

References Cited

Note: *Works in Greek are given translated titles and marked with an asterisk. Unpublished works, cited with authorial permission, are marked with a double asterisk (**).*

Agapitidis, Sotiris (1986), "Population Developments in the Dodecanese", *Dodecanesian Chronicles* 11: 9–34*

Aigaios, Yiannis (1992), *At Dieni and Other Stories.* Athens: Domos*

Allen, Peter (1986), "Female Inheritance, Housing, and Urbanization in Greece", *Anthropology* 10: 1–18

Alonso, Ana Maria (1994), "The Politics of Space, Time and Substance: State Formation, Nationalism and Ethnicity", *Annual Review of Anthropology* 23: 379–405

Alterman, Eric (1997), "Bosnian Camps: A Barbed Tale", *The Nation* 28 July/4 August.

Anawack, Jack (1989), "Inuit Perceptions of the Past", in Robert Layton (ed.), *Who Needs the Past? Indigenous Values and Archaeology*, 45–50. London: Unwin Hyman

Anderson, Benedict (1991), *Imagined Communities: Reflections on the Origin and Spread of Nationalism*, (Revised edition), London: Verso

Apostolopoulos, A. (1992), "War and Peace", *Avgi*, 21 June*

Apoyevmatini (1992), "Proof for Balkaners", 26 June*

Appadurai, Arjun (1981), "The Past as a Scarce Resource", *Man*, 16: 201–19

Argo Tis Kalymnou (1992), "Marks: The Women of Kalymnos", 8 December*

—— (1994), "The Theft of 7,000 Fireworks Seriously Defamed Kalymnos", 7 April*

Argyrou, Vassos (1996), *Tradition and Modernity in the Mediterranean: The Wedding as Symbolic Struggle*, Cambridge: Cambridge University Press

Augustinos, Gerasimos (1992), *The Greeks of Asia Minor: Confession, Community and Ethnicity in the Nineteenth Century*, Kent, Ohio: Kent State University Press

BBC (1994), "Report on Admiral Perry's Visit to the Balkans", *Mak-News Bulletin Board [Online]*, Available e-mail:MAKNWS-L–UBVM.CC.BUFFALO.EDU, 4 August

213

Badone, Ellen (1992), "The Construction of National Identity in Brittany and Quebec" (review of Handler and McDonald), *American Ethnologist* 19: 806–17

Bakalaki, Alexandra (1994), "Gender Related Discourses and Representations of Cultural Specificity in Nineteenth-Century and Twentieth-Century Greece", *Journal of Modern Greek Studies* 12: 75–112

Behar, Ruth (1986), *Santa Maria del Monte: The Presence of the Past in a Spanish Village*, Princeton: Princeton University Press

Ben-Amos, Dan (1976), "Analytical Categories and Ethnic Genres", in Dan Ben-Amos (ed.), *Folklore Genres* 215–42, Austin: University of Texas Press

Benjamin, Walter (1968), "Theses on the Philosophy of History", in *Illuminations* 253–64, translated by Harry Zohn, New York: Shocken Books

Bennett, Diane (1988), "'The Poor Have Much More Money': Changing Socio-Economic Relations in a Greek Village", *Journal of Modern Greek Studies* 6: 217–44

Bernard, H. Russell (1976a), "The Fisherman and his Wife", in W. Menard and J. Scheiber (eds), *Oceans: Our Continuing Frontier*, 304–9, Del Mar, California: Publisher's Inc

—— (1976b), "Kalymnos: The Island of the Sponge Fishermen", in Muriel Dimen and Ernestine Friedl (eds), *Regional Variation in Modern Greece and Cyprus: Toward a Perspective on the Ethnography of Greece* 291–307, New York: Annals of the New York Academy of Sciences

—— (1987), "Sponge Fishing and Technological Change in Greece", in H. R. Bernard and P. J. Pelto (eds), *Technology and Social Change* 168–206, Prospect Heights, Illinois: Waveland Press

Bialor, Perry (1967), "What's in a Name? Aspects of the Social Organization of a Greek Farming Community Related to its Naming Customs", in W. Lockwood (ed.), *Essays in Balkan Ethnology*, Berkeley: Kroeber Anthropological Society Publications 1: 95–108

Billiri, Niki (1982), *Our Kalymnos*, Athens*

—— (1986), *Of Sea and Land*, Athens*

Bloch, Maurice (1977), "The Past and the Present in the Present", *Man* 12: 278–92

Bodnar, John (1992), *Remaking America: Public Memory, Commemoration and Patriotism in the Twentieth Century*, Princeton: Princeton University Press

Booth, C. D. and I. B. Booth (1928), *Italy's Aegean Possessions*, London: Arrowsmith

Borneman, John (1992), *Belonging in the Two Berlins: Kin, State, Nation*, Cambridge: Cambridge University Press

Bosworth, R. J. B. (1979), *Italy, the Least of the Great Powers: Italian Foreign Policy Before the First World War*, Cambridge: Cambridge University Press

Bourdieu, Pierre (1966), "The Sentiment of Honour in Kabyle Society", in John G. Peristiany (ed.), *Honour and Shame: The Values of Mediterranean Society* 193–241, Chicago: University of Chicago Press

—— (1977), *Outline of a Theory of Practice*, Cambridge: Cambridge University Press

Bouvard, Marguerite G. (1994), *Revolutionizing Motherhood: The Mothers of the Plaza de Mayo*, Wilmington, Delaware: Scholarly Resources Inc

Brightman, Robert (1995), "Forget Culture: Replacement, Transcendence, Relexification", *Cultural Anthropology* 10: 509–46

Brow, James (1990), "Notes on Community, Hegemony, and the Uses of the Past", *Anthropological Quarterly* 63: 1–5

Brown, James (1991), "Turkey and the Persian Gulf Crisis", *Mediterranean Quarterly* 2(2): 46–56

Brown, Keith (1994), "Seeing Stars: Character and Identity in the Landscapes of Modern Macedonia", *Antiquity* 68: 784–96

—— (1995a), *Of Meanings and Memories: The National Imagination in Macedonia*, Doctoral Dissertation, Department of Anthropology, University of Chicago

—— (1995b), *The Oldest Profession: Post-Yugoslav Macedonian Historiography*, Paper presented at the American Association for the Advancement of Slavic Studies meetings, Washington DC, 27 October**

Buck-Morss, Susan (1987), "Semiotic Boundaries and the Politics of Meaning: Modernity on Tour – a Village in Transition", in Marcus Raskin and Herbert Bernstein (eds), *New Ways of Knowing* 200–36, Totowa, New Jersey: Rowman and Littlefield

Campbell, John (1964), *Honour, Family, and Patronage: A Study of Institutions and Moral Values in a Greek Mountain Community*, Oxford: Clarendon Press

—— (1966), "Honour and the Devil", in John G. Peristiany (ed.), *Honour and Shame: The Values of Mediterranean Society* 139–70, Chicago: University of Chicago Press

Caraveli, Anna (1986), "The Bitter Wounding: The Lament as Social Protest in Rural Greece", in Jill Dubisch (ed.), *Gender and Power in Rural Greece* 169–94, Princeton: Princeton University Press

Carrier, James (ed.), (1997), *Meanings of the Market: The Free Market in Western Culture*, Oxford: Berg

Casselbery, S. E., and N. Valvanes (1975), "'Matrilocal' Greek Peasants and a Reconsideration of Residence Terminology", *American Ethnologist* 3: 215–26

Clogg, Richard (1986), *A Short History of Modern Greece*, Cambridge: Cambridge University Press

—— (1992), *A Concise History of Greece*, Cambridge: Cambridge University Press

Collard, Anna (1989), "Investigating 'Social Memory' in a Greek Context", in Elizabeth Tonkin, Maryon McDonald and Malcolm Chapman (eds), *History and Ethnicity* 89–103, London: Routledge

Collingwood, R. G. (1939), *An Autobiography*, London: Oxford University Press

Collins, James (1995), "Literacy and Literacies", *Annual Review of Anthropology* 24: 75–93

Comaroff, John, and Jean Comaroff (1987), "The Madman and the Migrant: Work and Labor in the Historical Consciousness of a South African People", *American Ethnologist* 14: 191–209

—— (1992), *Ethnography and the Historical Imagination*, Boulder: Westview Press

Comaroff, John, and Jean Comaroff (eds), (1993), *Modernity and its Malcontents*, Chicago: University of Chicago Press

Connerton, Paul (1989), *How Societies Remember*, Cambridge: Cambridge University Press

Coufoudakis, Van (1987), "Greek Foreign Policy, 1945–85: Seeking Independence in an Interdependent World – Problems and Prospects", in Kevin Featherstone and Dimitrios Katsoudas (eds), *Political Change in Greece: Before and After the Colonels* 230–52, New York: St. Martin's Press

Couloumbis, T., Petropoulos, J., and H. Psomiadis (1976), *Foreign Intervention in Greek Politics: An Historical Perspective*, New York: Pella

Cowan, Jane (1988), "Folk Truth: When the Scholar Comes to Carnival in a 'Traditional' Community", *Journal of Modern Greek Studies* 6: 245–60

—— (1990), *Dance and the Body Politic in Northern Greece*, Princeton: Princeton University Press

—— (1992), "Japanese Ladies and Mexican Hats: Contested Symbols and the Politics of Tradition in a Northern Greek Carnival Celebration", in Jeremy Boissevan (ed.), *Revitalizing European Rituals* 173–97, London: Routledge

—— (1996), "Being a Feminist in Contemporary Greece: Similarity and Difference Reconsidered", in Nicki Charles and Felicia Hughes-Freeland (eds), *Practicing Feminism: Identity, Difference, Power* 61–85, London: Routledge

Danforth, Loring M. (1982), *The Death Rituals of Rural Greece*, Princeton: Princeton University Press

—— (1984), "The Ideological Context of the Search for Continuities in Greek Culture", *Journal of Modern Greek Studies* 2: 53–87

—— (1993), "Claims to Macedonian Identity", *Anthropology Today* 9: 3–10

—— (1995), *The Macedonian Conflict: Ethnic Nationalism in a Transnational World*, Princeton: Princeton University Press

Davis, John (1989), "The Social Relations of the Production of History", in Elizabeth Tonkin, Maryon McDonald and Malcolm Chapman (eds), *History and Ethnicity* 104–20, London: Routledge

Dede, Maria, and Ioanna Sotirhou (1997), "Night Schools: Tom Cruise and Che", *Eleftherotipia* 18 January: 23*

Delaney, Carol (1995), "Father State, Motherland, and the Birth of Modern Turkey", In *Naturalizing Power* 177–99, Sylvia Yanagisako and Carol Delaney (eds), London: Routledge

Denich, Bette (1994), "Dismembering Yugoslavia: Nationalist Ideologies and the Symbolic Revival of Genocide", *American Ethnologist* 21: 367–90

—— (1995), "Of Arms, Men and Ethnic War in (Former), Yugoslavia", In Constance Sutton (ed.), *Feminism, Nationalism, Militarism* 61–71, Washington DC: American Anthropological Association (Association for Feminist Anthropology)

Di Bella, Maria P. (1992), "Name, Blood and Miracles: The Claims to Renown in Traditional Sicily", in John G. Peristiany and Julian Pitt-Rivers (eds), *Honor and Grace in Anthropology* 153–65, Cambridge: Cambridge University Press

Diamandouros, P. Nikiforos (1993), "Politics and Culture in Greece, 1974–91: An Interpretation", in Richard Clogg (ed.), *Greece 1981–89: The Populist Decade*, New York: St. Martins Press.

Dimen, Muriel (1986), "Servants and Sentries: Women, Power and Social Reproduction in Kriovrisi", in Jill Dubisch (ed.), *Gender and Power in Rural Greece* 53–67, Princeton: Princeton University Press

Dimitriou-Kotsoni, Sibylla (1993), "The Aegean Cultural Tradition", *Journal of Mediterranean Studies* 3: 62–76

Dimokratiki Kalymnos (1980), Letters to the Editor, 31 May*

—— (1983), Letters to the Editor, 31 October*

Dimou, Nikos (1976), *The Misfortune of Being Greek*, Athens: Ikaros*

Diotsos, H. (1992), "Let's Govern Ourselves: Interview with Lakis Lazopoulos", *To Ethnos*, 20 April*

Doumanis, Nicholas (1997), *Myth and Memory in the Mediterranean: Remembering Fascism's Empire*, London: MacMillan

—— (n.d.), *Nationalism, History and Hegemony: Women's Protest in a Former Italian Colony (1935), and the Politics of Memory*, manuscript**

Drakos, Nikolas (1982), *On Kalymnos The Day Before Yesterday and the Day Before That*, "The Muses" literary publication series 8, Athens*

Dubisch, Jill (1974), "The Domestic Power of Women in a Greek Island Village", *Studies in European Society* 1: 23–33.

—— (1986), "Culture Enters Through the Kitchen: Women, Food and Social Boundaries in Rural Greece", in Jill Dubisch (ed.), *Gender and Power in Rural Greece* 195–214, Princeton: Princeton University Press

—— (1991), "Gender, Kinship and Religion: 'Reconstructing' the Anthropology of Greece", in Peter Loizos and Evthimios Papataxiarchis (eds), *Contested Identities: Gender and Kinship in Modern Greece* 29–46, Princeton: Princeton University Press

—— (1995), *In a Different Place: Pilgrimage, Gender, and Politics at a Greek Island Shrine*, Princeton: Princeton University Press

du Boulay, Juliet (1974), *Portrait of a Greek Mountain Village*, Oxford: Clarendon

—— (1986), "Women–Images of Their Nature and Destiny in Rural Greece", in Jill Dubisch (ed.), *Gender and Power in Rural Greece* 139–68, Princeton: Princeton University Press

Durrell, Lawrence (1953), *Reflections on a Marine Venus: A Companion to the Landscape of Rhodes*, London: Faber and Faber

The Economist (1993), Special Supplement on Greece, 22 May

Eikonomidis, Nikos (1993), "Byzantines and Serbs in the fourteenth Century", *To Vima*, 10 November*

Eisler, Rianne (1987), *The Chalice and the Blade: Our History, Our Future*, Cambridge: Harper and Row

Elefantis, Angelos (1992), "The Macedonian Question: From National Glorification to the Margins", *The Citizen* 120: 28–36*

Estevez-Weber, Leda (1983), *From Family Endowment to Self Endowment: The Dowry in Relationship to the Changing Roles of Women and Men among Messenian Migrants to Athens in Post-War Greece*, Ph.D. Dissertation, New York University

Evert, Miltiadis (1991), "Emerging Power Balances in the Mediterranean", *Mediterranean Quarterly* 2(3): 9–14

Fabian, Johannes (1983), *Time and the Other: How Anthropology Makes its Object*, New York: Columbia University Press

Fernandez, James (1986), *Persuasions and Performances: The Play of Tropes in Culture*, Bloomington: Indiana University Press

Fisher, Jo (1989), *Mothers of the Disappeared*, London: Zed Books

Fog Olwig, Karen, and Kirsten Hastrup (eds), (1997), *Siting Culture: The Shifting Anthropological Object*, London: Routledge

Foster, Robert (1991), "Making National Cultures in the Global Ecumene", *Annual Review of Anthropology* 20: 235–60

Fox, James (1979), "'Standing' in Time and Place: The Structure of Rotinese Historical Narratives", in Anthony Reid and David Marr (eds), *Perceptions of the Past in Southeast Asia* 10–25, Singapore: Heinemann

Frangopoulos, Hippocratis (1952), *History of Kalymnos, vols 1–3*, Athens*

—— (1986), "Resistance Organizations in the Dodecanese During the Second World War", *Kalymnian Chronicles* 6: 69–73*

—— (1994), "Bends in the Dodecanese Road Toward Freedom", *Kalymnian Chronicles* 11: 77–85*

Frangopoulou, Irini (1988), "The Legal Position of Women in Kalymnos During the Years of Roman Occupation", *Kalymnian Chronicles* 7: 100–5*

Friedl, Ernestine (1962), *Vasilika: A Village in Modern Greece*, New York: Holt, Rinehart and Winston

—— (1986), "The Position of Women: Appearance and Reality", In Jill Dubisch (ed.), *Gender and Power in Rural Greece* 42–52, Princeton: Princeton University Press

Friedman, Jonathan (1992), "The Past in the Future: History and the Politics of Identity", *American Anthropologist* 94: 837–59

—— (1996), "The Politics of De-Authentification: Escaping from Identity, A Response to 'Beyond Authenticity' by Mark Rogers", *Identities* 3: 127–36

Fukuyama, Francis (1992), *The End of History and the Last Man*, London: Hamish Hamilton

Garganas, Panos (1992), "Macedonia: New Chauvinist Mobilization", *The Crisis in the Balkans: The Macedonian Question and the Working Class*, International Socialist Organization pamphlet translated by Mark Matcott

Galani-Moutafi, Vasiliki (1993), "From Agriculture to Tourism: Property, Labor, Gender and Kinship in a Greek Island Village (Part One)", *Journal of Modern Greek Studies* 11: 241–70

Gavrilis, George (1997), "Reluctant Europeans: Greek Identity in the Context of the Macedonian Impasse", *Replika* 8: forthcoming

Geertz, Clifford (1987), *Works and Lives: The Anthropologist as Author*, New York: Basic Books

Gellner, Ernest (1983), *Nations and Nationalism*, Oxford: Basil Blackwell.

Glenny, Misha (1993), *The Fall of Yugoslavia: The Third Balkan War*, New York: Penguin

Glick-Schiller, Nina, Linda Basch and Cristina Szanton-Blanc (1995), "From Immigrant to Transmigrant: Theorizing Transnational Migration", *Anthropological Quarterly* 68: 48–63

Goddard, Victoria, Josep Llobera and Chris Shore (eds), (1994), *The Anthropology of Europe: Identities and Boundaries in Conflict*, Oxford: Berg

Goltsis-Rosier, Eleni (1993), *Autobiographical Memories for a Distant Time and Culture: Provincial Greece, 1941*, M.A. Thesis, Department of Psychology, Harvard University**

Goody, Jack (1976), *Production and Reproduction*, Cambridge: Cambridge University Press

Gottlieb, Alma (1992), *Under the Kapok Tree: Identity and Difference in Beng Thought*, Chicago: University of Chicago Press

Gould, Steven Jay (1987), *Time's Arrow, Time's Cycle: Myth and Metaphor in the Discovery of Geological Time*, Cambridge, Massachusetts: Harvard University Press

Gourgouris, Stathis (1992a), "Nationalism and Oneirocriticism: Of Modern Hellenes in Europe", *Diaspora* 2: 43–71

—— (1992b), "'Modern' Greece in the 'Third World'", *Journal of the Hellenic Diaspora* 18: 99–112

Graburn, Nelson (1995), "Tourism, Modernity and Nostalgia", in Akbar Ahmed and Chris Shore (eds), *The Future of Anthropology: Its Relevance to the Contemporary World* 158–78, London: Athlone

Gronborg, Ronni (1979), "Matriarchy – Why Not?" *Folk* 21–2: 219–28

Handler, Richard (1988), *Nationalism and the Politics of Culture in Quebec*, Madison: University of Wisconsin Press

Handler, Richard, and Jocelyn Linnekin (1984), "Tradition, Genuine and Spurious", *Journal of American Folklore* 97: 274–290

Hannerz, Ulf (1989), *Cultural Complexity: Studies in the Social Organization of Meaning*, New York: Columbia University Press

Hanson, F. Allan (1983), "Syntagmatic Structures: How the Maoris Make Sense of History", *Semiotica* 46: 287–307

—— (1989), "The Making of the Maori: Cultural Invention and Its Logic", *American Anthropologist* 91: 890–902

—— (1991), "Reply to Langdon, Levine and Linnekin", *American Anthropologist* 93: 449–50

Hart, Janet (1996), *New Voices in the Nation*, Ithaca: Cornell University Press

Hart, Laurie (1992), *Time, Religion, and Social Experience in Rural Greece*, Lanham, Maryland: Rowman and Littlefield

Harvey, David (1989), *The Condition of Postmodernity*, London: Basil Blackwell

Hayden, Robert (1996), "Imagined Communities and Real Victims: Self-Determination and Ethnic Cleansing in Yugoslavia", *American Ethnologist* 23: 783–801

Herman, Edward, and Noam Chomsky (1988), *Manufacturing Consent: The Political Economy of Mass Media*, New York: Pantheon

Herzfeld, Michael (1980), "The Dowry in Greece: Terminological Usage and Historical Reconstruction", *Ethnohistory* 27: 225–41

—— (1982a), *Ours Once More: Folklore, Ideology and the Making of Modern Greece*, Austin: University of Texas Press

—— (1982b), "When Exceptions Define the Rules: Greek Baptismal Names and the Negotiation of Identity", *Journal of Anthropological Research* 38: 288–302

—— (1985), *The Poetics of Manhood: Contest and Identity in a Cretan Mountain Village*, Princeton: Princeton University Press

—— (1987a), *Anthropology Through the Looking Glass: Critical Ethnography in the Margins of Europe*, Cambridge: Cambridge University Press

—— (1987b), "'As in Your Own House': Hospitality, Ethnography and the Stereotype of Mediterranean Society", in David D. Gilmore (ed.), *Honor and Shame and the Unity of the Mediterranean*, AAA Special

Publications 22, Washington DC: American Anthropological Association

—— (1991), *A Place in History: Social and Monumental Time in a Cretan Town*, Princeton: Princeton University Press

—— (1992a), "History in the Making: National and International Politics in a Rural Cretan Community", in Joao de Pina-Cabral and John Campbell (eds), *Europe Observed* 93–122, London: MacMillan

—— (1992b), *The Social Production of Indifference: Exploring the Symbolic Roots of Western Bureaucracy*, New York: Berg

—— (1992c), "Segmentation and Politics in the European Nation-State: Making Sense of Political Events", in Kirsten Hastrup (ed.), *Other Histories* 62–81, London: Routledge

—— (1995), "It Takes One to Know One: Collective Resentment and Mutual Recognition among Greeks in Local and Global Contexts", in Richard Fardon (ed.), *Counterworks: Managing the Diversity of Knowledge* 124–42, London: Routledge

Hill, Jonathan (1988), "Myth and History", in Jonathan Hill (ed.), *Rethinking History and Myth: Indigenous South American Perspectives on the Past* 1–17, Urbana, Illinois: University of Illinois Press

Hirschon, Renée (1978), "Open Body, Closed Space: The Transformation of Female Sexuality", in Shirley Ardener (ed.), *Defining Females: The Nature of Women in Society* 66–88, London: Croon Helm

—— (1983), "Women, the Aged and Religious Activity: Oppositions and Complementarity in an Urban Locality", *Journal of Modern Greek Studies* 1: 113–29

—— (1989), *Heirs to the Greek Catastrophe*, Oxford: Clarendon Press

—— (1992), "Greek Adults' Verbal Play, or, How to Train for Caution", *Journal of Modern Greek Studies* 10: 35–56

—— (1993), "Memory and Identity: The Asia Minor Refugees of Kokkinia", in Evthimios Papataxiarchis and Theodoros Paradellis (eds), *Anthropology and the Past: Contributions to the Social History of Modern Greece* 327–56, Athens: Alexandreia

—— (1995), *Individuals in the True Sense: The Significance of Personal Celebrations in Contemporary Greece*, Paper presented at the Modern Greek Studies Association Meetings, 3 November**

Hitchens, Christopher (1984), *Hostage to History: Cyprus from the Ottomans to Kissinger*, New York: Farrar, Straus and Giroux

Hobsbawm, Eric and Terence Ranger (eds), (1983), *The Invention of Tradition*, Cambridge: Cambridge University Press

Hoffman, Susannah, Richard Cowan and Paul Aralow (1974), *Kypseli: Women and Men Apart – A Divided Reality* (film), distributed by the University Extension Media Center, University of California, Berkeley

Hourani, Albert (1981), *The Emergence of the Modern Middle East*, Oxford: MacMillan

(Metropolitan), Bishop Hristodoulos (1993), "And Yet it Moves..", *To*

Vima, 27 June*

Huntington, Samuel (1993), "The Clash of Civilizations?" *World Policy Journal* 72: 22–49

—— (1996), *The Clash of Civilizations and the Remaking of World Order*, New York: Simon and Schuster

Ifeka-Moller, Caroline (1975), "Female Militancy and Colonial Revolt: The Women's War of 1929, Eastern Nigeria", in Shirley Ardener (ed.), *Perceiving Women* 127–57, London: J. M. Dent

Iossifides, A. Marina (1992), "Wine: Life's Blood and Spiritual Essence in a Greek Orthodox Convent", in Dimitra Gefou-Madianou, (ed.), *Alcohol, Gender and Culture* 80–100, London: Routledge

Just, Roger (1989), "Triumph of the Ethnos", in Elizabeth Tonkin, Maryon McDonald and Malcolm Chapman, (eds), *History and Ethnicity* 71–88, London: Routledge

—— (1994), "The Reformation of Class", *Journal of Modern Greek Studies* 12: 37–56

—— (1995), "Cultural Certainties and Private Doubts", in Wendy James (ed.), *The Pursuit of Certainties: Religious and Cultural Formulations* 285–307, ASA Decennial Conference, London: Routledge

Kalymnos Today (1997), Periodical Publication of the Kalymnian Mayorality, 1: April*

Kandiyoti, Deniz (1994), "The Paradoxes of Masculinity: Some Thoughts on Segregated Societies", in Andrea Cornwall and Nancy Lindesfarne (eds), *Dislocating Masculinity: Comparative Ethnographies* 197–213, London: Routledge

Kapella, Themelina (1983), *The Refugee Chronicle: Middle East 1943–1945*, Athens: Gnosis*

—— (1986), "The Women's Struggle of 1935 and the Rock War", *Kalymnian Chronicles* 6: 87–102*

—— (1987), *People and Things in Kalymnian Life*, "The Muses" literary publication series 15, Athens*

Kaplan, Robert (1993), *Balkan Ghosts: A Journey Through History*, New York: St. Martin's Press

Karakasidou, Anastasia (1993a), "Fellow Travellers, Separate Roads: The KKE and the Macedonian Question", *East European Quarterly* 27: 453–77

—— (1993b), "Politicizing Culture: Negating Ethnic Identity in Greek Macedonia", *Journal of Modern Greek Studies* 11: 1–28

—— (1994), "Sacred Scholars, Profane Advocates: Intellectuals Molding National Consciousness in Greece", *Identities* 1: 35–62

—— (1997), "Women of the Family, Women of the Nation: National Enculturation among Slav-Speakers in North-west Greece", in Peter Mackridge and Eleni Yannakakis (eds), *Ourselves and Others: The Development of a Greek-Macedonian Cultural Identity Since 1912* 91–110, Oxford: Berg

Kasperson, Roger (1966), *The Dodecanese: Diversity and Unity in Island Politics*, Department of Geography Research paper 108, The University of Chicago

Katris, John (1971), *Eyewitness in Greece: The Colonels Come to Power*, St. Louis: New Critics Press

Kearney, Michael (1995), "The Local and The Global: The Anthropology of Globalism and Transnationalism", *Annual Review of Anthropology* 24: 547–65

Keesing, Roger (1989), "Creating the Past: Custom and Identity in the Contemporary Pacific", *Contemporary Pacific* 1: 19–42

Kemp, Amanda, et al. (1995), The Dawn of a New Day: Redefining South African Feminism, in Amitra Basu (ed.), *The Challenge of Local Feminisms* 131–62, Boulder, Colorado: Westview

Kenna, Margaret (1976), "Houses, Fields and Graves: Property and Ritual Obligation on a Greek Island", *Ethnology* 15: 21–34

Kitromilidis, Paschalis (1990), "'Imagined Communities' and the Origins of the National Question in the Balkans", in Martin Blinkhorn and Thanos Veremis (eds), *Modern Greece: Nationalism and Nationality* 23–66, Athens: Sage-Eliamep

Koester, David (1989), *Saga and Metasaga: Reputation in the Icelandic Conception of Honor*, Paper presented to the Charles Darwin Society, Purdue University, 20 October**

Kofos, Evangelos (1964), *Nationalism and Communism in Macedonia*, Salonica: Institute for Balkan Studies

Korkoli, Anastasia (1990), "Kalymnian Emigration: Theses and Estimations", *Kalymnian Chronicles* 9: 406–17*

Kyriakidou-Nestoros, Alki (1986), "Introduction to Modern Greek Ideology and Folklore", *Journal of Modern Hellenism* 3: 35–46

Lampsas, Yiannis (1992), "Danish Europeanism", *Eleftheros Tipos*, 13 May: 2*

Leacock, Eleanor (1981), *Myths of Male Dominance: Collected Articles on Women Cross-Culturally*, New York: St. Martin's Press

Lee, Dorothy (1959), *Freedom and Culture*, New York: Prentice Hall Inc

Leontis, Artemis (1995), *Topographies of Hellenism: Mapping the Homeland*, Ithaca: Cornell University Press

Liakos, Andonis (1993), "Nationalism and the Balkan Crisis", in *The Janus-Face of Nationalism and Greek Balkan Politics*, Athens: Politis, 9–30*

Linnekin, Jocelyn (1990), "The Politics of Culture in the Pacific", in Jocelyn Linnekin and Lynn Poyer (eds), *Cultural Identity and Ethnicity in the Pacific* 149–73, Honolulu: University of Hawaii Press

—— (1991), "Cultural Invention and the Dilemma of Authenticity", *American Anthropologist* 93: 446–9

Llobera, Josep (1986), "Fieldwork in Southern Europe", *Critique of Anthropology* 6: 25–33

Logothetis, Miltiadis (1983), "Trade in the Southern Sporades (Dode-canese), During the Final Years of Turkish Rule", *Dodecanesian Chronicles* 8: 137–66*

Loizos, Peter (1994), "A Broken Mirror: Masculine Sexuality in Greek Ethnography", in Andrea Cornwall and Nancy Lindesfarne (eds), *Dislocating Masculinity: Comparative Ethnographies* 66–96, London: Routledge

Loizos, Peter, and Evthimios Papataxiarchis (eds), (1991), *Contested Identities: Gender and Kinship in Modern Greece*, Princeton: Princeton University Press

MacDonald, Sharon (ed.), (1992), *Inside European Identities*, Oxford: Berg

Maïllis, Sakellaris (1992), "Kalymnos as a Self-Governing State", *Kalymnian Chronicles* 10: 244–8*

Marcus, George (1993), "Introduction", in George Marcus (ed.), *Perilous States: Conversations on Culture, Politics and Nation* 1–16, Chicago: University of Chicago Press

Marcus, Greil (1995), *The Dustbin of History*, Cambridge, Massachusetts: Harvard University Press

Martis, N., and S. Papathemelis (1992), "Open Letter to De Michelis", *Athens News*, 5 May: 2–3

Mavroidi, Iro (1992), "With The Scandalous Tolerance of the 'Civilized' World: The Spiritual Genocide of the Serbs Continues", *Avgi*, 21 June: 25*

Mba, Nina (1982), *Nigerian Women Mobilized: Women's Political Activism in Southern Nigeria, 1900–1965*, Berkeley: University of California Press

Mertzanis, Fotis (1994), "The Endogenous Dynamism of Kalymnos", *New Ecology*, February: 16.*

Mestrovic, Stjepan (1995), "After Emotion: Ethnic Cleansing in the Former Yugoslavia, and Beyond", in Akbar Ahmed and Chris Shore (eds), *The Future of Anthropology: Its Relevance to the Contemporary World* 251–71, London: Athlone

Mitropoulos, Kostas (1993), "Cartoon", *To Vima*, 20 June*

Moran, Mary (1989), "Collective Action and the 'Representation' of African Women: A Liberian Case Study", *Feminist Studies* 15: 443–60

Mouzavizadeh, Nader (ed), (1996), *The Black Book of Bosnia: The Consequences of Appeasement*, New York: Basic Books

Mouzelis, Nikos (1992), "Greece on the Threshold of the 21st Century: Institutions and Political Culture", *To Vima*, 23 August*

—— (1993), "Nationalism (Part 1)", *To Vima*, 16 May: B4–5*

Munn, Nancy (1990), "Constructing Regional Worlds in Experience: Kula Exchange, Witchcraft and Gawan Local Events", *Man* 25: 1–17

Myers, Linnet (1994), "Serbs' Baffling Defiance Has Ancient Roots", *Chicago Tribune*, 21 July: 1

(Metropolitan) Bishop Nektarios (1986), "Kalymnos" (poem), *Kalymnian Chronicles* 6: 268*

New York Times (1994a), "Mr Clinton's Risk in Macedonia", 30 April: 22

—— (1994b), "Edessa Journal: Real "Macedonia" Issue is Real Estate", 12 March: 4

—— (1995), "In Macedonia, New Fears of a Wider Balkan War", 9 April: 12

Olujic, Maria (1995), "The Croatian War Experience", in Carolyn Nordstrom and Antonius C. G. M. Robben (eds), *Fieldwork Under Fire: Contemporary Studies of Violence and Survival* 185–204, Berkeley: University of California Press

Ong, Aihwa (1996), "Anthropology, China and Modernities: The Geopolitics of Cultural Knowledge", in Henrietta Moore (ed.), *The Future of Anthropological Knowledge* 60–92, London: Routledge

Orthodox Christian Brotherhood Lidia (1993), *Learn Justice*, Pamphlet distributed by the Christian Bookstore "I Alithia," Kalymnos*

Ortner, Sherry (1984), "Theory in Anthropology Since the Sixties", *Comparative Studies in Society and History* 26: 126–66

Panourgia, Neni (1995), *Fragments of Death, Fables of Identity: An Athenian Anthropography*, Madison: University of Wisconsin Press

Papadimitropoulos, Damianos (1993), "The Balkans and Us", in *The Janus-Face of Nationalism and Greek Balkan Politics* 77–94, Athens: Politis*

Papataxiarchis, Evthimios (1995), "Male Mobility and Matrifocality in the Aegean Basin", in S. Damianos et al. (eds), *Brothers and Others: Essays in Honor of John Peristiany* 219–39, Paris: Ecole des Hautes Etudes

Parmentier, Richard (1987), *The Sacred Remains: Myth, History and Polity in Belau*, Chicago: University of Chicago Press

Patellis, Yiannis (1994), "The Period of Greek Statehood in Kalymnos (1828–29)", *Kalymnian Chronicles* 11: 41–9*

Pavlowitch, Stevan (1994), "Who is 'Balkanizing' Whom? The Misunderstandings Between the Debris of Yugoslavia and an Unprepared West", *Daedalus* 123: 203–23

Peel, J. D. Y. (1984), "Making History: The Past in the Ijesha Present", *Man* 19: 111–32

—— (1989), "The Cultural Work of Yoruba Ethnogenesis", in Elizabeth Tonkin, Maryon McDonald and Malcolm Chapman (eds), *History and Ethnicity* 198–215, London: Routledge

Peletz, Michael (1995), "Kinship Studies in Late Twentieth Century Anthropology", *Annual Review of Anthropology* 24: 343–57

Pina-Cabral, Joao de (1989), "The Valuation of Time among the Peasant Population of Alto Minho, Northwestern Portugal", in

Robert Layton (ed.), *Who Needs the Past?* 59–69, London: Unwin Hyman

Ploritis, Marios (1994), "Blockades and Exclusivities", *To Vima*, 17 April: A20*

Politis, Nikos (1993), "One for Us and One for Them", *To Vima*, 18 July*

Pollis, Adamantia (1992), "Gender and Social Change in Greece: The Role of Women", in Theodore Kariotis (ed.), *The Greek Socialist Experiment: Papandreou's Greece 1981–1989* 279–304, New York: Pella

Poppi, Cesare (1992), "Building Difference: The Political Economy of Tradition in the Ladin Carnival of the Val di Fassa", in Jeremy Boissevan (ed.), *Revitalizing European Rituals* 113–36, London: Routledge

Poulton, Hugh (1995), *Who are the Macedonians?* Bloomington: Indiana University Press

Pratt, Mary Louise (1986), "Fieldwork in Common Places", in James Clifford and George Marcus (eds), *Writing Culture: The Poetics and Politics of Ethnography* 27–50, Berkeley: University of California Press

Price, Richard (1983), *First-Time: The Historical Vision of an Afro-American People*, Baltimore: Johns Hopkins University Press

Psychogios, D. K. (1994), "Orthodoxy: Leavening of War or Spiritual Shield?" *To Vima*, 24 April: B32–33*

Ranger, Terence (1993), "The Invention of Tradition Revisited: The Case of Colonial Africa", in Terence O. Ranger and O. Vaughan (eds), *Legitimacy and the State in Twentieth Century Africa* 62–111, London: MacMillan

Rappaport, Joanne (1994), *Cumbe Reborn*, Chicago: University of Chicago Press

Ricoeur, Paul (1981), "Narrative Time", in W. J. T. Mitchell (ed.), *On Narrative* 165–86, Chicago: University of Chicago Press

Roessell, David (1994), *"Cut in Half as it Was": Editorial Excisions and the Original Shape of Lawrence Durrell's* Reflections on a Marine Venus, paper presented at the Next Wave Conference on Byzantine and Modern Greek Studies, Columbus, Ohio, 30 October**

Rofel, Lisa (1992), "Rethinking Modernity: Space and Factory Discipline in China", *Cultural Anthropology* 7: 93–114

Rogers, Susan Carol (1975), "Female Forms of Power and the Myth of Male Dominance: A Model of Female/Male Interaction in Peasant Society", *American Ethnologist* 1: 727–756

Rosaldo, Renato (1980), *Ilongot Headhunting 1883–1974*, Stanford: Stanford University Press

—— (1989), *Culture and Truth: The Remaking of Social Analysis*, Boston: Beacon Press

Rossi, Alice (1965), "Naming Children in Middle-Class Families", *American Sociological Review* 30: 490–513

Rossos, Andrew (1991), "The Macedonians of Aegean Macedonia: A British Officer's Report, 1944", *The Slavonic and East European Review* 69: 282–309

Safire, Willliam (1997), "History is Toast", *New York Times Magazine*, 20 April: 22

Sahlins, Marshall (1985), *Islands of History*, Chicago: University of Chicago Press

—— (1993), "Goodbye to <u>Tristes Tropes</u>: Ethnography in the Context of Modern World History", *Journal of Modern History* 65: 1–25

Sahlins, Peter (1989), *Boundaries: The Making of France and Spain in the Pyrenees*, Berkeley: University of California Press

Sakellaridis, Yiorgos (1986a), "Self-administration during the years of Slavery", *Kalymnian Chronicles* 6: 61–8*

—— (1986b), "Antonio Ritelli", *Kalymnian Chronicles* 6: 151–69*

Sakellarios, Yiorgos (1977), *The National-Religious Resistance of Kalymnos: 1935, vol. 1*, Athens*

Salamone, S. D., and J. B. Stanton (1986), "Introducing the Nikokyra: Ideality and Reality in Social Process", in Jill Dubisch (ed.), *Gender and Power in Rural Greece* 97–120, Princeton: Princeton University Press

Samuel, Rafael, and Paul Thompson (eds), (1990), *The Myths We Live By*, London: Routledge

Sant-Cassia, Paul, (with Constantina Bada), (1992), *The Making of the Modern Greek Family: Marriage and Exchange in nineteenth Century Athens*, Cambridge: Cambridge University Press

Schneider, Jane (1971), "Of Vigilance and Virgins: Honor, Shame, and Access to Resources in Mediterranean Societies", *Ethnology* 10: 1–24

Schneider, Jane, and Rayna Rapp (eds), (1995), *Articulating Hidden Histories: Exploring the Influence of Eric R. Wolf*, Berkeley: University of California Press

Scott, David (1990), "The Demonology of Nationalism: On the Anthropology of Ethnicity and Violence in Sri Lanka", *Economy and Society* 19: 491–510

Seferis, George (1967), *Collected Poems (1924–1955)*, translated by Edmund Keeley and Philip Sherrard, Princeton: Princeton University Press

Seidman, Gay (1993), "'No Freedom without the Women': Mobilization and Gender in South Africa, 1970–1992", *Signs* 18: 291–320

Seremetakis, C. Nadia (1991), *The Last Word: Women, Death and Divination in Inner Mani*, Chicago: University of Chicago Press

—— (1994), *The Senses Still: Perception and Memory as Material Culture in Modernity*, Chicago: University of Chicago Press

Sharma, Ursula (1980), "Dowry in India: its Consequences for Women", in Renée Hirschon (ed.), *Women and Property, Women as Property* 62–74, London: Croon Helm

Shaw, Rosalind, and Charles Stewart (1994), "Introduction: Problematizing Syncretism", in Charles Stewart and Rosalind Shaw (eds), *Syncretism/Anti-Syncretism: The Politics of Religious Synthesis* 1–26, London: Routledge

Shore, Chris (1995) "Usurpers or Pioneers? European Commission Bureaucrats and the Question of 'European Consciousness.'" in Anthony P. Cohen and Nigel Rapport (eds), *Questions of Consciousness* 217–36, London: Routledge

Skardhasis, Mihalis (1979), *Kalymnian Everyday Life*, Anagnostirio folklore series 1: Athens*

Skiada, Virginia (1990), *Gender and Material Culture: The Social History of Wealth in Olymbos, A Greek Insular Village*, Doctoral dissertation, Department of Anthropology, the New School for Social Research

Skilakakis, Thodoros (1995), *In the Name of Macedonia*, Athens: Greek Europublishing*

Someritis, Ricardos (1994), "A European Patriarch", *To Vima*, 30 April: B6*

Spencer, Jonathan (1990), "Writing Within: Anthropology, Nationalism, and Culture in Sri Lanka", *Current Anthropology* 31: 283–300

Stamiris, Eleni (1986), "The Women's Movement in Greece", *New Left Review* 158: 98–112

Stewart, Charles (1991), *Demons and the Devil: Moral Imagination in Modern Greek Culture*, Princeton: Princeton University Press

—— 1995 *Rethinking Cultural Continuity: The Historical Anthropology of Dreams in Greece*, Paper delivered at the Modern Greek Studies Association Meetings, Cambridge, Massachusetts, 3 November**

Strathern, Marilyn (1992), "Reproducing Anthropology", in Sandra Wallman (ed.), *Contemporary Futures: Perspectives from Social Anthropology* 172–89, London: Routledge

Sutton, Constance (1984), *Africans in the Diaspora: Changing Continuities in West Indian And West African Sex/Gender Systems*, paper presented at the Conference on New Perspectives in Caribbean Studies, New York, 29 August**

Sutton, Constance, and Elsa Chaney, (eds), (1987), *The Caribbeanization of New York City: Transnational Perspectives*, New York: Center for Migration Studies

Sutton, David (1994), "'Tradition and Modernity': Kalymnian Constructions of Identity and Otherness", *Journal of Modern Greek Studies* 12: 239–60

Talbot, Strobe (1992), "Greece's Defense Seems Just Silly", *Time* 12 October: 49

Tanner, Nancy (1974), "Matrifocality in Indonesia and Africa and Among Black Americans", in Michelle Rosaldo and Louise Lamphere (eds), *Woman, Culture and Society* 129–56, Stanford: Stanford University Press

Tatakis, A. (1993), "Makriyiannis and the Bosnian Serbs", Letter to the Editor, *Kathimerini*, 23 June*

Tavuchis, N. (1971), "Naming Patterns and Kinship Among Greeks", *Ethnos* 36: 152–62

Taylor, Diana (1994), "Performing Gender: Las Madres de la Plaza de Mayo", in Diana Taylor and Juan Villegas, (eds), *Negotiating Performance: Gender, Sexuality, and Theatricality in Latina/o America* 275–305, Durham and London: Duke University Press

Terdiman, Richard (1993), *Past Present: Modernity and the Memory Crisis*, Ithaca: Cornell University Press

Terkel, Studs (with Ronald Grele), (1975), *Envelopes of Sound: The Art of Oral History*, New York: Praeger

Terkel, Studs (1988), *The Great Divide: Second Thoughts on the American Dream*, New York: Avon Books

Thomas, Nicolas (1992), "The Inversion of Tradition", *American Ethnologist* 19: 213–32

Thomassen, Bjørn (1996), "Border Studies in Europe: Symbolic and Political Boundaries, Anthropological Perspectives", *Europaea* 2: 37–48

Thompson, Mark (1992), *A Paper House: The Ending of Yugoslavia*, London: Vintage

Todorova, Maria (1994), "The Balkans: From Discovery to Invention", *Slavic Review* 53: 453–82

To Vima (unsigned newspaper articles), (1993), September 12:38*
—— (1994a), Who is Killing Africa? 3 July: 26*
—— (1994b), Rwanda: Who Prepared the Genocide", 4 September: 32–3*

Tsing, Anna L. (1993), *In the Realm of the Diamond Queen*, Princeton: Princeton University Press

Tsoucalas, G. M. (1989), *Dodecanesian National Resistance 1940–1945*, Athens*

Valeri, Valerio (1990), "Constitutive History: Genealogy and Narrative in the Legitimation of Hawaiian Kinship", in Emiko Ohnuki-Tierney (ed.), *Culture Through Time: Anthropological Perspectives* 154–92, Stanford: Stanford University Press

Vansina, Jan (1990), *Paths in the Rainforest: Toward a History of Political Tradition in Equatorial Africa*, London: Currey

Veremis, Thanos (1997), " The Revival of the 'Macedonian' Question, 1991–1995", in Peter Mackridge and Eleni Yannakakis (eds), *Ourselves and Others: The Development of a Greek-Macedonian Cultural Identity Since 1912* 227–34, Oxford: Berg

Verney, Susannah (1996), "The Greek Socialists", in John Gaffney (ed.), *Political Parties and the European Union* 170–88, London: Routledge

Vernier, Bernard (1984), "Putting Kin and Kinship to Good Use: The Circulation of Goods, Labour, and Names on Karpathos (Greece)", in Hans Medick and David W. Sabean (eds), *Interest and Emotion: Essays on the Study of Family and Kinship* 28–76, Cambridge: Cambridge University Press

—— (1987), "Filiation, Regles de Residence et Pouvoir Domestique dans les Iles de la Mer Egee", in G. Ravis-Giordani (ed.), *Femmes et Patrimoine* 365–93, Paris: C. N. R. S

—— (1991), *La Genese Sociale des Sentiments*, Paris: Ecole des Hautes Etudes

Voice of America (1994), "Macedonia Embargo", *Mak-News Bulletin Board [Online]*, Available e-mail: MAKNWS-L–UBVM.CC.BUFFALO.EDU. 25 April

Walker, Anita (1989), *What is your Fortune, My Pretty Maid*, Paper Delivered at the Modern Greek Studies Association Meetings, Minneapolis, Minnesota**

Wambaugh, Sarah (1944), "The Dodecanese Islands", in N.G. Mavris (ed.), *The Greek Dodecanese* 14–22, New York: Dodecanesian National Council

Weismantel, Mary (1995), "Making Kin: Kinship Theory and Zumbagua Adoptions", *American Ethnologist* 22: 685–703

White, Hayden (1978), *Tropics of Discourse: Essays in Cultural Criticism*, Baltimore: Johns Hopkins University Press

Wilford, John (1990), "Anthropology Seen as Father of Maori Lore", *New York Times*, 20 February

Wilkinson, Henry (1951), *Maps and Politics: A Review of the Ethnographic Cartography of Macedonia*, Manchester: Manchester University Press

Williams, Brackette (1995), "Classification Systems Revisited: Kinship, Caste, Race, and Nationality as the Flow of Blood and the Spread of Rights", in Sylvia Yanagisako and Carol Delaney (eds), *Naturalizing Power* 201–36, London: Routledge

Woodhouse, C. M. (1990), "The Greek Psyche", *International Minds* 1: 5–9

Woost, Michael (1993), "Nationalizing the Local Past in Sri Lanka: Histories of Nation and Development in a Sinhalese Village", *American Ethnologist* 20: 502–21

Yanagisako, Sylvia, and Carol Delaney (eds), (1995), *Naturalizing Power: Essays in Feminist Cultural Analysis*, London: Routledge

Yang, Mayfair (1996), "Tradition, Travelling Theory, Anthropology and the Discourse of Modernity in China", in Henrietta Moore (ed.), *The Future of Anthropological Knowledge* 93–114, London: Routledge

Yiannopoulos, K., and Tz. Pantelis (1992), "The Gulf War", *E Magazine: Eleftherotipia tis Kiriakis*, 22 March*

Zairi, Maria (1986), "On the Educational Question in the Dodecanese during the years of Italian Occupation", *Kalymnian Chronicles* 6: 106–24*

—— (1989), "The Kolliva", *Kalymnian Chronicles* 8: 247–53*

—— (1992), "Dowry Agreements from the End of the nineteenth Century (1890–1900)", *Kalymnian Chronicles* 10: 155–63*

—— (1995), "Custom?" *The Kalymnian*. May 5*

Author Index

Subject Index

57–8, 74, 76, 112, 205
see also otherness
imagined communities 5–7, 123
Imia 14n12, 168n3, 196n15
Industrial Revolution 8, 23,
  174
infighting 46, 122, 138–40
inheritance 4, 117n23, 185,
  199n27
  dual primogeniture 106–7,
    199n28
  equal 108, 113, 116n8, 186
  matrilineal 105–10, 185, 209
interpretivism 13n6

Jehovah Witnesses 92

Karamanlis, Konstantinos 19,
  76, 129–30, 140
Karpathos 106–7, 184, 189,
  199n28, 200n32
kinship 4, 40, 54n7, 83, 100,
  124–5, 180, 201n36
  and nationalism 174–5, 195n3
  see also naming practices
Knights of Saint John 16, 33n3
Kos 16, 18, 25–6, 29, 33n3,
  39–41, 44–5, 52, 54n9, 76
Koskotas affair 123, 127

Ladin carnival 58, 112
Lago, Mario 87
landscape 27–33
Lazopoulos, Lakis 123
Leros 18, 29, 40–1, 54n9
Levi-Strauss, Claude 170
literacy 49, 58, 76n2
local
  as domain of experience/
    meaning 121–5, 127, 135,
    140–1, 151, 167–8, 174–5,
    180, 193, 195n3, 205, 207
  discourses 8–9, 150–2, 155–8,
    163, 174, 192–4
  identity 50, 53, 70, 75–6, 123

see also globalization,
  resistance

Macedonian question 175–94
  and anthropologists 178
  Former Yugoslav Republic of
    Macedonia (FYROM) 173,
    176–7, 182, 189–90, 199n30
  Greek Macedonia 190,
    196n10, 200n33
  and Greek state 178–9
  Kalymnian perceptions of
    180–94, 197n17
  in media 175–8, 186, 196n9
  national consciousness
    196nn4–5
Madres of the Plaza de Mayo 89,
  96
male authority 103, 110–11
Markezinis, Spyros 20
marriage 106, 24, 48, 101–02,
  117n20, 187
Marx, Karl 10
master narratives 9, 14n13
matriarchy 82, 97, 99–115
matrifocality 183
matrilocal residence 80, 83,
  100–2, 209
memory 7, 14n11, 65–71, 120,
  160–3
  gendered 92–3, 97
men
  and movement 85
  and sexual activity 40, 44
  see also dynamite throwing,
    sponge-diving
metaphors in discourse 123–8,
  146n9
Metaxas, Ioannis 125, 146n10
migration 18, 23, 46–8, 55n21,
  99, 108
  remittances 24
  see also return migration
Mitsotakis, Constantine 123,
  176

tanzimat reforms 17
television 48–9
Theodorakis, Mikis 123
Thessaloniki 176
Thessaly 92
Thucydides 130
toughness 42–3, 45, 62
tourism 24, 25–6, 28, 34n21, 40,
    44–5, 48, 75, 115
tradition 3, 36, 52, 58–9, 67–9,
    74, 76n1, 105, 111-15,
    136–7, 143–4
    invention of 5–7, 58, 112, 179
Treaty of Paris, 1947 19
Tsovolas, Dimitris 21, 127,
    147n13

United States 1, 4, 13, 82, 122–3,
    130, 166, 210, 212n11

Varvitsiotis, Yiannis 126
Vathi 22, 29
Venizelos, Eleftherios 19, 130,
    140
Venizelos, Sophocles 130, 140
Viale, Admiral 17
video clubs 30
virilocal community 83
voting patterns 19–22

Vouvali, Katerina 94–5

women
    and collective action 79–80,
        88–9, 91–2, 96
    and employment 24–5, 44
    and house ownership 34n21,
        100–02
    and leisure activity 85–6
    and religion 86, 89, 98n9
    and restrictions on movement
        47, 54n12, 84–7, 89, 97n5,
        112
    during Roman Empire 109
    and speech 82–4, 96
    see also female power, Rock
        War

Yugoslav war
    in Greek media 150, 154
    Kalymnian perceptions of 149,
        152–68
    role of Great Powers 155–7,
        159–60
    Vance-Owen Plan 157,
        169n12
    in Western media 149, 152–3,
        159, 169n5

Zervos, Skevos 139–40